HELEN HUNT JACKSON AND HER
INDIAN REFORM LEGACY

AMERICAN STUDIES SERIES
WILLIAM H. GOETZMANN, EDITOR

VALERIE SHERER MATHES

HELEN HUNT JACKSON

AND HER INDIAN REFORM LEGACY

UNIVERSITY OF TEXAS PRESS, AUSTIN

First Edition, 1990

Requests for permission to reproduce material from
this work should be sent to Permissions, University
of Texas Press, Box 7819, Austin, Texas 78713-7819.

⊗ The paper used in this publication meets the
minimum requirements of American National
standard for Information Sciences—Permanence
of Paper for Printed Library Materials, ANSI
Z39.48-1984.

Library of Congress Cataloging-in-Publication Data
Mathes, Valerie Sherer, 1941–
    Helen Hunt Jackson and her Indian reform legacy
/ by Valerie Sherer Mathes.—1st ed.
        p.   cm.—(American studies series)
    Includes bibliographical references.
    ISBN 0-292-73056-x (alk. paper)
    1. Jackson, Helen Hunt, 1830–1885—Political
and social views.   2. Jackson, Helen Hunt, 1830–
1885—Influence.   3. Indians of North America—
California—Civil rights.   4. Ponca Indians—Government relations.   5. Indians in literature.
6. Authors, American—19th century—Biography.   7. Social reformers—United States—
Biography.
I. Title.   II. Series.
PS2108.M37   1990
818'.409—dc20   89–29116
                                            CIP

Dedicated to my father
and my sister, Pat,
and to the memory
of my mother,
who loved history

Contents

ILLUSTRATIONS

Preface

When I began research on Helen Hunt Jackson, I knew little about her except that she had written two books and numerous articles criticizing the government's Indian policy. Through her letters, I came to know her, to admire and respect her. Although confined and restricted by the separate sphere assigned women during the Victorian era, she was, nevertheless, able to burst the bonds and make a profound impact upon Indian reform.

Few people today have ever heard of Jackson, let alone her historical novel, *Ramona*. This became painfully apparent during a trip to San Diego and its environs to photograph and follow in her footsteps. People in the very same places that she had traveled a century ago were totally unaware of her historical existence or importance. The intent of this biography, therefore, is to faithfully present her influence upon her contemporary Indian reformers, thus restoring her to her rightful position as a prominent nineteenth-century author and reformer.

My "hobby" of Jackson began a decade ago in the Huntington Library in San Marino, California. Since then Jackson has led me to Colorado Springs and Washington, D.C. The letters discovered there inspired various interesting research projects. For example, in a letter to William Hayes Ward, superintending editor of the *New York Independent*, she expressed a hope to be one hundredth as successful in behalf of the Indians as Harriet Beecher Stowe had been in behalf of the slave. Here was an interesting challenge. Did *Ramona* have as much impact upon the reading public as *Uncle Tom's Cabin?*

A comparison of the lives and careers of these two women illustrated much in common, including a feeling of being possessed while writing their masterpieces. And Jackson did get her wish. *Ramona* is at least one hundredth as successful as *Uncle Tom's Cabin.* After a century, it is still in print, and Hollywood has made several versions of it—whether the latter is a measure of literary success or not, I am not sure.

Jackson's literary works on Indians interested me, but my original intent was to explore the role of numerous women reformers working among the California Indians. Jackson interfered with this concept. She seemed to guide my work much as she believed someone had guided her while writing *Ramona.* A decade of research resulted in much information on her and not enough on other women reformers. For a more balanced study on Jackson alone, I asked myself: did her writings impact at all on other reformers—men and women? Individual members of all three of the major Indian reform groups— the Women's National Indian Association, the Indian Rights Association, and the Lake Mohonk reformers—had indeed personally taken up Jackson's campaign following her death. Thus, the study had come full circle—beginning with Jackson, it had ended with her influence on other reformers.

Jackson continued to draw me into her world, and during the summer of 1988, a friend and I toured the very same places that she had visited a century ago while researching and writing her magazine articles and a government report. Comfortably driving along in an air conditioned automobile and eating fresh cherries, I reflected back on Jackson's journey. Our trip took about a day and a half, but she endured long, hot, dusty days and even weeks bouncing along in a wagon over tortuous mountain roads—possibly along some of the very same roads we sped over. My admiration for her grew.

Some of the reservations she visited still exist today; Jackson, however, would never recognize them. She most certainly would have been appalled at the bingo parlor and the fancy country club on the Saboba reservation. At Warner Springs, elegant condos with a lush green golf course replaced the Indian villages that she knew and respected. Probably the one bright spot in the trip was a visit to the lovely restored mission at Pala, which was in ruins during her visit— this most assuredly would have pleased Jackson.

I have tried to tell her story through her words, quoting when appropriate from letters. I have also chosen to use her spelling of the various groups as well as her term "Mission Indians." This usage may displease some readers, but, after all, this is her story from her point of view—that of a nineteenth-century Indian reformer.

Jackson's writings portrayed a romantic, kindly atmosphere in the California missions. She wrote affectionately of Father Junípero

Serra and the mission era, unlike some writers today who view this period as one of pain and suffering for Indian neophytes. As Jackson's storyteller, I am not interested in judging the mission era. My goal is to document her total dedication to protect former Mission Indians whom she felt had been dispossessed of their land not by Catholic Spain but by Protestant America. Worse yet, she believed that the federal government had neglected them. This, then, is her story.

During my decade of research, I have had to depend heavily upon photocopies and microfilm copies of her letters. Without the help of the staff at the following archives, historical societies, and libraries, I would have been unable to accomplish my task: Amherst College Library, Jones Library, Milton E. Eisenhower Library at Johns Hopkins University, Bancroft Library, Boston Public Library, Bowdoin College Library, Houghton Library at Harvard University, Clifton Waller Barrett Library at the University of Virginia, Charles Leaming Tutt Library at Colorado College, New Hampshire Historical Society, Watkinson Library at Trinity College, Los Angeles County Museum of Natural History, Morristown National Historical Park, Butler Library at Columbia University, New York Public Library, Pierpont Morgan Library, Women's History Archive at Smith College, Princeton University Library, Minnesota Historical Society, San Diego Historical Society, San Francisco Public Library, Huntington Library, Holt-Atherton Pacific Center for Western Studies, the Library of Congress, and the National Archives.

In addition, various articles by me on Jackson's Indian reform work and legacy have appeared in *South Dakota History, Montana: The Magazine of Western History, Essays and Monographs in Colorado History, Southern California Quarterly,* and *The Californians.* Acknowledgement is also due them.

I am further indebted to friends and colleagues who have listened to my ramblings about Jackson for a decade but especially to Drs. Robert Trennert, Albert Hurtado, and Bradford Luckingham at Arizona State University who patiently read and reread my dissertation. Finally I owe much to Don Beilke, instructor of English at my college who painstakingly read my manuscript and made valuable suggestions, to Dr. W. Michael Mathes who helped me on the California Mission phase, and especially to Sarah Buttrey, my copy-editor at the press. Any and all mistakes that remain are my sole responsibility.

Introduction

In the summer of 1880, Helen Hunt Jackson, a middle-aged, New England-born writer, described the federal government's dealings with the American Indian as "a shameful record of broken treaties and unfulfilled promises." Indian/white relations presented a "sickening record of murder, outrage, robbery, and wrongs committed by the former, as the rule, and occasional savage outbreaks and unspeakably barbarous deeds of retaliation by the latter, as the exception."[1] Her indictment of federal Indian policy was not the mere rambling of a misguided busybody but a thoughtful exposé written after months of extensive research through government documents and other sources in New York City's Astor Library.

Her initial introduction to the condition of the American Indian occurred in November 1879 when she attended a lecture in Boston given by Chief Standing Bear of the Ponca tribe. Standing Bear related the poignant story of his tribe's loss of ancestral land and their eventual banishment to the inhospitable climate of Indian Territory. The sad condition of the Ponca tribe prompted Jackson to commit her formidable writing and research talents to their cause and eventually to that of other beleaguered Indian groups.

Jackson's book, *A Century of Dishonor*, a scathing study of the government's treatment of the Ponca and other tribes, was published in January 1881 by Harpers. At her own expense, Jackson sent copies to every member of Congress in hopes that they would end the country's mistreatment of the Indians, thus becoming the first congress "to redeem the name of the United States from the stain of a century of dishonor!"[2] Congress declined to accept Jackson's challenge.

Between the publication of *A Century of Dishonor* and her death in August 1885, Jackson wrote incessantly about the American Indian. Hundreds of letters, several magazine articles, a government report on the condition of the California Mission Indians, and her protest-novel *Ramona* followed. Jackson hoped that *Ramona* would be the *Uncle Tom's Cabin* of the Indian reform movement. It failed to accomplish her original intent. Instead of being perceived as an indictment of the assault of Anglo-California society upon the California Indians, it was seen as a romantic love story that become a stock symbol of southern California chambers of commerce and tourist bureaus.

Despite the public's perception of her work, Jackson's vivid writing revealed her total commitment to the Indian cause. Because she was a widely published and well-received author, Jackson was acquainted with many of the country's best known government officials and literary figures. Those to whom she wrote on behalf of the Indians included jurist Oliver Wendell Holmes, poet Henry Wadsworth Longfellow, clergyman Moncure Daniel Conway, editor William Hayes Ward of the *New York Independent,* Richard Watson Gilder of *Century Magazine,* and publisher Whitelaw Reid of the New York *Daily Tribune.*

Jackson possessed a remarkably strong personality and made tremendous demands upon friends in behalf of the Indians. Moreover, she did not hesitate to engage in verbal battle with Secretary of the Interior Carl Schurz, calling him, among other things, "an adroit liar." While serving as a special agent to the California Mission Indians, she turned to Secretary of the Interior Henry Teller and Indian Commissioner Hiram Price for assistance when convinced that the agent for the California Mission Indians was not doing an adequate job.

Jackson's articles and books so moved members of the Women's National Indian Association (WNIA), the Indian Rights Association (IRA), and the Lake Mohonk Conference that, following her death, these organizations and various individual members continued her work in behalf of the California Mission Indians. When Charles C. Painter, Washington, D.C., lobbyist for the Indian Rights Association, completed eleven months of surveying California Mission Indian reservations, he informed Herbert Welsh, secretary of the organization, that he had carried out his promise made to Jackson on her deathbed. Osia Jane Joslyn Hiles, a member of a Women's National Indian Association auxiliary, was personally drawn to the Mission Indians after reading a copy of *Ramona.* She, too, carried on Jackson's crusade, as did Amelia Stone Quinton, the spirited president of WNIA. Finally, Albert K. Smiley, founder of the Lake Mohonk Con-

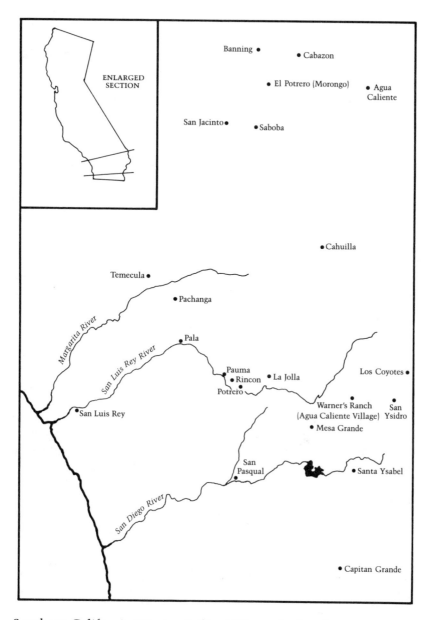

Southern California Mission Indian Villages during the 1880s

ference and a member of the California Indian Commission, personally visited Mission Indian villages. Following the 1891 passage of the Act for the Relief of the Mission Indians in the State of California, Smiley remarked that this bill was based largely on the recommendations Jackson made during her tenure as agent to the Mission Indians.

In comparing Jackson with those reformers who, after her death, carried on the crusade for the California Mission Indians, it becomes apparent that she was more of a muckraker than a missionary reformer. Incensed with the mistreatment of the Indian, particularly the illegal seizure of their land, she was interested in generating pro-Indian public sentiment and forcing Congress to implement existing treaties, thereby preventing the future theft of Indian land. Jackson did not appear to be overly committed to the destruction of Indian culture and their acculturation into American society.

The reformers who carried on her legacy were imbued with evangelical Protestant Christianity and strongly anti-Catholic. Jackson, on the other hand, was not driven by evangelicalism and did not appear to be anti-Catholic. In a *Century Magazine* article devoted to Franciscan Father Junípero Serra and in her portrayal of Father Salvierderra in *Ramona* she presented a sympathetic picture of the role of the Catholic church.

Jackson's Indian legacy therefore had an ironic twist. Interested primarily in preserving the land base for future generations of the California Mission Indians, she opened the door to reformers who were much more divisive and destructive of Indian culture. The women of the WNIA were strongly interested in turning Indian women and girls into typical nineteenth-century Victorian women, while their counterparts in the IRA were interested in turning the men and boys into farmers.

Jackson's premature death in 1885, only a scant six years into the Indian reform movement, clouds any strong definition of her attitude toward Indian culture. She died two years before the passage of the General Allotment Act which divided tribal reservations into small privately held parcels. Her opinion of this legislation remains unknown, although she knew and respected its author, Henry Lauren Dawes. One wonders if, had she lived beyond 1885 and continued her membership in the WNIA, she might have accepted their attitude that only they knew what was best for the Indians. All Indian reform groups, including the WNIA, viewed Indian acculturation as the solution to the problem, much as other contemporary reformers viewed Americanization of the immigrants as the solution to the influx of thousands of Europeans.

To understand Helen Hunt Jackson's Indian legacy, it is necessary to look at the failure of Indian policy during the nineteenth century which prompted her to write *A Century of Dishonor;* the resulting reform movement, particularly the emergence of Jackson and other women reformers; the importance of evangelical Christianity; and the condition of the California Mission Indians at the time of Jackson's appointment as their special agent. Only then can the importance of Jackson's Indian writings and her legacy be understood.

I

Indian Policy, Christian Reformers, and the California Mission Indians

Two decades before Helen Hunt Jackson wrote *A Century of Dishonor*, Indian/white relations on the Plains had disintegrated into a continual battle over Indian land. Ineffective government policy, exacerbated by the patronage system in the Indian Office, resulted in the appointment of incompetent Indian agents, graft, and fraud. The building of the first transcontinental railroad and the disruption caused by the Civil War, which necessitated the replacement of regular western army units by volunteers, made an already unworkable system impossible. At war's end, the federal government finally focused attention on Indian affairs.

In March 1865, Wisconsin Senator James R. Doolittle, member of the Senate Committee on Indian Affairs, introduced a resolution creating a joint congressional committee to investigate conditions of western tribes. Following his suggestion that activities of unscrupulous military officers and fraudulent practices of superintendents and agents were responsible for Indian wars, the joint committee of three senators and four representatives headed west to investigate.

Committee members reported on January 26, 1867, that Indians were decreasing in alarming numbers, that their hunting grounds were disappearing, and that most of the Indian wars were traced to the lawless white aggression found on the frontier.[1] To improve current Indian policy, they urged the creation of appointed boards of inspection as a way to promote greater efficiency and to prevent useless wars.

These recommendations, which marked a new direction in Indian relations, were soon to be criticized by western residents as too lenient. Instead, westerners urged that Indian agencies be eliminated, that Indian land be divided into militarily controlled districts, and that the Office of Indian Affairs be transferred back to the War Department. In agreement, General William T. Sherman believed that the utilization of army officers as Indian superintendents would prove more cost effective and create a system free of political patronage.[2]

Many reformers believed that consolidating Indians upon reservations would accelerate their civilization and provide new lands for white expansion. However, the eighteenth-century theory of containing Indians on one large reservation west of white settlements had failed, largely because of the demand by whites for Indian land. In addition, the removal policy begun by President Thomas Jefferson and carried out by Andrew Jackson had also proven ineffective. By mid-nineteenth century, a shift from removal to creating smaller fixed reservations appeared to be working. In 1859 Secretary of the Interior Jacob Thompson noted that the gathering of Indians on small tribal reservations and the assignment of tracts of land in severalty to individual tribal members was working well.[3]

Thus, by the approach of the Civil War, numerous small tribal reservations were scattered across the West. But settlements soon surrounded these areas, and the inevitable friction resulted. Therefore, William P. Dole, commissioner of Indian affairs during the administration of Abraham Lincoln, questioned the use of small reservations and suggested instead that larger areas be designated for Indian occupancy. By the Civil War it became common practice to settle northern Plains tribes north of Nebraska and west of the Missouri River and southern Plains tribes in Indian Territory or parts of the Southwest as needed.[4]

During the summer of 1867 the House of Representatives passed legislation creating a Peace Commission comprised of four civilians and three generals. They were directed to establish peace with hostile tribes, settle them on reservations, remove the causes of Indian wars, provide for the safety of frontier settlements and transcontinental railroads, and finally institute a plan for civilizing the Indians. Commission members, believing that the "civilization" process must concentrate on turning the Indians into farmers, renewed efforts to protect native land base. They were also confident that teaching English to Indian children would lessen cultural differences and rapidly bring them into the civilized world.[5]

To implement this new "peace policy," commissioners concluded treaties with the southern Plains tribes in 1867 and with the northern Plains the following year. This approach reached its zenith with the inauguration of Ulysses S. Grant in 1869 and was commonly referred to as "Grant's Peace Policy."[6] The president, who believed in Indian "civilization" and citizenship, worked closely with the nation's churches to create a Christian approach to Indian affairs.[7]

The proposed transfer in 1867 of the Indian Office from the Department of the Interior to the War Department caused many of the country's religious leaders to take more interest in Indian reform.[8] Quaker leaders, who believed that only Christian influence and civilian control could save the Indians from extermination, became alarmed. Fortunately, both Grant and the Quakers were in agreement with the Peace Commission's recommendation that restricting the tribes to a clearly defined reservation and protecting them from white encroachment was the requisite to civilizing and assimilating them.

The success of this new policy hinged upon the quality of Indian agents assigned to assist the Indian in the transformation from nomadic to "civilized" life. The patronage of the spoils systems, however, had resulted in agencies being assigned as repayment for political loyalties. Because the final report of the Peace Commission had recommended the replacement of current superintendents and agents by competent appointees, Grant, at the urging of Quaker leaders, requested that Christian and philanthropic organizations suggest the names of good Christians willing to serve.

By 1872 members of thirteen different denominations became Indian Office field officers in charge of over 70 agencies with an estimated 239,000 resident Indians. Episcopalians, Methodists, Presbyterians, and Quakers received almost two thirds of all agencies. If Grant's policy "was a mission policy,"[9] it was primarily a Protestant one. The Catholic church received only seven agencies. Antagonism, competition, and distrust over apportionment of agencies soon emerged between denominations.

In addition to drawing agents from the various churches, President Grant, in the spring of 1869, selected religious leaders and noted philanthropists to serve without compensation as members of the Board of Indian Commissioners.[10] This nine-member board, nominated by various Protestant denominations, was authorized to exercise joint control with the Interior Department in the purchase and inspection of goods and the disbursement of funds, including a two million dollar "Civilization Fund." However, they were not given power to direct Indian policy, they had insufficient funding for annual tours of inspection, and their recommendations were subject to approval by the president and secretary of the interior.

The ultimate goal of the Board of Indian Commissioners and other reformers was to assimilate the Indians into mainstream American culture. This was to be accomplished by creating a reservation system and civilizing the Indians through education, Christianization, and citizenship legislation. In addition, the most important panacea to the Indian problem was the promotion of private property. To help achieve this, Congress in 1875 passed the Indian Homestead Act— legislation intended to weaken the tribal structure by stressing individual land ownership instead of communal holdings. Under the Indian Homestead Act, the Indians were provided all the benefits of the 1862 Homestead Act without loss of tribal funds.

Despite wide support among eastern reformers and humanitarians, Grant's policy soon came under severe criticism. The appointment of honest church men as agents and commission members did not necessarily prevent hostilities. And, although reservations were under civilian control, it was still necessary for the military to serve as a police force to keep whites out and Indians inside.

By the close of Grant's second term, hostilities, including the Red River War of 1874–1875 on the southern Plains and the 1872–1873 Modoc War in Northern California, as well as the Battle of the Little Bighorn, marred the record of the peace policy. Western governors, legislators, and newspaper editors continually called for more aggressive military action. Other critics demanded that Indian control be returned to the War Department, although humanitarians and eastern reformers unanimously supported civilian control. The latter prevailed, and the Office of Indian Affairs continued under the Interior Department.[11]

Although the "peace policy" was pronounced a failure by the late 1870s, some ideas did make headway. For a time the quality of agents was upgraded, although Christian agents were not necessarily more knowledgeable about Indian culture. And more monetary support reached church missions and schools, resulting in the education of some Indian children. In addition, the Board of Indian Commissioners initially played an invaluable role. During their first three years, members traveled 250,000 miles to negotiate treaties and make inspection tours.

The inauguration of Rutherford B. Hayes as president and his appointment in 1877 of Carl Schurz, a reform-minded liberal, as secretary of the interior resulted in a policy change. Although Hayes assured concerned Quakers and other religious leaders that he did not intend to alter Grant's policy, Schurz, nevertheless, cleaned out the Indian Office and established an aggressive policy of individualizing the Indian. Although the reservation system in general did not come under attack, the new secretary emphasized smaller reserves where private land ownership and farming could be promoted.

Secretary Schurz, believing in separation of church and state, disliked government support of denominational mission schools. Religion alone was not enough to stop the corruption in the Indian Office. In addition, his personal selection of Ezra Ayers Hayt as commissioner in the fall of 1877 alienated the religious community. Hayt in his first year removed thirty-five church-nominated agents. Thereafter, churches became less involved in the selection of agents. Grant's policy weakly survived Hayt, but the appointment of Henry Teller in 1882 as secretary of the interior "buried the Peace Policy."[12]

During the Hayes/Schurz administration the forced removal of the small, peaceful Ponca tribe from their Missouri River Reservation in present day South Dakota to Indian Territory[13] sparked considerable interest in Indian policy. In early 1879 Ponca Chief Standing Bear, with the body of his only son, and a small band of followers headed north to their former burial grounds. By March they had traveled as far as the Omaha Reservation in Nebraska when they were arrested for leaving Indian Territory without permission. They were subsequently freed by a decision in *Standing Bear v. Crook*, won with the help of Thomas Henry Tibbles, assistant editor of the *Omaha Daily Herald*, who had hired two Omaha lawyers. As a consequence of this courtroom victory,[14] Tibbles resigned his position and organized an eastern lecture tour for Standing Bear and other Indians. The recounting of this tragic story made Ponca removal a popular public issue.

The tour was most successful in the Northeast where prominent citizens organized the Boston Indian Citizenship Committee to fight for the rights of the Ponca and other tribes.[15] Among these individuals was Helen Hunt Jackson. She supported the efforts to return the Ponca to their original reservation in South Dakota, promoted Indian equality in the courts, and advocated fulfillment of all treaty obligations and voluntary allotment of land.

Prior to the Ponca tragedy, Jackson[16] had never before identified with any humanitarian reform. After listening to Standing Bear's tale, she totally immersed herself in their cause, devoting the rest of her life to helping Indians in general. She campaigned for money, encouraged her friends to hold receptions, helped organize the Boston Indian Citizenship Committee, and affiliated with the Women's National Indian Association. Her involvement was so strong that she noted to a friend: "I shall be found with 'Indians' engraved on my brain when I am dead.—A fire has been kindled within me which will never go out."[17]

The work of Jackson and her fellow reformers ultimately resulted in a government inspection of Indian Territory, the appointment of a commission to confer with Poncas living both in Indian Territory and Nebraska, and the appropriation of $165,000 by Congress as indemnity for losses sustained during removal. Congress also recommended that each tribal member select 160 acres either in Indian Territory or Dakota Territory and receive a patent to the land, inalienable for thirty years.

Prior to the Ponca removal, humanitarian reformers lacked the direction and leadership to implement Indian reform policies. That changed, however, with the strong public interest generated by the Ponca tour. The creation of the Boston Indian Citizenship Committee was soon followed by other organizations including the Philadelphia-based Women's National Indian Association (WNIA) founded by Mary Lucinda Bonney, principal of the Chestnut Street Female Seminary. Although she was more influenced by unauthorized white settlement in Indian Territory than the Standing Bear tour, Bonney, nevertheless, benefited from the new interest in the condition of all Indians. Aided by the organizational skills of Amelia Stone Quinton, later president of the national organization, WNIA members participated in spectacular petition drives, circulated literature on Indian topics, furnished information to the press, and established branches throughout the country.[18]

By 1883 WNIA members began to shift their emphasis from civil and political activities to educational and missionary work. This change was possible because of the December 15, 1882, establishment in Philadelphia of the male-dominated Indian Rights Association (IRA) by Herbert Welsh. Although the women had taken the initial step in founding a national reform organization, they were relieved to have the support of the IRA. Like WNIA members, Welsh assumed that cultural assimilation would benefit the Indians. Furthermore, he was also personally aware of the inefficient management of Indian affairs. His uncle William had served as the first chairman of the Board of Indian Commissioners in 1869. Thus Welsh took the Indian cause before the public.

Initial IRA efforts were devoted to investigative tours of Indian country and the publication of reports. Politically oriented from the start and armed with the franchise, which WNIA members were not, the IRA sought to civilize the Indians and prepare them for eventual participation in mainstream American culture. Members hoped to achieve their goals through land allotment, an educational system for all Indian children, political and civil rights for the Indians, and the break-up of tribal organizations, which members believed to be "the real citadel of savagery."[19]

The IRA, following the lead of the WNIA, established branch associations and sent representatives to reservations to obtain firsthand knowledge. In addition, they embarked on a publication program, circulated reports of members' trips of inspection, and reprinted newspaper articles, speeches, and other materials. Welsh, like Quinton, often spoke before interested groups to explain his ideas and elicit support. The organization also employed a full-time lobbyist in the nation's capital. Until his death in 1895, Charles C. Painter guided legislation through Congress, closely followed the progress of Indian legislation, brought information to the attention of congressional members, and pushed for measures deemed beneficial to the Indians. He also made frequent visits to reservations to obtain firsthand insight on conditions.[20]

In 1883 a forum for discussing various reform ideas was established at Lake Mohonk near New Paltz, New York, by Quaker schoolteacher Albert K. Smiley. Smiley, a member of the Board of Indian Commissioners, felt that meetings of the board with missionary society representatives were too short. He decided to host a three-day conference where ideas could be discussed in detail. The first Lake Mohonk Conference of the Friends of the Indians, which included Welsh, General Clinton B. Fisk (president of the Board of Indian Commissioners), and ten others, was held in October 1883. Although this group was small, during the 1890s more than 150 gathered annually at Lake Mohonk to hear suggestions of Indian experts and government officials. Congressmen, reformers, philanthropists, government officials, clergymen, and editors of leading eastern newspapers, all carefully selected to unite the best minds, became a dominant force in formulating Indian policy for the next three decades.[21]

Another common interest that connected members of the WNIA, IRA, and Mohonk conferences was their strong religious beliefs. The WNIA had grown out of the Women's Home Mission Circle of the First Baptist Church in Philadelphia but later became nondenominational. The women drew heavily upon church support, and, when various mission stations became self-sustaining, they were turned over to an established church to run.

The IRA was strongly motivated by the Christian beliefs of Herbert Welsh, an active member of the Episcopalian Church to which he contributed money, time, and operational skill. Finally, the religious atmosphere at Lake Mohonk was due in part to the influence of the Quaker host but also to heavy clerical participation. Between

1883 and 1900 more than one-fourth of the members represented various religious groups or were ministers. In addition, editors of leading religious journals and papers attended.

According to Francis Paul Prucha, S.J., an authority on Indian policy, participants at Lake Mohonk represented "a powerful segment of Protestant church membership, and thereby of late nineteenth- and early twentieth-century American Society." They "reflected the concepts of rugged individualism and a faith in the saving grace of honest work [and] . . . brought the finest traditions of Christian altruism and spirit of progressive reform," notes historian Larry Burgess.[22] Not only were reformers influenced by religion but also three Indian commissioners were ordained ministers.[23]

These reformers who set out to do God's work were part of the strong evangelical movement that dominated the country during the nineteenth century. They reflected a large segment of Protestant America and spoke for the majority of society. Evangelical religion molded America "into a unified, pietistic-perfectionist nation, and spurred them on to those heights of social reform, missionary endeavor, and imperialistic expansionism which constitute the moving forces of our history in that century,"[24] writes William G. McLoughlin, a prominent religious scholar, echoing the beliefs that nineteenth-century reformers held about themselves.

These evangelical Christian reformers were missionary minded, for "by Biblical injunction it was the duty of the saved to save others."[25] Seeing no redeeming value in Indian culture, they set out to save the Indians—to force them to give up their communal lifestyle and adopt the sedentary individualist ways of American society. Individuality was important to Indian reform, for the "distinguishing mark of American evangelicalism was its insistence on individual salvation."[26] Thus reformers deliberately set out to destroy tribal relations and replace communally held tribal lands with allotments in severalty to individual Indians, who in turn were expected to become self-supporting farmers like the rest of rural America.

Reformers believed these goals were possible since Indians were assumed to be different only because their environment was different. These reformers accepted the view that humanity had passed through stages of society beginning with savagery and ending with civilization. They only wanted to speed up the process by educational and other civilizing programs—to accomplish in one generation what Indians had taken generations to achieve. No mere sentimentalists, these reformers were sincere but narrow-minded and often lacked any appreciation of Indian culture. As arbiters of society, they shared complete confidence in their beliefs, finding the source of their obligations toward the Indians in religion. With the frontier disappearing, they argued, unless the Indian accepted the ways of the predominant culture, they would surely be exterminated.[27]

Secretary of the Interior Carl Schurz also believed that Indians faced either extermination or civilization. He argued that "to civilize them, which was once only a benevolent fancy, has now become an absolute necessity, if we mean to save them."[28] Similarly, the IRA Executive Committee in its second annual report declared that "the Indian as a savage member of a tribal organization cannot survive, ought not to survive the aggressions of civilization."[29] Reformers often viewed Indians as children of nature to be led by the hand to civilization. Compulsory education, Christianization, allotment, and citizenship were the methods used to bring these unworldly "children" into American society, whether they wanted to or not.

These Indian reformers, so willing to force their beliefs upon another culture, were, according to Herbert Welsh, the elite of New England, New York, and Philadelphia.[30] They were generally past forty and mostly eastern, urban dwellers. One quarter of them were women.

The participation of middle- and upper-class women in the Indian reform movement was a logical outgrowth of nineteenth-century America's perception of women's role as a "separate sphere" from that of men. The "Cult of True Womanhood"—piety, purity, submissiveness, and domesticity—enveloped these women.[31]

Domesticity was by far the most important element. "To render *home* happy is a woman's peculiar province, home is *her world*," noted a contributor to a ladies' magazine in 1830.[32] Even contemporary religious sermons were often devoted to motherhood and the Christian home, and leading clergymen promoted women's role. Henry Ward Beecher believed that women were, by far, men's superior as "molder and trainer of children in the household."[33] This emphasis on the role of domesticity would later be important to WNIA members when working with Indian women who were expected to learn the proper homemaking skills of the nineteenth-century Victorian woman.

Catharine Beecher, eldest daughter of clergyman Lyman Beecher and sister to Henry Ward Beecher, believed that to American women "more than to any others on earth is committed the exalted privilege of extending over the world those blessed influences, which are to renovate degraded man."[34] Her views were reinforced by William W. Fowler in his popular study, *Women on the American Frontier*, first published in 1876. Fowler viewed women as capable of refining and humanizing society as well as carrying civilization into the wilderness. A woman, he noted, was a *"civilizer par excellence."*

According to Fowler, "that state of man which is best ordered and safest, is only where woman's membership is most truly recognized."[35]

Fowler also believed that woman's influence was necessary for the Indians; she could prepare them for Christianity "by her kind and placid ministrations." He concluded that, "with her heart full of love and pity for her dark-browed brethren, woman as a missionary to the Indians is a crowning glory of her age and sex."[36]

Constantly told by contemporaries of their responsibilities toward society and the Indians, ideas reinforced by the novelists of the day, upper- and middle-class American women ventured forth into Indian reform to work among women and children.

Although home was woman's "proper sphere," the nineteenth-century woman also ventured into church work. Church work would not take her from her sphere and would not make her less domestic or submissive. Woman's piety obviously made her "naturally prone to be religious," noted one contemporary cleric.[37] Another clergyman believed that woman was "fitted by nature" for Christian benevolence[38] while a third wrote: "Religion is far more necessary to . . . a woman . . . than a self-sufficient man. In . . . the woman it would be not only *criminal*, but *impolitic* to neglect it."[39] Clerics were not alone in this belief. Catharine Beecher noted: "It is Christianity that has given to women her true place in society. And it is the peculiar trait of Christianity alone than can sustain her therein."[40]

Women in increasing numbers flocked to join various congregations and church-related organizations. Their participation resulted in more genteel, less rigid church institutions—thus emerged the "feminization of American religion."[41] In due time, as these women became involved in church-related reforms, they were able to assert themselves in both private and public ways.[42] Benevolent societies were established in various evangelical Protestant churches, and soon women established orphan asylums, charity schools, homes for the indigent, and Sunday schools—all tasks traditional to woman's sphere. They ventured into the issue of morality, then into the abolition movement. Finally, to protect husband, hearth, and home, they became dedicated temperance workers.

Ironically, the Victorian woman was viewed by contemporaries as defenseless and possessed of a mind too weak for serious thought. Her body was too frail for strenuous work, and her emotional makeup too brittle to cope with reality, yet she was expected to take on the tasks of guardian of the home's fires and controller of the wilder nature of man. As a consequence of these powerful obligations, the Victorian woman not only was in charge of the destiny of every community but also assumed the role of special guardian of democracy. She was responsible "for the moral sustenance of the nation."[43] This expanded role of wife, mother, homemaker, and protector of society had forced women to enter the reform arena via their religious commitments. And aided by their respective churches and ministers, women made marked contributions to reforming America.[44]

The skills that they had learned over a half century of experience in moral reform, anti-slavery, and temperance work gave women the tools and expertise to undertake Indian reform. They had learned to chair business meetings, to raise funds, and to speak before large audiences. Armed with the right of petition, so gallantly protected for them by John Quincy Adams, who believed that women were "by the law of their nature, fitted above all others for that exercise,"[45] late-nineteenth-century women began the task of turning Indian women into their Victorian counterparts while male reformers worked to change Indian men into contemporary Jeffersonian yeoman farmers.

The founding of the Women's National Indian Association marked the beginning of seven decades of labor in behalf of the American Indian by middle- and upper-class women. In the spring of 1879, Mary Lucinda Bonney stood before the monthly meeting of the Women's Home Mission Circle of the First Baptist Church in Philadelphia and informed them that railroads and settlers were clamoring to enter Indian Territory in direct violation of federal treaties. Bonney believed that this action "would greatly hinder the work of Christianizing the Indians, and would also be a vast moral evil to [the] nation."[46]

She came by her reform-minded, missionary attitude naturally. Founder of the Chestnut Street Female Seminary, member of the Woman's Union Missionary Society of America for Heathen Lands (which sent missionaries to work with women in the Orient), and president of the Women's Home Mission Circle,[47] Bonney, in combining a strong religious conviction with a solid background in education, concluded that the way to civilize the Indian was through the process of education and Christianization. Skilled in both areas, she became the initial driving force of the WNIA.

Bonney's early attempt to encourage her mission circle to aid the Indians was thwarted when her petition protesting the invasion of Indian Territory was ignored when the circle adjourned for the summer. Unwilling to let the matter drop, she enlisted her friend Amelia Stone Quinton, who was more skilled in bringing a cause before the public. Quinton, who taught one year at the Chestnut Street Female Seminary following the death of her first husband, Reverend James

Franklin Swanson, had always devoted her time to the less fortunate. She had helped the inmates of New York City's charity asylums, worked in almshouses, infirmaries, prisons, and women's re-
formatories as well as conducted weekly Bible classes for sailors
docked at the city's pier. In 1874 she joined the Women's Christian
Temperance Union and organized local and later state unions.[48]

The work proceeded slowly. Bonney paid all expenses for the first
two years while Quinton supplied research and organizational skills.
The first petition requested that the president and Congress prevent
white encroachment in Indian Territory and protect Indian rights
guaranteed in federal treaties.[49] Seven thousand copies, accompanied
by Quinton's article, *An Earnest Petition Needed,* detailing the
forced removal of the Five Civilized Tribes from their southern
homeland to Indian Territory, were circulated to various women's
missionary groups and other benevolent societies during the summer.

The final petition, measuring 300 feet and signed by 13,000 citizens in 15 states, was carried by Bonney and two members of the
missionary circle to Washington, D.C. President Rutherford B. Hayes,
in accepting the petition on February 14, 1880, expressed "his sense
of the timeliness of the memorial."[50] Hayes turned the petition over
to William D. Kelly of Pennsylvania, who presented it before the
House on February 20.

Encouraged by the successful petition drive, the following May,
Bonney and Quinton, now joined by others from the mission circle,
organized a Committee of Ways and Means to distribute petitions
and tracts. Meanwhile, Quinton continued investigating official
records, writing leaflets, and attending meetings at missionary
circles, anniversary associations, and pastors' conventions. At her
insistence, the committee secured a release from the First Baptist
Church and became nonsectarian. They reorganized on December
11, 1880, changing their name to the Central Indian Committee.
Four new members joined, one each from the Presbyterian, Methodist Episcopal, and Episcopal churches as well as the Society of Friends,
or Quakers.[51]

In January 1881, Quinton and the chairman of the committee presented the second annual petition with 50,000 signatures representing every state. Again these women requested the prevention of
encroachments on all reservations and the retention of all treaties
until changed by mutual consent. Both the petition and accompanying memorial letters were presented to the Senate by Massachusetts
Senator Henry Lauren Dawes, chairman of the Senate Indian Committee, on January 27, 1881. Four days later the Honorable Gilbert
DeLaMatyr of Indiana presented it to the House.

In her memorial letter, Quinton noted that the petition signatures represented people of all occupations, including judges, governors, pastors, bishops, ambassadors, authors, editors, and university presidents. She believed that it revealed "that the *moral sentiment* of those classes who largely make and control public opinion already requires governmental faithfulness to our Indian treaties."[52]

Probably because these women were still unsure about themselves—their power, their position, and probably even their skill—this petition did "not suggest any political policy to be pursued, leaving such matters to wise statesmanship."[53] This attitude changed as they gained more expertise, and as early as 1883 they united to secure the adoption of "a just, protective and fostering Indian policy."[54]

Leading clergymen soon took notice of the work of this small but determined group of women. Bishop Henry B. Whipple of Minnesota, personally active in Indian reform since the Civil War, noted that "the Women have builded [*sic*] larger than they know."[55] Another clergyman commented that "when Christian women pray and labor for any great interest of public righteousness, the Christian ministry may be counted in their following."[56] And counted they were. As the membership grew, the advisory board included the names of many of the country's leading clergymen.

In March 1881 Bonney was elected president of the group, with Quinton as secretary. On June 3 they changed their name to the Indian Treaty-Keeping and Protective Association and drew up a new constitution providing for auxiliaries, or associate committees. However, the executive board, now representing eight different denominations, remained in Philadelphia with branches elsewhere. Although second in command, Quinton continued to be the driving force. The previous year alone she delivered 150 addresses before women's groups, church associations, ministers' conferences, and missionary groups. During the summer of 1881 she began organizing outside Philadelphia. By August 1, the work of the association had reached twenty different states, including Connecticut, Massachusetts, Rhode Island, New York, and New Jersey. Quinton continued as its energy source even after it became a diversified, loosely federated organization.[57]

During her second year of research, Quinton became convinced that law, education, and citizenship were the tools needed to rescue the Indian from oppression. In addition, lands should be distributed in severalty, and treaties that hindered the process of civilization should be abrogated by consent of both Indians and government officials.[58]

The reservation system was also severely criticized by Quinton. Enlarged during Grant's Peace Policy, tribal reserves were viewed by many whites as degrading to the Indians, relegating them to the position of paupers. Reservations required "super human wisdom and goodness" for success. "Even if the angelic guard has been detailed to administer" them, the women reformers believed that "no broad and wholesome civilization could ever result from permanent imprisonment and segregation."[59] Eventually, most nineteenth-century Indian reformers viewed the reservation system as both perpetuating Indian culture and acting as a boundary to keep out law and social order.

Therefore, the organization's third annual petition not only urged the gradual destruction of the reservation system but also called for universal common-school education, industrial training, and allotment in fee-simple title, along with a twenty-year period of inalienability, of at least 160 acres to any Indian. In addition, the WNIA urged the maintenance of all treaties until changed by the consent of the Indians and the recognition of Indian rights under the law.[60]

Circulated in every state and territory, the third petition was signed by 100,000 citizens, including the entire ministry of three Philadelphia denominations and professors and students from Yale, Harvard, Brown, and Cornell, as well as editors of leading periodicals and boards of hundreds of missionary and benevolent societies. The immense petition, wrapped in white bunting and tied by red, white, and blue ribbons, was presented on February 21, 1882, to President Chester A. Arthur by Quinton and five other women, including Mrs. Hawley, president of the Washington auxiliary and wife of a Connecticut senator, and Mrs. Keifer, wife of the Speaker of the House. The great roll was then carried to the Marble Room of the Senate, where Dawes presented it while the ladies in the gallery eagerly listened to his speech.[61]

The concepts detailed in this third petition eventually became governmental policy. Herein lies one of the more important legacies of the WNIA: not only were they the first major national Indian reform group organized but also they initially formulated policies that were later endorsed by other groups and adopted by the government. Among those who recognized the value of these ideas was Senator Henry L. Dawes, author of the 1887 General Allotment Act, also called the Dawes Act, which incorporated the concept of land allotment. Dawes once noted that the new government Indian policy "was born of and nursed by the Women's National Indian Association."[62]

Infused with renewed vigor, members held more meetings, wrote more press articles, and prepared and circulated new leaflets. Meanwhile, Quinton continued her arduous rounds, organizing more state branches and auxiliaries. During an October 3, 1882, executive meeting, the constitution was again revised, and the name was changed to the National Indian Association. Furthermore, it was decided that an educational and missionary department be established. These two areas would soon consume most of the energy of the association.[63]

The timing for the new department was propitious. Two months later, in December 1882, Herbert Welsh, returning to Philadelphia from a visit in Dakota, founded the Indian Rights Association, which soon took over some of the work previously done by the women. Now WNIA members were free to devote part of their time "to uplifting Indian homes; [and] to aiding the vastly needed work within Indian hearts, minds and souls, while not intermitting the effort to secure to the race civil rights."[64]

Indian Rights Association members, who intended to use public pressure to bring civil rights, citizenship, and general education to the Indian population,[65] were received "with joy" by the WNIA membership during their January meeting in Philadelphia. These women recognized male members of the IRA as an associate society working toward obtaining for the Indians the same opportunities as granted to other races in the country.[66]

In the third annual report, IRA members praised the women of the association, giving them credit for "having both planned and begun the execution of the work, which now in some of its phases is more fully carried out by the Indian Rights Association."[67] Out of recognition and courtesy, the women again changed their name, becoming the Women's National Indian Association. Both organizations resolved that a representative from each executive board would attend the other's meetings.

The formation of the IRA allowed the women of WNIA, in addition to their original activities, to take up the missionary work that had first been proposed in October 1882. As Quinton aptly expressed it, the IRA could now pursue "as their chosen work, and with far greater facilities than we could command, the very objects which had previously wholly occupied our attention."[68] Thus while male members of the IRA, armed with the franchise, promoted citizenship, allotment, and political rights for the Indians, the women of WNIA could continue to do what they had done in early reform groups—minister to women and children, continuing the traditional Victorian role of "true womanhood."

On February 13, 1883, the first WNIA resolution adopting missionary work was formally presented. Soon thereafter, General Samuel C. Armstrong, founder of Hampton Institute, suggested that the Apaches of Arizona be the first to be provided missionary service, but too many obstacles emerged. In 1884, Indian Territory became WNIA's first field, and two missionaries were soon busy among the Ponca, Oto, and Pawnee.

By the end of the third year, the Missionary Department had opened eleven stations and was working not only among the Ponca, Oto, and Pawnee but also among the Sioux of Dakota, the Bannocks and Shoshoni of Idaho, the Omaha of Nebraska, and six small tribes near Round Valley, California. In 1894 alone, they sponsored fourteen missionary workers in Florida, Alabama, Indian Territory, Arizona, Idaho, Washington, Montana, and California.[69]

To clarify their missionary activities, the executive board on January 12, 1884, resolved that work be undertaken only where no missionary currently resided and where government help could be obtained. The board finally agreed that their work would be only temporary; when a missionary station was well established, it would be turned over to a missionary society to run.[70] In the meantime, while the mission was in their hands, the WNIA women would engage in one of their traditional societal roles—caring for women and children.

In the 1882 memorial letter accompanying the third petition to government officials, Quinton noted it was the responsibility of WNIA to secure legislation for the legal protection of suffering Indian women and children. The "plea of Indian women for the sacred shield of law is the plea . . . of all womanhood, indeed, on their behalf to you as legislators and as men," she wrote.[71] Two years later she noted that to minister to Indian women's "great sufferings from barbarism, to enlighten their physical, mental and spiritual ignorance, to win heart and confidence by kind charities, . . . to teach them as opportunity constantly offers, . . . is a work . . . imperatively needed."[72] Quinton, Bonney, and others intended to continue their work until the Indian woman and her home were removed from pagan darkness into the "light of Christian faith."[73]

The Christian women of the WNIA saw their work as two-fold. First, they intended to awaken public sentiment, which they hoped would aid the government in the adoption of a policy bringing the principles of equity and justice to Indian affairs. This, they believed, would gradually lead to the abolition of the reservation system and give all Indians the same laws, education, and citizenship enjoyed by all other races. Second, through educational and missionary work, they hoped to hasten the civilization, Christianization, and enfranchisement of the Indians.[74]

The various WNIA branches and state associations worked with the Indians of many western states. Their work in California would be extensive and strongly influenced by Helen Hunt Jackson. Shortly after beginning her work in behalf of the Ponca, Jackson visited the WNIA office in Philadelphia and expressed delight in finding earnest women hard at work acquainting the public with the Indian situation.[75]

Jackson's untimely death in 1885 removed her as a direct influence upon the reform movement. But her poignant novel *Ramona*, numerous articles, and a government report on the condition of the Mission Indians of Southern California prompted members of the Women's National Indian Association, as well as of the Indian Rights Association and the Lake Mohonk Conference, to become concerned about the condition of the California Mission Indian. These groups, in effect, carried on her crusade until it was substantially completed.

Actually, WNIA educational and missionary work in California began in the northern part of the state in the year of Jackson's death. At the suggestion of Senator Dawes in 1885, Round Valley, California, became the first WNIA state mission.[76] Although at the time of her death, Jackson was aware of the efforts of the WNIA in Round Valley, she was much more personally concerned with the Mission Indians.

During her stay in Southern California, Jackson visited many of the villages occupied by descendents of Indians who had once been neophytes in Spain's Franciscan missions. This mission system had been devised to both create a frontier settlement in areas unattractive to civilian population and acculturate neighboring native peoples.[77] In California, Franciscan missionaries had selected locations suitable for mission establishments with ample water and lands for agriculture and stock raising. The missions consisted of churches, residences for missionaries and Indians or neophytes who were incorporated into the mission, and various outbuildings.

The neophytes were not only given religious instruction but also taught the Spanish "way of life" as well as manual arts, livestock husbandry, and agriculture. Under Spanish law, within ten years of a mission's foundation, the neophytes and their offspring were expected to be sufficiently acculturated, and the mission was then to become the nucleus of a civil settlement surrounded by fields and grazing pastures to be divided among the Indian families. The missionary would then move on and be replaced by a secular or parish priest.

In most instances the system was less than perfect. In the case of California, the ten-year goal was not met. Fearful that their charges would become influenced by sinful outsiders who would retard their cultural evolution, some missionaries assumed an attitude of excessive paternalism.

Numerous factors that neither the missionaries nor the neophytes could have anticipated, including the spread of contagious disease, which frequently brought death because of the Indians' lack of immunity, also had an effect upon the mission. Furthermore, any hope for the evolution of mission centers into civil settlements ended with the secularization decree of August 1833, which ordered instant conversion of mission religious buildings to parish churches, released the neophytes, and distributed their lands to others. The twenty-one Franciscan missions in California, located along the coast between San Diego and Sonoma and with an estimated population in 1823 of over 21,000 neophytes,[78] were secularized between 1834 and 1836.

Thus, by decree, California Mission Indians became homeless, landless vagabonds. Peonage was an answer to the latter problem, as some former neophytes remained on old mission ranchos to work for new owners and others chose instead to move to interior areas not under Mexican control. Some rejoined their old rancherías, or villages, although non-mission (gentile) Indians sometimes rejected the neophytes. Still others moved into towns such as Los Angeles to find work. The years between 1833 and 1850 proved even more difficult for California Indians. Anglo-Americans who settled in Mexican California readily adopted the prevailing system of Indian labor. The change to American sovereignty did not substantially improve the Indians' situation.[79]

Statehood resulted in the passage in 1850 of the Act for the Government and Protection of Indians (sometimes known as the Indian Indenture Law), which allowed a vagrant Indian or an Indian guilty of a crime to be hired out by local authorities to settlers. Furthermore, an apprenticeship system allowed the use of the labor of males under eighteen and females under fifteen, which in turn resulted in the kidnapping of Indians, especially children. The demand for cheap agricultural and domestic labor resulted in the extension of this apprenticeship system, which was abolished in 1863.[80]

Statehood subjected the Indians not only to an extension of the peonage system, which had continued from the period of Mexican rule, but also to control by the federal government. In February 1851 three federal commissioners negotiated eighteen treaties involving some twenty-five thousand Indians, who gave up land claims in return for reservations. Congress rejected the eighteen treaties.[81] Many Californians would have preferred to see the Indians entirely removed from the state. Others pursued wars of extermination against the Indians, conflicts that the state underwrote and the federal government paid for.[82]

In the spring of 1852, Congress established an independent Indian Superintendency and appointed Edward Fitzgerald Beale as the first California superintendent.[83] His solution was to place the Indians not on large reservations, as proposed by the three federal commissioners, but on a number of smaller reservations created without benefit of treaties, on existing government lands. Eventually, these small reservations were expected to become self-supporting, much like the former Franciscan missions. In 1853, Congress appropriated money for the establishment of five reservations, the first at Tejon Pass at the southern end of the San Joaquin Valley.

The removal of Beale in May 1854 as superintendent brought no policy change. His successor, Thomas J. Henley, established several additional reservations.[84] During an 1858 tour of the California reservations, J. Ross Browne, a special agent of the United States Treasury Department, not only witnessed poor living conditions but also uncovered evidence of fraud and misuse of funds. Henley was subsequently removed, and by the early 1860s most of the original reservations were closed or abandoned.

Reservation conditions were often aggravated by fiscal problems in the California Indian Superintendency.[85] In addition, few qualified agents were appointed. By the early 1870s, reports of the Board of Indian Commissioners reflected the deplorable condition of the former Mission Indians, who were little more than vassals to white settlers. Since the federal government had failed to recognize Indian land rights under Mexican rule, the report suggested that the Indians be allowed to homestead, "securing to those who now occupy them the little homes and patches on which they or their forefathers have lived for so many years, and allowing those who have none to select them upon any unoccupied land."[86]

The Board of Indian Commissioners' annual reports during the era of Grant's Peace Policy reflected the role of the Methodist Episcopal Church in the selection of agents for California reservations. Under these agents' influence, church services among Indians increased. However, the seven thousand Cahuilla and San Luis Rey Mission Indians in Southern California had neither churches nor schools.[87] With the appointment of Ezra Ayers Hayt as commissioner of Indian affairs during the Hayes administration, church mission boards lost all control over reservations as Hayt removed a

Helen Hunt Jackson, New England author and prominent nine-teenth-century Indian reformer. (Special Collections, Tutt Library, Colorado College)

A young Helen Hunt Jackson as she appeared in the 1860s before she became involved in Indian reform.

Apocryphal postcard claiming that Jackson had written her protest novel *Ramona* in Colorado Springs. In fact, *Ramona* was written in New York City and her inspiration came not from the beauty of Seven Falls but from her travels in Southern California.

Standing Bear, shown here with his family, was the catalyst for Jackson's Indian reforming career. (Special Collections, Tutt Library, Colorado College)

Henry M. Teller, senator from Colorado, secretary of the interior (1882–1885), and friend to Jackson, supporting her activities in behalf of the California Mission Indians. (Special Collections, Tutt Library, Colorado College)

The Reverend Antonio D. Uback, parish priest in San Diego and guide and friend to Jackson during her Southern California trips. (San Diego Historical Society Research Archives)

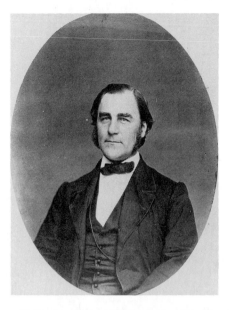

Maj. Edward Bissell Hunt, Helen Hunt Jackson's first husband. (Special Collections, Tutt Library, Colorado College)

Jackson fell down this staircase in her Colorado Springs home and broke her leg. (Special Collections, Tutt Library, Colorado College)

William Sharpless Jackson, Colorado banker and railroad promoter and Helen Hunt Jackson's second husband. (Special Collections, Tutt Library, Colorado College)

The home of Helen Hunt Jackson and William Sharpless Jackson on the northwest corner of Kiowa and Weber in Colorado Springs. Built in 1873, it was purchased the following year by Mr. Jackson, who six years later added one of the first bathrooms in Colorado Springs to the second floor. The house no longer exists, but a re-creation of one of the rooms can be seen at the Colorado Springs Pioneers Museum.

number of church-nominated agents and refused to appoint ministers as agents.[88] The government appointed civilian agents to handle
Indian affairs in California.

By the 1870s, the situation of the California Indian, and especially
that of the Mission Indians, had become critical. The Indian population in the state had declined from approximately 150,000 in 1845 to
a low of 30,000 in 1870.[89] According to an 1852 government report,
the Mission Indians living in Tulare, Santa Barbara, Los Angeles, and
San Diego counties were estimated at about 15,000. Twenty years
later their numbers had dropped to about 5,000, and in his 1881 annual report to the Indian commissioner, Mission Agent S. S. Lawson
estimated that the Indians under his charge numbered only 3,010.[90]

Subjected to a system of apprenticeship approaching slavery and
driven off their lands by encroaching white settlers, the California
Indians, drastically reduced in numbers, faced a dismal future. At
this point in time, Helen Hunt Jackson, fresh from her victories in
behalf of the Ponca, shifted her interest to the Mission Indians. Her
reforming activities in behalf of the Poncas and the California Indians and the work carried on by members of the Women's National
Indian Association, the Indian Rights Association, and the Lake
Mohonk Conference members in her behalf will be the subject of
the remainder of this work.

2

Early Indian Reform Work of Helen Hunt Jackson

By the time Helen Hunt Jackson became interested in the Indians of California, she was already a veteran Indian reformer.[1] Unlike many nineteenth-century reformers, however, Jackson did not have a history of participation in previous humanitarian movements. Instead, her involvement dated from her fall 1879 attendance at one of Standing Bear's lectures in Boston. From the day she first saw the dignified sixty-year-old Ponca chief whose gentle face was "stamped with unutterable sadness"[2] until her death in 1885, she "became what . . . [she] said a thousand times was the most odious thing in life, 'a woman with a hobby.'" She confided to a former abolitionist: "I think I feel as you must have felt in the old abolition days. I cannot think of anything else from morning to night."[3] Longtime friend Thomas Wentworth Higginson, in writing of her commitment, noted that her sympathy for the Indians was natural, "but it was hardly foreseen how strong and engrossing that interest would become."[4]

Jackson's childhood foretold the powerful personality that would later emerge and enable her to become a prominent Indian reformer. She was born Helen Maria Fiske on October 14, 1830,[5] in Amherst, Massachusetts, where her father was a professor of languages at Amherst College. Described as "a child of dangerous versatility and vivacity,"[6] her inquisitive nature enabled her to fit comfortably into the academic circle at the college,[7] as well as in the literary circles of Newport, Boston, and New York. Most importantly, her curiosity served her well during her Indian affairs research.

Well educated and described by some as brilliant, she was not a beautiful woman, although she dressed fashionably. She was, however, a captivating woman because of her "sweet and gracious womanhood, her capacity for love and friendship, her deep sympathy and her immense tenderness." Another described her as possessing a distinguished appearance "with candid beaming eyes, in which kindliness contented with penetration."[8] She was witty, generous, impetuous, and charming.

But Jackson possessed other traits which enabled her to become a noted reformer. To Higginson, she possessed a "soul of fire,"[9] while her good friend Sarah Chauncey Woolsey (who used the pen name of Susan Coolidge) described her as a born radical, accepting "nothing that she had not tested and made sure of."[10] "Tenacity and impulse ruled her fate," and she possessed both "the velvet scabbard and the sword of steel" with the ability to "strongly love, to frankly hate!"[11]

Jackson's inquisitive nature, tenacity, fiery soul, strong emotional feelings, and investigative spirit served her well. Lovingly working in behalf of the oppressed Indians, she sometimes viciously turned upon government officials or others who did not agree with her. She possessed "strong likes and dislikes and some unnecessary prejudices,"[12] which she was at times too quick to act upon. Thus, Jackson seemed obsessed with her new-found cause and acted impetuously, bumping heads with officials. Spirited debates with editors as well as Secretary of the Interior Carl Schurz resulted. Her letters to acquaintances and friends condemned government policies and officials in strong terms.

By the time Jackson embarked upon her crusade in behalf of the Indians, her husband, Edward Bissell Hunt, and both her sons had died. As an escape from personal tragedy, she turned to writing prose and poetry for a living. Ralph Waldo Emerson called her the "greatest American woman poet" and carried one of her sonnets in his pocket.[13] Higginson believed that her poetry "unquestionably" ranked above that of any American woman, with the possible exception of her childhood friend Emily Dickinson.[14]

Needing something else in her life besides her poetry and prose, Helen Maria Fiske Hunt married William Sharpless Jackson in a Quaker ceremony in October 1875. While her second husband, a Colorado Springs banker and railroad promoter, attended to his various business ventures, she continued writing from her new home in Colorado. Missing the stimulating literary excitement of her New England days, in the fall of 1879 she boarded the train for a trip east. Besides visiting friends, she planned to attend Oliver Wendell Holmes's seventieth birthday celebration, hosted by the publishers of the *Atlantic Monthly*, at Boston's Hotel Brunswick on Wednesday, December 3, 1879. Holmes had served as the first editor of the monthly, and most of the guests were contributors to the magazine. Jackson was seated between poet John Greenleaf Whittier and her good friend Charles Dudley Warner, co-proprietor and co-editor of the *Hartford Courant*. Before the distinguished group, Warner read a birthday poem of Jackson's, which incorporated quotations from the more celebrated works of Dr. Holmes.[15]

The month before the birthday party, Jackson had attended the lecture by Ponca chief Standing Bear. This lecture was part of a well-orchestrated tour of various eastern cities to elicit support and to present the Indians' anguish over the loss of their homeland. Indian delegations had toured American cities in the past, but this tour served as a catalyst that launched the Indian reforming careers not only of Jackson but of Thomas Henry Tibbles, assistant editor of the *Omaha Daily Herald*, and Massachusetts Senator Dawes.

The Poncas, living on a 96,000-acre reservation in South Dakota, were a small, semisedentary agricultural Plains tribe whose villages had been visited by such notables as the Lewis and Clark expedition and artists George Catlin and Karl Bodmer. For eight years following the mistaken inclusion in 1868 of their reservation into the Great Sioux Reservation, the peaceful Ponca tribe were plagued by floods, droughts, locust infestations, and continued attacks by both Brulé and Oglala Sioux. Finally, in 1876 Congress appropriated $25,000 to remove them to Indian Territory.

The Poncas resisted, but under strong pressure ten headmen, including Standing Bear, accompanied officials to Indian Territory in early February 1877 to select lands for a new reservation. Disheartened by what they saw, Standing Bear and seven others returned home on foot after being refused transportation. The remaining chiefs, too elderly to travel, were forced to make a selection of land.

Standing Bear's small group struggled home, enduring bitter cold with only thin blankets for warmth. They slept in haystacks when available, ate raw corn, and walked barefoot in the snow when their moccasins fell apart. Barely able to stand on their bloody feet, they struggled onto the Otoe Agency in southern Nebraska. The Indian agent provided them with food and horses. Returning home, Standing Bear continued to oppose removal. He was arrested but later freed by a sympathetic commander who suggested to officials that the removal be abandoned. However, Carl Schurz, secretary of the interior, determined there would be no reprieve, and in April the first party of Poncas headed south. They endured a fifty-nine-day journey in stormy, cold weather. The remaining Poncas suffered a much longer trek marred with heavy rain storms, a tornado, and numerous deaths.

In the fall of 1877, Standing Bear and other headmen met with President Rutherford B. Hayes and Secretary Schurz to ask that they be allowed either to return to their old reservation or join their Omaha kinsmen in Nebraska. Denied both requests, the old chief helplessly stood by as 160 of his people died, including his only remaining son, a victim of malaria. Accompanied by a small party of 30 followers, Standing Bear with the body of his son, who had requested to be buried in the land of his birth, slipped away on the night of January 2, 1879. Often befriended and fed by white settlers, the small group traveled for ten weeks before reaching the Omaha reservation in March. Chief Joseph LaFlesche welcomed them and offered food, land, and seeds.

Troops commanded by Brigadier General George Crook, commander of the Department of the Platte, on orders of Secretary Schurz, arrested the Poncas for leaving Indian Territory without permission. They were temporarily detained at Fort Omaha because their weakened physical condition made it impossible to return them immediately to Indian Territory. During this detention, Crook, accompanied by newspaper editor Thomas Henry Tibbles, interviewed the Indians. Both men were deeply moved by the dignified Indian chief. Crook commented how odd it was that the only people without rights in the country were the original inhabitants. "An Irishman, German, Chinaman, Turk or Tartar will be protected in life and property," he wrote, "but the Indian can command respect for his rights only so long as he inspires terror for his rifle."[16]

Tibbles hired lawyers and through editorials acquainted the public with the Poncas' condition. In *Standing Bear vs. Crook*, Nebraska District Court Judge Elmer S. Dundy declared the Indian a legal "person" with a right to sue for a writ of habeas corpus in federal courts. Once the Indians were freed, Tibbles resigned his editorial post and organized a six-month lecture tour to Chicago, Boston, New York City, Philadelphia, and Baltimore to generate support for their cause.[17] The small tour included Standing Bear, nineteen-year-old Omaha Indian Frank LaFlesche, or "Woodworker," and his twenty-five-year-old sister, Susette, known as "Bright Eyes,"[18] who served as the old chief's interpreter.

The tour began in October 1879 and had its greatest success in Boston where residents opened their hearts and their purses to the visiting delegation. Within two weeks, the tour raised a large sum of money, generated a number of public meetings, and interested prominent citizens, including Massachusetts Governor John D. Long, Boston Mayor Frederick O. Prince, poet Henry Wadsworth Longfellow, Massachusetts Senator Dawes, and Helen Hunt Jackson, in their cause. The city's acceptance of the Poncas was due in part to the personal interest of Delano Goddard, editor of the *Boston Daily Advertiser*. Impressed by the Indian delegation, Goddard made sure his paper covered their daily activities.

In mid-November Jackson showed up at Tibbles' Boston hotel room. He described her as close to fifty, of extraordinary intelligence, and fascinating, "with swiftly changing expressions."[19] Tibbles immediately realized he had an ally. She had come to ask him to look over her *New York Independent* article on the Poncas. Reflecting back over this initial meeting, Tibbles doubted that the Indian's cause would have been so successful without her influence in dealing with congressmen, senators, and editors. Her sharp wit and guile successfully drew supporters to the cause, and her campaigning for money made the tour a success.

According to poet and author Joaquin Miller, Jackson influenced Wendell Phillips to work in behalf of the Indians just as he had worked for the slaves.[20] In December 1879 Phillips wrote a dedication to Tibbles' *The Ponca Chiefs: An Indian's Attempt to Appeal from the Tomahawk to the Courts*. Phillips described this book, which included the full text of Judge Dundy's decision, as "a fair specimen of the system of injustice, oppression, and robbery which the Government calls *its Indian policy*."[21]

Jackson was not averse to making strong demands upon her editorial friends either. To prove that she was "the most prudent woman alive," she asked Warner of the *Hartford Courant* to reprint a Ponca article that had appeared earlier in the *New York Independent*. She admonished him not to be "funny" about the Indians. To make her stand absolutely clear, in a postscript she wrote, "If you're 'agin' the Indians, don't mention the subject when we meet."[22] A month later she demanded that Whitelaw Reid, managing editor and owner of the *New York Daily Tribune*, print an article on the Poncas in a conspicuous place.[23] However, for some unexplained reason, Jackson became annoyed with Reid and in January 1880 angrily wrote to Warner that she would give a thousand dollars for access to a newspaper. "I can't make Reid print my things, and I am chafing under the misery of not saying half I want to."[24]

Jackson continued to rain verbal blows upon friends. She had difficulty understanding why Reverend Moncure Daniel Conway, former Unitarian minister and an abolitionist, did not work in the Indian's behalf. She felt Indians were "higher nobler creatures" and that their condition was far worse than that of the average slave. The Indian was "a prisoner in fact—left to starve—and forced into poisonous climates to die."[25]

In addition to raising money and encouraging her friends to hold receptions in behalf of the Indians, in late November 1879 Jackson decided to use her literary skills to arouse the public. Writing to the editor of the *Tribune,* she called the plight of Standing Bear "a striking illustration of the working of our Indian policy." After recounting his trip from Indian Territory and the final removal, she noted that all he wanted was monetary help to enable his tribe to appeal to the courts for restoration of their lands "from which they had been so unjustly and barbarously expelled."[26]

The Poncas arrived in New York City on December 5 and settled into the Fifth Avenue Hotel.[27] Reporters covered receptions and public meetings, but New Yorkers were not as generous as Bostonians. Jackson, who had energetically thrown herself into her new "hobby" and was busy researching at the Astor Library, was angered. Her dislike "of New York [would] crystallize into a morbid mania at this rate," she wrote. The Indians had come to the city, but the citizens were uncaring. "I have walked, talked, written & spent myself all in vain," she continued. "The Tribune will not say a word for them."[28] However, her accusation seemed unwarranted in view of the newspaper's coverage of the Poncas on December 8, 9, 13, and 15.

Jackson possessed a sharp tongue which she used liberally when she felt she was not getting her way. Whatever the problem was with the *Tribune,* it was soon over. She apologized to Reid for attacking his paper and asked if he would see Tibbles. Her change of heart partially resulted from the newspaper's publication of a letter from her to the editor and an editorial calling attention to it. Jackson's daily research at the Astor Library on various Western tribes had resulted in a wealth of historical information, and she had spent her evenings writing letters to the editors to publicize her findings.[29]

This particular letter, dated December 11, presented ten questions to the public. Jackson asked if the readers were aware that a reservation Indian when raising sheep could not sell the wool nor keep the proceeds? "How many farmers in Vermont or Massachusetts would become, or continue industrious, hard working and contented, under such conditions as these?" she queried. Were the readers aware of the condition of the White River Utes? They were starving, "not simply suffering hunger—starving, dying for want of food," because their annual supplies had been deliberately withheld. She offhandedly wondered if the intention of the government was to "keep the Indians as National paupers."[30]

Jackson also inquired if the public was aware of the condition of the Poncas, whom Schurz in his recently published annual report claimed were now perfectly content and acclimated to Indian Territory. They were not contented, Jackson noted emphatically; instead, they were waiting like exiles while Standing Bear tried to obtain legal redress. Their appeal to the Supreme Court would, if successful, "do for the Indian race precisely what the Emancipation act did for the negro." She wondered how Americans could be so blind to this oppression.[31]

Reading this letter, Secretary Schurz immediately telegraphed the *Tribune* for an interview. His rebuttal, addressing each one of Jackson's ten questions, appeared in the newspaper on December 19. The following day Jackson wrote William Hayes Ward, editor of the *New York Independent*, that she was "about wild with delight." Calling the secretary a blockhead, she was curious if his answer had "helped his cause?"[32] "What glory to have Schurz answer me by telegraph," she confided to Warner. "I had hardly hoped I could do anything for the Indians. Now I see that I can."[33]

The resulting verbal conflict, published in the *Tribune* and the *Boston Daily Advertiser* and later in the appendix of *A Century of Dishonor*,[34] was inevitable, given Schurz's past history as a reformer and Jackson's incredible stubbornness once she began a crusade. In a moving tribute written after her death, Higginson as kindly as possible noted that she was "impulsive in her scorn of mean actions" and "sometimes very unjust to those whom she simply did not understand."[35] Possibly she did not understand the point of view that Schurz was operating from.

Ironically, Jackson had been both a strong and "enthusiastic admirer" of Schurz, refusing initially to believe anything bad of him or allow anyone to say a negative word in her presence. As she continued her research and as the secretary challenged her, her attitude changed. She criticized Schurz in letters to close friends, and before long, letters to powerful members of the literary community reflected her vindictiveness. To Oliver Wendell Holmes and Henry Wadsworth Longfellow in March 1881, she noted her research had prompted her to criticize Schurz. She enclosed one of her articles and a newspaper editorial and added that recently Schurz had developed "such malignity towards innocent people, and such astounding and wholesale lying" that true friends of the Indians should denounce him and his methods.[36] Her crusade seemed not only to be in behalf of the Ponca but against the secretary of the interior.

Schurz was in a somewhat awkward situation. His goal as secretary of the interior was to end incompetence and corruption, not to defend the policies of previous administrations nor to publicly defend the government's Indian policy. In all fairness to him, the Ponca removal, which had created the initial furor, was well underway before he assumed office in 1877. The following year, Indian Commissioner Hayt even admitted the error and asked for restitution; Schurz agreed. Unfortunately, the bill presented by the Interior Department on February 3, 1879, for relief of the Ponca tribe failed to pass Congress.[37] As the condition of the tribe improved, both Schurz and Hayt felt the Poncas should remain in Indian Territory, an opinion strongly supported by the Board of Indian Commissioners in their 1879 report. These Christian philanthropists believed the Poncas were safer in Indian Territory than they had been on their old reservation.[38]

On November 28, 1879, the *Tribune* liberally quoted from the newly released report of the secretary of the interior. Because ample evidence was presented to show that the Poncas were sufficiently acclimated to their new home, Schurz recommended that they probably should be left alone.[39] He also warned against misplaced agitation on their behalf—a reference to the court case and tour. Thus Schurz was already well sensitized and defensive, which probably accounted for his strong reaction to Jackson's letter to the editor.

In his defense, Schurz explained carefully that orders for the Ponca removal were enacted before he assumed office, and since then, both he and the commissioner were doing everything in their power to indemnify the Indians for their losses.[40] Furthermore, they were the first to bring the Ponca problem to the attention of the public. He also refuted Jackson's statement that Indians could not sell their wool.

Jackson's reaction was immediate. Writing to Ward, she noted that "for the statement about the sheep, I had the authority of a former Head Clerk in the Ind. [Indian] Bureau!"[41] Schurz also explained that supplies for the Utes were held up because of an incompetent contractor who had since been tried, convicted, and sentenced to jail. Jackson wanted to know what difference that made to Indians who were starving.

After reading Schurz's reply in the *Tribune,* on December 23 Jackson scribbled another letter answering him point by point. Tibbles and the two Omaha lawyers, not Schurz and the commissioner, were the first to acquaint the public of the issue. She did, however, concede that Schurz's letter of August 23, 1879, which had appeared in the *Advertiser,* "was one of the next noticeable instrumentalities in bringing the 'wrongs inflicted on the Poncas to public notice.'"[42]

Instead of denouncing the secretary and presenting the plight of the Poncas in the newspapers, on January 9, 1880, Jackson wrote him directly, enclosing excerpts from the letter of a Boston woman willing to contribute the remainder of the money needed to prosecute a suit to regain Ponca lands. By February, Bostonians had already contributed over $6,000.[43] Jackson asked if the secretary approved of such a suit, and if not, would he be willing to give his reasons in a clear and explicit form.[44]

Schurz replied that, because the Supreme Court had decided that tribes could not sue in federal courts, any monies collected might be better spent on Indian schools. Furthermore, the solution to the problem of Indian landholding was in legislation transforming tribal title into individual title giving Indians the same protection as white landowners over property.[45] Jackson then inquired if such legislation had ever been presented. The secretary responded in the affirmative, explaining that such bills were now up for consideration. He only hoped the current congress would pass this legislation.[46]

Still not convinced of his culpability, Jackson apologized, noting that her strong interest in the Indians prompted her to write. Less than a week later she informed Ward she would like to show him the long letter from "false souled" Carl Schurz. "I am almost appalled at the way things are pouring in.—& the way the people are waking up at last . . . to our infamy—& the Indians' sufferings," she noted. "The air is thickening with the smoke of this battle for the oppressed," and they were on the "threshold of a great revolution." Then she smugly concluded, "the thieves who have been fattening on the seven millions a year short in our Indian policy, will do well to make all they can this year for the next year they will have small chance."[47]

During the controversial Jackson/Schurz exchange, Tibbles, through his well-staged presentations, continued to keep the Ponca controversy before the public. At the same time, Jackson gained much needed support from a *New York Times* editorial which observed that Schurz had given the impression he did not approve of the attempt to gain legal rights for the Indians through court action. The editor cynically noted that it was regrettable that Schurz did not adequately show "how the giving to an Indian of 160 acres of land can clothe him with civil rights which he does not now possess"— rights which the secretary "thinks that the courts cannot give him."[48]

In early February 1880, a Senate committee began investigating the Ponca situation. Agents, inspectors, prominent clergymen, and Indians, including Susette LaFlesche and Standing Bear, testified. About the same time that the young Omaha Indian woman was on the witness stand, a *New York Times* editorial praised Jackson's efficient activities in behalf of the Indians—work that had attracted public attention.[49]

Jackson's self-satisfaction with her success was expressed in a letter to her sister, Ann Scholfield Fiske (Mrs. Everett Colby Banfield): "I cannot but think that I have already accomplished something in the way of rousing public attention to the outrageous in-justice of our treatment of those poor creatures."[50]

As her research at the Astor Library intensified, Jackson uncov-ered important bits of information about other tribes. The White River Utes caught her attention. In the fall of 1879 they attacked their agency, killing several people, including Agent Nathan Meeker, whose arbitrary policies appeared to be a contributing factor in the uprising. To strengthen the Utes' case, Jackson published provisions of their Brunot Treaty of 1873, explaining how the government failed to remove white trespassers from the reservation as promised. She also inquired if the only resource left to the government to satisfy justice against the twelve men who had attacked the agency and murdered the agent was to fight against "four thousand men, women, and children who not only have done us no wrong but have been for ten years this patient and long suffering under the wrongs we have done to them."[51]

To elicit more sympathy for the Utes, Jackson discussed the Janu-ary 1880 murder of Henry Harris, a Winnebago, by D. Balinska. Ba-linska was arrested, tried, and freed because, according to Jackson, "it was only an Indian that was killed." To show the inequity of pun-ishment for the murder of an Indian as opposed to a white man, she asked if it would be "worth while to ask the Government to com-bine with its efforts to apprehend the murderers of Mr. Meeker some attention to D. Balinska, the murderer of Henry Harris?"[52]

The public outcry against the Ute uprising continued to intensify. To lessen the outrage and gain a more sympathetic following, Jack-son recounted the activities of the Third Colorado Volunteers who under Colonel John M. Chivington had attacked Black Kettle's peace-ful band of Cheyenne and Arapaho in 1864. In a January 31 letter to the *Tribune*, she described atrocities committed by the troops. "Shall we apply the same rule of judgement to the white men of Colorado that the Government is now applying to the Utes?" she inquired. She then compared the 130,000 residents of Colorado, hundreds of whom had participated in the Sand Creek Massacre—and others who had applauded the action—to the 4,000 Utes in Colorado, a dozen of whom had committed murder and rape and some 300–400 of whom had gone to war to prevent soldiers from entering their lands. She wondered if the public could justify Schurz's policy of cutting guaranteed rations of 1,000 helpless Utes. Chivington's meth-ods, at least, were less inhumane: "To be shot dead is a mercy," wrote Jackson, "and a grace for which we would all sue if to be starved to death were our only other alternative." The Utes were being starved not because of weather, blight, or pestilence "but because it lies within the promise of one man, by one word, to deprive them of one-half of their necessary food for as long a term of years as he may please."[53]

Jackson's sympathetic view of the Cheyenne and Arapaho Indians and critical view of Chivington did not find wide support in her home state of Colorado, which less than two decades before had endured Indian hostilities. Furthermore, her pro-Indian writings embroiled her in a controversial exchange of heated letters with the former editor of the *Rocky Mountain News*, William N. Byers. In a letter to the *Tribune* in February 1880, Byers explained that Jackson had ignored much of the background to the Sand Creek Massacre in order to dramatize the condition of the Utes. The Indians at Sand Creek were not under government protection, nor were they peaceful. Instead, Byers explained, they had engaged in plundering along the length of the Platte River Road, evidence of which had been found in their camp. If Jackson had only been in Denver in 1864 to witness the mutilated, scalped, and bloated bodies of the Hungate family, she would have regarded the punishment at Sand Creek as justified. Byers concluded that Colorado soldiers had "again covered themselves with glory."[54]

Unsympathetic to the present condition of the Utes, Byers challenged Jackson, or anyone else, to find a dozen White River male Utes who were not guilty of the massacre at the agency. "I know these Indians well enough to know that these attacks were perfectly understood and deliberately planned," he wrote.[55] Therefore, he strongly believed that Schurz was obeying the law by withholding supplies from the tribe.

In her rebuttal letter dated February 22, Jackson used testimony from the Senate investigation of Sand Creek as proof that the Cheyenne and Arapaho had indeed been under government protection and had committed no depredations. Furthermore, ample testimony for Chivington's defense had been gathered, disproving Byers's accusation that the investigation had been deliberately one-sided. Finally, in refuting Byers's statement that Schurz was obeying the law in withholding rations, she quoted from Schurz's annual report of 1879 in which he had stated that crimes committed by others should not affect the innocent. Any Indians who had remained peaceful and abided by the terms of their treaty were entitled to all benefits and provisions.[56]

This controversial exchange of letters with Byers again forced Jackson to make heavy demands upon her editor friends. On February 22 she visited the *Tribune* office in the hopes of personally delivering to Reid her reply to Byers's "most astounding letter," which had appeared that day. Because his letter was filled with misstatements, she wanted to reply promptly and forcibly. "I am sure as Byers' letter was so direct & gross an attack on me & my statements," she implored, "you will allow me this privilege of an immediate defense of both."[57] Reid, of course, granted her wish.

In a March 4, 1880, letter to Tibbles she noted: "[Byers's] lies have been more astounding even than Kembles [an Indian agent] and Schurz's. I think he will not reply to my last letter." She continued: "If he does, I shall take no notice of him. I have covered all the ground."[58]

In a final attempt to exonerate the white people of Colorado from any blame for Sand Creek, Byers sent a postal card to the editor of the *Tribune*. He not only continued to complain that Colorado never had a fair hearing but also denied that in the case of the White River Utes only twelve men were guilty.[59] Two days after the publication of Byers's letter, Jackson privately wrote Reid that she had overlooked it. "How pitiful and at the same time audacious the man is." She called the situation "simply ludicrous," and asked Reid if he would print her rebuttal.[60]

In her *Tribune* letter, Jackson stressed that Colorado had ample time to present its case on Sand Creek. A congressional investigation and a seventy-three-day military commission held at Denver and Fort Lyon had given Chivington ample time to cross-examine his witnesses. She had also discovered over two hundred pages of testimony to verify her point of view. To elicit more pro-Indian sympathy, she related the cruel incident of an Indian woman who, after catching a soldier's runaway horse, handed the reins to him only to be shot by the soldier who later boasted of his heroic act. "It was by such deed as this that the Colorado soldiers acquitted themselves well, and covered themselves with glory," she concluded sarcastically.[61] This shocking story had been told to her by a senator named Foster who, fifteen years later, trembled when he spoke of it.[62]

This particular rebuttal prompted Jackson's husband, Will, who generally stayed out of his wife's affairs, to comment that it was "a controversial weapon . . . worth all . . . [she] ever did before, put together." Jackson agreed, thanked Reid for publishing it so quickly, and then asked if he wished to take her on as a "fencing pupil." If she were drawn into any more controversies, she definitely wanted him as an instructor.[63]

Jackson's letters reflected hope for the Indian's future. In late January 1880, she commented to William Hayes Ward that reformers were "on the threshold of a great revolution."[64] Success was also represented by her first full-length article on the Indians in *Scribner's*

Monthly in March. Not only did she mention her beloved Poncas, but also she included the sufferings of the Nez Perce during their flight to Canada. Although a positive public sentiment was emerging, Jackson realized the struggle was not yet won, for "arrayed on the other side are the colossal forces of selfishness, greed, love of power; and . . . our national lack of a sense of honor."[65] For the past one hundred years, the country had broken Indian treaties, and she wondered if that meant the country was to continue in the same manner and experience two centuries of dishonor instead of one.

By late March she was again writing to the *Tribune* editor. She listed eleven laws that if enforced would have protected the Indians and resulted in the arrest of unauthorized individuals in Indian Territory. Curiously, she noted, the government had ignored these "dead letter laws."[66] The following month, pleased with a *Tribune* editorial on the Northern Cheyennes and their flight from Indian Territory, she supplied additional facts. Their situation was reminiscent of the Poncas. After suffering needlessly from malaria and other illness following their removal to Indian Territory, they fled in 1878. One of the two bands had been captured and imprisoned. When their food, water, and fuel had been cut off, they escaped, only to find death in their frantic flight.[67]

On May 5, 1880, between hurried letters to editors, she finished a long manuscript, which she called a sketch to avoid criticism for not writing a history which would be too long. "I have put an enormous amount of solid work in it . . . & all the heart & Soul I possess," she wrote Ward, hoping he would publish the five completed chapters as a series in the *Independent*.[68] As early as December 21, 1879, she had confided to Warner that she wanted to write "simply & *curtly* a Record of our Broken Treaties—& call it "A Century of Dishonor." She intended it to be factual not sentimental. "I never so much as dreamed what we had been guilty of," she concluded.[69]

Beginning with a legal brief, which had been sent to two lawyers for approval, on the original right of Indian occupancy, Jackson followed with seven tribal histories and a chapter on massacres of Indians by whites. She criticized the government for repeatedly breaking treaties and allowing frontiersmen to practice "murder, outrage, robbery, and wrongs" against the Indians. She hoped that publication would give Congress the opportunity "to cover itself with a lustre of glory, as the first to cut short our nation's record of cruelties and perjuries!" and to redeem the country's name from the stain of a century of dishonor.[70]

Physically exhausted from her intensive seven-month work in behalf of the Indians, Jackson left the proofreading to Higginson and joined friends on a European tour. Nevertheless, the Indians were seldom far from her thoughts. In a letter from Norway, she thanked a friend for sending along some newspaper clippings about her "beloved Indians" and lamented: "Nothing puts the Indians out of my mind. Except that I know there is nothing to be done this summer."[71] She would take up the fight in the autumn and work until something was accomplished.

Upon returning in early October 1880, Jackson began work on the appendix. Reverend Whipple, Episcopal bishop of Minnesota and a longtime supporter of Indian rights, agreed to write the preface which she felt would "double the value" of the book. In addition, President Julius H. Seelye of Amherst College agreed to prepare the introduction.[72]

During early and middle November, the importance of the presidential elections kept the columns of the New York papers closed to lesser issues. The appearance, however, of a November 22 *Tribune* article, quoting the 1880 annual report of the Indian Office, prompted Jackson to write Reid for space for the Indians. The report mentioned that "meddlesome persons" were trying to encourage the Poncas to leave Indian Territory and return to Dakota, but tribal leaders had assured the agent they were satisfied and did not wish to return. To prove their sincerity, the Indians signed a petition on October 25, 1880, relinquishing all rights to their Dakota lands, requesting in return a title to their present lands.[73]

After reading this article, Jackson angrily wrote Reid how "truly artful, how artistically artful" the secretary had become. The petition was "the climax of the Dept's infamous cunning," she noted.[74] Since over one hundred of the Poncas in Indian Territory had already fled to Dakota, obviously they really were not pleased with that reservation despite what Schurz reported. She noted to another friend, she was glad he saw through that "audacious" annual report. "For pure cheek and lying I never saw its equal," she concluded.[75]

By late November and early December, Jackson's efforts were beginning to pay off, and the public had awakened to the Indian's problem. "I have great hopes," she noted to a friend, but at other times it looked to her "as if Carl Schurz and Satan were a match for God."[76] On a more positive note, she wrote Reid that she was beginning to believe that her *Tribune* articles and the *Tribune* editorials were really aiding the Indian cause.[77] A committee of four men from Boston were looking into the fraud of the "pretended petition," while a committee of bishops, clergymen, and lay people appointed by the Episcopal Convention were to monitor congressional action during the coming winter.

The condition of the Ponca had finally come to the attention of President Rutherford B. Hayes, who on December 8, 1880, noted in his diary, "a great and grievous wrong has been done to the Poncas."[78] Shortly thereafter, he appointed a special commission composed of Generals George Crook and Nelson A. Miles and two civilians, William Stickney of the Board of Indian Commissioners and Walter Allen of the Boston Indian Citizenship Committee, to confer with the Poncas living in Indian Territory and in the Dakotas. After consultation with both groups, in late January the commission recommended that they be allowed to choose whichever reservation they preferred. In March, 1881, Congress appropriated $165,000 as an indemnity for losses sustained during their unfortunate and unnecessary removal. In May, Indian Commissioner Hiram Price authorized the distribution of $10,000 to Standing Bear's group in Dakota because it was the more destitute of the two.[79]

Initially, Jackson reacted strongly against the composition of this commission. In December 1880 she wrote Senator Dawes: "For God's sake . . . don't let that committee go, as it stands." Since Schurz organized it, she was certain that "not a man in it can be absolutely trusted not to be either hoodwinked or influenced, except Gen. Crook."[80] Not only was she unhappy with the commission's membership, but also she was afraid that Schurz intended to "bully, or intrigue, or bayonet" through Congress a bill that would give the Poncas no choice.[81] Fortunately, this did not occur. Jackson's reaction to the final settlement remains unknown. A severe case of chronic bronchitis along with anxiety over her long-delayed trip to California dominated her letters during the early part of 1881.

About the time that the solution to the Ponca controversy was emerging, Jackson's letters reflected an intensification of her dislike for Secretary Schurz. Calling him an "arch hypocrite" in a December 3 letter to Warner, she accused the secretary of presenting himself publicly as an advocate of land allotment "when for *twenty* years the poor creatures have been *begging* for all these things!" She was tired of Schurz flaunting his "philanthropic policy."[82] Three days later when writing Warner about the presidential endorsement of Schurz's plan for Indian education as the only solution to the Indian problem, she vehemently explained: "His plan!—I declare I think I shall burst a blood vessel some day in my indignation at the cheek of that man."[83] Several days later in a letter to Massachusetts Senator Dawes, she called Schurz "a very stupid man" for making false accusations that could be "so easily disproved by his own words."[84]

Her distrust of Schurz continued to grow. She was soon calling him "an unprincipled liar" and hoped that within the next two months the truth about the Poncas would be known and he would "be shown up in a most unenviable light."[85] That same day she wrote Warner that Schurz was "trying to go out in a blaze of glory," blinding people to the "enormities 1st of the System under which he has had his power—second, of the use he has made of that power."[86]

Jackson, in Washington, D.C., during the early part of 1881, accused the secretary of being engaged in a desperate fight because the settlement of the Ponca controversy was her victory. Writing to Ward, she noted that, despite all of his various tricks and lies, Schurz was worse off than before. As an afterthought, she added, "but not nearly so badly off as he deserves to be."[87] Seeing Schurz in attendance at governmental hearings, she wrote she would never forget the "malignity & craft of [his] face—never.—It was a study. I could *paint* it, if I knew how to paint."[88]

Because of her sympathy for the Poncas, Jackson mildly rebuked Ward when he sided with Schurz at one point. She assured Ward if she had time and opportunity, she would convince him how "wicked, insincere, and hypocritical" the secretary had been. As the most "adroit liar" she had ever known, Schurz was posing as a friend and champion of the Indian. But after all, he was "the man who murdered the Cheyennes—the Nez Perces—robbed the Poncas—& cheated the Utes!—all in one four years!"[89]

In early January, Jackson had received a "wet copy" of *A Century of Dishonor*, the first work which openly carried her name. She read it fondly, "but with some terror," she noted to Warner. "I don't know what they'll do to me."[90] The previous May 21, she had signed a contract with Harper & Brothers that guaranteed her ten percent.[91] At first she had not been pleased with the contract, calling its three pages "ponderous" and complaining there was much she did not understand. In addition, some points seemed "hardly fair" to her. Nevertheless, she signed it.[92]

To gain support for the Indian cause, Jackson, accompanied by her husband, interviewed representatives and army officers. In addition, at personal expense she sent copies of her book, bound in blood-red cloth, to each congressman. Embossed on the cover were the words of Benjamin Franklin: "Look upon your hands! They are stained with the blood of your relations."

Neither Congress nor the public responded to *A Century of Dishonor* with much enthusiasm. However, as she mentioned to Warner, some book reviews were better than her wildest hopes, and Schurz had not yet attacked her. Nevertheless, she remained suspicious, afraid he might have something brewing.[93] Later she confided: "My book did not sell—but somehow it stirred things—for you see books, pamphlets, & mag. articles are steadily pouring out on the subject. . . . The world moves."[94]

Although *A Century of Dishonor* did not immediately become a best seller and did not bring about an improvement in Indian affairs, it did lay the groundwork for Jackson's next Indian crusade, that of the Mission Indians of Southern California. Her work had definitely acquainted the public with the deplorable condition of the American Indian and was read with interest by humanitarian reformers who would eventually take up her crusade. But more importantly, her months of research at the Astor Library, her letters to the editors, and her controversies with both Secretary Carl Schurz and former editor William N. Byers gave her the determination and the skills necessary to defend the Mission Indians. This work would prove to be her most lasting legacy.

3

Helen Hunt Jackson's First Visit to the Mission Indians

With the publication of *A Century of Dishonor* completed, Helen Hunt Jackson decided in the spring of 1881 to visit California to study and write several articles about the Franciscan missions. Her trip was unexpectedly delayed until that fall. Making up for the lost time, she visited numerous Mission Indian villages only to learn that their occupants were in danger of losing their lands. Her concerned letters to government officials in behalf of these Indians resulted in her appointment as an official agent commissioned to locate permanent homes for them. Thus, a mere magazine project to pay for her trip west had resulted in an important government appointment.

Jackson's fascination with California began in May 1872 when she and Sarah Chauncey Woolsey headed west for a vacation. Needing a respite from strenuous literary efforts undertaken to assuage the death of her second son, Jackson, accompanied by her friend, had embarked on a two-month trip by train. Jackson's expenses were paid by the *New York Independent*, a widely read weekly that agreed to publish accounts of her trip in sixteen installments.

At Stockton, California, in mid-June the two women transferred from the Central Pacific to a smaller line and finally to a stagecoach. Traveling through old mining towns and scattered vineyards and fruit orchards, they came upon a small Indian settlement, which Jackson described as "too loathsome to be looked at." Shortly after settling into their hotel in Yosemite, she saw an old, half-naked, dirty Indian woman with a child on her back walking along the road. Jackson compared her "vicious-looking hair" to "fringed eaves" and noted that "her soulless eyes dart[ed]. . . . to right and left, in search

of a possible charity."[1] Only a decade later, Jackson would dedi-
cate the rest of her life to helping the Mission Indians of Southern
California.

Yet in the summer of 1872, the California Indians she viewed received much less praise than the climate and the scenery. While describing the Indians she saw in derogatory terms, she described the
days at Yosemite as bursting, flashing, and beginning like "a trumpet
peal."[2] Less than a year later, while incapacitated by a severe case
of diphtheria, she fondly remembered the mild California weather.
Writing to a friend, she declared that during the past eight months
her health had been better than she had ever known. "My trip to
California seemed to have absolutely made me over in all ways. If
ever you get run down go there," she exclaimed, "the air of the
Sierras is enough to revive the dead!"[3]

Almost ten years later, Jackson set about preparing to return to
California, this time accompanied by her husband. "Don't you envy
us the Sun and flowers?" she wrote Warner, informing him she had
been commissioned to write four articles for *Harper's*, which would
pay for the luxuries of the trip. Having suffered from chronic bronchitis for a month, she was looking forward to the warmer climate.
And in her usual humorous way, she informed Warner that "her
bronchial tubes smack their mouths at the thought of the soft air,"
for the climate in New York was fit only for bears and tigers.[4]

On April 2, Jackson's husband, who was to have joined her on
the western trip, telegraphed he was unable to do so because of important bank business in Leadville. Jackson spent days frantically
writing her husband and wildly telegraphing friends, trying to find
someone willing to accompany her west. She wrote Warner that she
was so mad she could not unpack or even work. Generally demoralized, she was spending money wildly. "Total inanition" stared her
in the face.[5]

Not wanting to go alone, she turned down the California sketches
for *Harper's*, which were immediately assigned to another author.
By June, Jackson had left New York and was home in Colorado
Springs. During the summer, she and her husband, accompanied by
a friend, took several trips. With her Indian interest a high priority,
they traveled to New Mexico to see some Pueblo Indians dance on
St. John's Day. In August the couple took a second trip into New
Mexico where they again visited some old pueblos.[6]

In the fall of 1881, Jackson received an assignment from Richard
Watson Gilder to write several articles on California for *Century
Magazine*, which, unlike the *Harper's* articles, would be illustrated
with engravings. The magazine hired an artist to join her.[7] Accom-

panied by her husband, she traveled to New York in late September for six to eight weeks, presumably to continue her research on California before heading West. In early December she left New York by train, arriving in Los Angeles on the 20th.

Jackson's arrival in Los Angeles in the winter of 1881 profoundly affected the lives of the descendants of former Mission Indians from the Franciscan missions of San Diego de Alcalá (established 1769), San Gabriel Arcángel (1771), San Juan Capistrano (1775), and San Luis Rey de Francia (1798). Named by the Spaniards after the missions in which they had once lived, the Diegueño, Gabrieliño, Juaneño, and Luiseño Indians became the beneficiaries of her reforming activities, as would other nearby groups including the Cupeño, Serrano, Ipai, and Cahuilla.[8]

Jackson visited and revisited the Luiseño villages of Pala, Temecula, Pauma, Rincon, Pachanga, Potrero, and La Jolla; the Cahuilla villages; the Cupeño village of Agua Caliente (Kupa) on Warner's Ranch; the Ipai villages of Mesa Grande and Santa Ysabel; and the Serrano village of Saboba.[9]

Their valiant effort to eke out a meager living raising cattle and farming on poor land evoked in Jackson great sympathy, causing her to write of them as a helpless, docile, passive people.[10] But they had not always been docile, for three decades earlier some of these Indians had participated in raids in Southern California. Missionization and acculturation were not readily accepted by all Indians. Many resisted by running away or showing little interest in learning Spanish or steadfastly continuing their traditional customs. Following secularization, the neophytes continued to resist. Some joined in raiding ranchos and running off cattle and horse herds. Others followed emerging new Indian leaders, some of whom were former neophytes, on devastating raids in the southern part of the state during the 1850s. Still others joined in alliance with owners of land-grant ranchos and fought against their own kind.[11]

By the late nineteenth century, however, the former Mission Indians had been subdued, and to Jackson their condition was much worse than that of the Poncas. Although driven from their designated reservation, the Ponca tribe at least was given a new one, albeit not to their liking. The Mission Indians, on the other hand, were not given reservations until 1870. Their former mission lands had been secularized by the Mexican government, and what little tracts they were able to cultivate were often taken by settlers.

Jackson was not the only individual interested in protecting the former Mission Indians. Less than a decade before she arrived in California to write her mission articles and during the same year the

Ponca removal controversy began, J. E. Colburn was trying desperately to aid the Mission Indians. Colburn was in charge of the U.S. Mission Indian Agency in San Bernardino, which served the Indians of San Bernardino and San Diego counties. These Indians had always been self-supporting, but because of increased encroachment upon their dwindling lands, they needed more assistance than in the past. To establish a priority list, the agent divided his charges into those living near or on various ranches and working as day laborers, those living in small, self-sufficient agricultural Indian communities, and finally those few who lived in towns as vagrants. He strongly recommended that the Indian Office help the self-supporting agricultural group. The Indians had already been driven from the best places years ago, and Colburn feared that most of the few tracts they now held could not be preserved. Therefore, he highly recommended the establishment of permanent reservations.[12]

In August 1877, Colburn wrote to John Q. Smith, commissioner of Indian affairs, that John, captain, or leader, of the Morongo band of Mission Indians, had traveled almost one hundred miles to Los Angeles for advice. John and a few families had lived for a number of years in El Potrero, a small village protected by a Mexican grant and located in San Gorgonio Pass near Banning. Carefully utilizing the nearby creek water for irrigation purposes, the Indians had successfully raised a few crops. However, under the terms of the 1877 Desert Land Act,[13] an American named Helmick had acquired land nearby and monopolized the water, rendering El Potrero uninhabitable. Colburn recommended that an executive order be issued immediately, setting this land aside as a reservation.[14] Eventually, the Morongo Reservation was created but not without numerous challenges from and direct trespass by local white settlers.

Colburn's replacement, S. S. Lawson, echoed similar sentiments. In the fall of 1878, the new commissioner, Hayt, informed Lawson that there already was sufficient land set aside for the El Potrero group. New at the position and unfamiliar with the topography, Lawson consulted with the deputy U.S. surveyor and made a personal tour of the area east of San Bernardino. In a November 28, 1878, letter to Hayt, Lawson described the terrain as a sandy desert with no water or vegetation within thirty miles, an area not suitable for agriculture. He also urged Hayt not to insist upon the Indians' removal yet. In the meantime, Lawson had located suitable land to the east with a splendid stream and sufficient arable and pasture land for a reservation, but the government would have to buy out the claimants—an expense Lawson estimated at $5,000.[15]

Within three weeks, Lawson forwarded a letter from the attorney of the woman who had inherited the rancho surrounding El Potrero and currently held a patent issued in July 1878 to village lands. Claiming the Indians were monopolizing the land, she totally disregarded the fact that they had lived there for generations. Already, two cases against the Indians were pending in federal court, one for ejectment and a second for forcible trespass. Lawson's letter to the commissioner reflected his personal frustration. "Between thieving white men who would defraud them of their rights, and avaricious lawyers who have robbed them of their money," he wrote, "the Indians were being ground between two mill stones."[16] Lawson criticized the legal profession. In the past two years certain San Diego lawyers had already charged over two thousand dollars in money and stock for services rendered to the Indians. Extortion, Lawson called it, and his suit against the lawyers was still pending.[17]

To generate support for a Mission Indian reservation, Lawson explained to Representative P. D. Wiggington that only a fraction of tillable land had been reserved for Indian use. Believing that a "crisis" had been reached, Lawson was "utterly unable to account for the indifference with which their situation has been regarded by the Government."[18] He insisted that, to enable the Indians to become self-sufficient, land must be purchased. But no action was taken.

Agent Lawson persisted in his attempt to convince the commissioner of the aridity of the desert. In January 1879, he visited lands suggested by Hayt as suitable for the El Potrero Indians. Whenever he found sufficient water, however, that water was owned or utilized by white settlers. Other than the land the El Potrero group currently occupied, Lawson could find no place to relocate them.

Again he reminded Commissioner Hayt of the area only five miles from the present El Potrero location and large enough to accommodate all the Mission Indians in the southern part of the state. This tract called San Gorgonio was adjacent to the Southern Pacific Railroad lands. Although desert, water was available on nearby government-owned timber land and could easily be obtained. Lawson tried to convince Hayt that with irrigation the Indians could raise crops, run stock, and cut timber for the railroad as an additional source of employment. Unfortunately, several claimants would have to be bought out. In closing, Lawson apologized for his "persistent endeavors," but he sincerely wanted to help these Indians.[19] Believing so strongly in the reservation, he even offered to appear personally before the House Committee on Indian Affairs if it would help expedite matters.[20]

Lawson may have approved of the location for his proposed reservation, but the former San Luis Rey Mission Indians and others did not. Over one thousand Indians from the villages of Temecula, La Jolla, Saboba, Pauma, Pala, Potrero, Rincon, and San Luis Rey signed a petition requesting the right to continue living on lands peacefully occupied for generations. They described San Gorgonio as a sterile, unfit country.[21] Although he bitterly criticized this action, Lawson nevertheless forwarded the petition to the commissioner on March 26, 1879.

When the House committee recommended the passage of a March 1878 Bill to Provide for the Consolidation of the Mission Indians of California, calling for the creation of a reservation, Lawson wrote Hayt expressing his satisfaction.[22] Yet Congress was not willing to pass legislation to guarantee former Mission Indian lands.

In February 1879, Lawson informed Commissioner Hayt of the possible ejectment of the San Jacinto Indians from their village on the San Jacinto Ranch. The mission agent requested that these Indians be protected in their homes and land.[23]

Two months later he wrote of the possible ejection of additional Indians. Captain Wilcox, the owner of the Santa Ysabel Ranch, demanded the removal of Indians from his land within the year so he could rent it out. In addition, John Gately Downey, governor of California from 1859 to 1861, demanded the removal of the Agua Caliente Indians from Warner's Ranch, which he had recently purchased in April 1880.[24] Already those Indians at San Pasqual had been removed by the sheriff and forced into the mountains. And finally, the Potrero group were still in danger. Prostitution, disease, and drunkenness merely added to their deplorable situation. Lawson wanted to know what was going to happen to the Indians when driven out of their homes with no other place to go now that Congress had not acted on the reservation.[25] No one seemed to care about the gravity of this situation but Lawson, who continued to push for a reservation.

In April 1879, Hayt was advised of the problems of the Cahuilla Indians whose village, when surveyed, was found to be on a railroad section. A local white man had filed on this section, had taken possession of the chief's house, and was threatening to drive all the Cahuilla from their village. After communicating with the Southern Pacific Railroad, Lawson learned that the man really had no "reserved right" and because the Indians had a history of long residence and improvements, they had a prior claim. He informed Hayt: "Now [the Indians] . . . stand in the same relation to the land on which their village is located as the white man—with this advantage, that they were there first and have made the improvements."[26] When the man was notified to leave and refused, Lawson requested advice.

Still persistently trying to secure a reservation, Lawson informed Roland E. Trowbridge, Hayt's replacement, that three years ago lands cultivated for a dozen years by eighteen families of San Luis Rey Indians had been fraudulently entered upon by whites under the Desert Land Act. The agent requested this land be set aside by executive order.[27] On March 8, 1881, Lawson learned that his request had finally been granted.[28]

By summer 1881 Lawson was actively protecting the land of the Capitán Grande Indians of the Diegueño tribe whose reserve had been set apart on December 27, 1875. Because the original grant of land was uninhabitable, the Indians had moved off the reservation. Now trespassers were encroaching upon these new lands, especially those belonging to Ignacio, the band's leader, or captain. Lawson requested additional sections be set aside by executive order. After some investigation, Commissioner Hiram Price, appointed in May 1881, finally explained in March 1883 that Charles Hensley had homesteaded part of the land on June 1, 1881, followed by James Mead on February 1, 1882. Since this was the same land occupied by Ignacio, Price noted that the entries could be contested.[29]

Although both Colburn and Lawson had actively worked in behalf of the Mission Indians, they had been generally unsuccessful, partially because Grant's Peace Policy was coming to an end and reformers had not yet taken up the Mission Indian's cause. That changed in the winter of 1881 when Helen Hunt Jackson arrived in Southern California. She found the most miserable of the few remaining Mission Indians living near San Diego in shapeless mounds of "refuse and brush, old blankets, old patches of sailcloth, old calico, dead pine boughs, and sticks." She had never seen "so loathsome" living conditions, even in the wilds of Italy, Bavaria, Norway, or New Mexico.[30]

Arriving in Los Angeles on December 20, 1881, she settled into the elegant, three-storied Pico House. A month later she set out for Santa Barbara and then to San Diego, Riverside, and San Bernardino. Jackson then returned to Los Angeles in April 1882 to await the arrival of the artist hired to illustrate her four *Century* articles.

Her impressions of California were vividly expressed in letters to friends. To William Hayes Ward, she noted she wished she could write a book instead of magazine articles, for she found the old missions to be of "inexhaustible interest."[31] To Thomas Bailey Aldrich, editor of the *Atlantic Monthly*, she described California as a "topic of color and song." "It is real pain to have to skim over it flying as I do," she continued. "Whoever will come & live on this coast, can make a book of romance which will live."[32] Two years later her own prophesy came true as she began writing her romantic novel, *Ramona*. In another letter to Aldrich she wrote of picturesque Franciscan missions every thirty miles and brown faces with their dark eyes. "I did not dream how much those old Friars had done," she remarked.[33]

Although fascinated by the missions, Jackson was more interested in the condition of their former occupants. Following secularization, the parceling out of small tracts of former mission lands to heads of households and adult Mission Indians did not occur. In addition, those lands held in common for grazing purposes were not turned over to the Indians. Mission administrators could not bring themselves to give up such valuable land to the Indians. Since many original Mexican land grants included clauses protecting the Indians on the lands they occupied, some continued to live and farm lands tenuously protected by these clauses, yet others scattered to inaccessible fertile valleys and mountains. When the "easy-going, generous" Mexican sold his land to the American, the position of the Indian worsened. Thus Jackson, in her 1883 report to the commissioner of Indian affairs, summarized the history between secularization and the conquest of California as "a record of shameful fraud and pillage, of which the Indians were the most hapless victims."[34]

During her first Los Angeles visit, Jackson, through the auspices of the Right Reverend Francis Mora, bishop of Monterey and Los Angeles, met Antonio F. Coronel, former inspector of the southern Indian missions for the Mexican government and a lifelong friend of the Indians. She described the old gentleman as sixty-five years of age, yet young in spirit, with a "memory like a burning-glass bringing into sharp light and focus a half century as if it were a yesterday."[35] She sat for hours in the Coronel family's comfortable adobe home in the western suburbs of Los Angeles, surrounded by orchards, vineyards, and orange groves, listening to him relate the past while his wife, Mariana, translated.

Antonio Coronel entertained Jackson with stories of his travels from Mexico to California and his adventures during the American conquest. Sometimes he strummed his guitar and sang. His vivid stories of early California and its Indian inhabitants stirred her conscience. He helped draw up an itinerary of old ranches and missions she could visit to gain materials for her *Century* articles.

Jackson left Los Angeles in late January 1882 for Santa Barbara. Along the way she visited San Fernando Mission and was received cordially by the custodian, who was a friend of Antonio Coronel. At the suggestion of the Coronels, she next stopped at Camulos, the ranch owned by the del Valle family, which later figured so prominently as the Moreno home in *Ramona*. Located near Piru, some sixty miles northwest of Los Angeles, this ranch still retained much of the old California rancho charm. She also visited the Elwood Cooper Ranch some fourteen miles from Santa Barbara.[36] Arriving in Santa Barbara in late January, she remained a month.[37] A visit to the Santa Bárbara mission not only acquainted her with the Franciscans, who lent her books for further study from their library, but also Father Francisco de Jesús so impressed her that, when writing *Ramona*, she used him as a model for Father Salvierderra.[38]

Jackson arrived in San Diego aboard a steamer from Santa Barbara[39] the first week of March 1882 and settled in at the Horton House, the finest hotel in the area. A letter of introduction to David Cronyn, minister of the Unitarian church, enabled her, through him, to meet prominent citizens including businessman Ephraim W. Morse and his wife, who gave her valuable information for her articles.

The vicinity of San Diego offered tremendous research potential for both old Spanish missions and their former residents.[40] The first Franciscan mission in upper California, San Diego de Alcalá, had been established in San Diego. Neighboring San Luis Rey, founded three decades later, was one of the most beautiful in Alta California.[41] As San Luis Rey Mission extended its influence twenty miles away to the Pala Valley, a granary and later a chapel, or *asistencia*, were established on the San Luis Rey River in the summer of 1816 and called San Antonio de Pala.[42] By the time Helen Hunt Jackson arrived at Pala, the chapel and other church buildings had fallen into ruin. In addition to San Diego and San Luis Rey, San Juan Capistrano, founded in 1776, was not too far distant. Finally, the hills and valleys surrounding San Diego held remnants of the Mission Indians.

Accompanied by Father Anthony D. Ubach, parish priest in San Diego and later model for Father Gaspara in *Ramona*, Jackson got a firsthand look at the villages of Temecula and San Pasqual. The San Pasqual Valley, set aside by executive order in 1870 as a reservation, had been recently preempted by white settlers following the revocation of the order a few years later. Father Ubach could remember when the village had a population of three hundred and over six hundred acres of good farm land.

In the winter of 1882, however, all Jackson and Ubach found of the former Indian village in the beautiful valley with its "soft-contoured hills" was the chapel and cemetery and a dozen adobe houses all but one occupied by white intruders. A small white settlement now occupied the village site. Only one native labored for the farmers who had dispossessed his people; the remainder had "fled into secret lairs like hunted wild beasts."[43] However, the Indians respected and trusted Father Ubach, and when he came to say Mass, several hundred came out of hiding.

Claims to the Temecula Valley, the home of descendents of the San Luis Rey Mission Indians, had been based on a protective clause in an old Mexican land grant; but a suit was brought by settlers in a San Francisco district court in 1873 to recover certain lands, including the Temecula Valley. The Indians unsuccessfully pleaded their case. Ordered to leave by the sheriff, they carried their roof tiles as they walked behind their wagons. Some moved three miles away to Pachanga Canyon, described by Jackson as a "dreary, hot little valley, bare, with low, rocky buttes . . . [and] not a drop of water in it." Only sadness "stamped indelibly by generations of suffering, [and] immovable distrust" showed in the faces that Jackson saw.[44]

She watched the women of the village carry water jugs on their heads or busily make baskets or beautiful handmade lace for sheets and pillow cases, an art learned during the mission era. On June 27, 1882, Pachanga was set aside as a reservation by an executive order of President Chester A. Arthur. When Jackson returned the following May 1883, her first thought was that "all persons who still hold to the belief that Indians will not work" should see the valley.[45] Four times the amount of grain had been planted, corrals built, orchards started, and a government school constructed.

Unknown to Jackson, in 1882 and 1885 the government issued patents to two tracts of land within the reservation to Peter Mouren, a French immigrant who had been grazing his sheep at Pachanga for several years. In 1894 the government instituted a suit against Mouren to revoke the patents because an Indian agent alleged that they had been obtained fraudulently. The case was dismissed in 1901; in November 1978 the Pachanga band of Mission Indians filed a case in the District Court in Los Angeles to regain these two tracts of land.[46]

Totally unaware of the potential future controversy for those at Pachanga, Jackson was more interested in the current condition of the Indians at San Pasqual and Temecula. She believed that a "monstrous injustice" had resulted from a combination of events—the cruelty and greed of Americans and ignorance, indifference, and neglect by government officials.[47] Her sentiments closely echoed those of Agent Lawson who, after touring San Jacinto, Temecula, Pala, and Rincon, wrote Commissioner Hayt in December, 1878, that the wrongs inflicted upon these Indians marked "the blackest page in our Indian history."[48]

While Jackson was writing about the Indians in Pachanga Canyon, Mission Agent Lawson was actively trying to help another group of

Temecula refugees. The captain of a band of thirty families, who had settled on government land on a mesa adjacent to the Temecula Ranch, came to the agency to consult Lawson. About 1880, these San Luis Rey Indians moved onto the mesa, sunk wells, and began farming. Their first crop yield was good, but they were now fearful they might be driven off. Lawson was well aware of the government policy against creating numerous small, isolated reservations, but he nevertheless informed Commissioner Price that this tract should be reserved. Angered by years of apparent government neglect, Lawson, rather than see injustice continue, threatened to personally reserve government land now occupied by the Indians.[49] Whether or not he attempted to carry out his threat is unknown, but his sheer frustration was apparent.

Ironically, both Jackson and Lawson wanted the same thing for the Mission Indians, but as in her dispute with Carl Schurz and William Byers, Jackson soon came to view Lawson as an enemy, not an ally. She began a letter-writing campaign against him that may possibly have been a factor in his resignation in the fall of 1883.

In April 1882, Jackson visited Saboba, in the San Jacinto Valley, at the foot of the San Jacinto Mountains. She found fields of wheat, peaches, and apricot orchards, irrigation ditches, and substantial adobe houses belonging to the 157 residents, members of the Serrano tribe, who had lived in the mountains for decades. The Mexican government had issued a grant of land near their village to José Antonio Estudillo on December 21, 1842. In March 1851 this grant was confirmed to Estudillo's survivors by the United States District Court. The initial survey had not included the Indian village, but the 1878 survey, patented on January 17, 1880, mistakenly included all the farms, streams, and the village itself. Part of the original grant had recently been sold to M. R. Byrnes, a San Bernardino merchant, who wanted the Indians removed. Jackson feared that the residents at Saboba were in danger of losing their lands like those at Temecula and San Pasqual, "just as truly as if at the point of the bayonet."[50]

At the time of Jackson's visit there were some thirty to forty students enrolled in the government school at Saboba. Mary Sheriff, the Pennsylvania teacher who had formerly taught freedmen, escorted Jackson around the village and encouraged the children to come forth with offers of candy. One evening the two women drove the three miles to Corove, the home of Victoriano, his daughter Rosaria, and grandson José Jesús Castillo. The boy's great-grandfather had settled in the valley more than one hundred years before. The Castillo family owned a good adobe home with livestock, a vineyard, and two orchards located in a beautiful canyon.[51] Realizing that Jackson was sympathetic, Mary confided her fears that the Indians would soon lose their village.

Faced with a new dilemma, Jackson returned to Los Angeles by April 10 to await the arrival of Henry Sandham, the young Canadian artist hired to illustrate the *Century* articles, and to reflect upon Mary Sheriff's fears. With the fate of the Saboba village foremost in her mind, in early May, Jackson wrote Henry Teller, secretary of the interior. After relating the condition of the Mission Indians, she explained that without government protection they would be driven off their lands.[52]

In late April, accompanied by Sandham who needed to do some sketching, Jackson took a ten-day jaunt to Temecula, Mission San Juan Capistrano, and the Pala Valley. Watered by both the San Luis Rey River and the Pala Creek, the valley was, like Temecula, a mission outpost. Within the valley were the settlements of Pala, Pauma, Apeche, La Jolla, and Rincon. Pala was a favorite spot of the Indians, and in the 1830s over a thousand would gather at the chapel for weekly Mass. Now the dilapidated old church was only half full during service.

The trip to Pala had been a difficult one, requiring a full day's travel by horse from San Juan Capistrano. Following a faintly worn trail up sloping cliffs, Jackson and Sandham entered a mesa carpeted with flowers of yellow, blue, lavender, white, and scarlet. The thousands of acres they journeyed through were owned now by one man, whose father had originally stolen it from the Indians. Passing his buildings and herds, the weary travelers arrived at Pala late at night. The pealing of the old bronze mission bell led them to the few remaining houses. Unable to find accommodations at the small adobe building which served as store and inn, they tried a second house and were invited to spend the night by the old woman, the widow of an Austrian colonel, and her son.[53]

While Jackson and her party were in Pala, a memorial service was being held for an old Indian woman. One of her daughters invited them to Potrero for the night of April 25, 1882. Located in a mountain meadow some ten miles from Pala, Potrero (not to be confused with El Potrero) was reached only by a difficult trail. Once there, however, Jackson settled down comfortably in a neatly made bed with lace-trimmed sheets and pillow cases, unaware until morning that most of the family had spent the night on the earthen floor in the kitchen. In the morning she was handed a gilt-edged mug with water to brush her teeth and ate a meal of chicken, rice, and chile set out on a clean tablecloth and served on china. Her host saw them safely on their way early in the morning.[54]

The villages of Rincon and Pauma lie between Potrero and Pala. At Rincon, a village of two hundred, Jackson and Sandham found fields of barley, wheat, hay, and peas, as well as flocks of sheep and a herd of cattle peacefully grazing. The Pauma village on the San Luis Rey River was located at the Pauma Ranch. The Indians' right to the free use of arable lands as well as pasturage for livestock was tenuously guaranteed by a clause in the original 1844 land grant to José Antonio Serrano.[55]

At the end of the month, the travelers headed back to Los Angeles where Jackson again settled into the comfortable Kimball Mansion boardinghouse. Another resident was Abbot Kinney. One evening the young man was seated beside her at supper.[56] After a long visit with him, Jackson realized she had found another sympathetic ear as well as a good friend.

Born in New Jersey, Kinney possessed a vast fortune acquired when the family cigarette business was purchased by a New York trust.[57] Educated in France and Germany, he was a well-read, experienced world traveler. Since Jackson had also visited Europe twice, once in 1868 and a second time recuperating from researching and writing A Century of Dishonor, the two dinner companions discussed the sights of Europe. But Kinney, much to Jackson's delight, was also interested in the Indians. He not only spoke Spanish but was acquainted with California land laws. She inquired if he would be willing to accompany her on another tour of the Indian villages; he agreed. A very strong bond was soon forged between this wealthy young man and the tiny, matronly New England author.

In early May, now joined by Will Jackson, they made preparations for a twenty-day journey to Monterey. Before setting out, however, her concern for the Indians at Saboba prompted Helen Jackson to write Mary Sheriff requesting that she have José Jesús Castillo write a letter to Secretary Teller about the Saboba land; the two women had discussed this idea during their April visit. Jackson requested the letter be sent to Monterey prior to June 7 to insure its safe arrival.[58]

From San Francisco in mid-June, Jackson wrote Teller that she hoped he would be able to do something "sharp and decisive for the protection of all these old Mission Indians." But more importantly, she wanted to do something herself. She assumed it would be out of the question and even preposterous for the Interior Department to send a woman to investigate the conditions of the Indians and write the report, but she added, "That is what I would like above all things, and I believe I am capable of writing judiciously and with exactness, even when I feel intensely."[59]

Upon receipt of her letter, Teller wrote Commissioner Price requesting him to reply to Jackson's letter and authorize her to visit the Mission Indians for the federal government. Her task was to locate suitable lands within the public domain that could be set aside as permanent reservations for those Indians who did not yet have a reservation. Jackson should also furnish detailed descriptions of any lands, thereby enabling the department to draft executive orders setting them aside.[60]

Price, following an informal examination at the General Land Office of the Interior Department in order to respond to Jackson's letter, discovered that the grant of land at Saboba to the Estudillo family had been confirmed. Nevertheless, he agreed that Jackson should visit the grant and try to find suitable lands for the Indians after the completion of a grant survey. In the event she did not find sufficient lands in that area, she was authorized to locate other lands that would be set aside by executive orders. He even suggested some grantees might be willing to at least sell lands including Indian villages.[61]

Unaware of the positive reception of her letter by both Secretary Teller and Commissioner Price, Jackson, accompanied by her husband, Kinney, and Sandham, boarded the steamer *Los Angeles* for Santa Barbara. Both Kinney and Will Jackson were interviewed by a *Santa Barbara Daily Press* reporter, who, impressed by the distinguished group, informed his readers that only good will would result from their Southern California visit.[62]

Jackson and her friends were the guests at the Elwood Cooper Ranch for two days before heading overland to Monterey. A few miles from the mission of San Carlos Borromeo on the Carmel River, they found "the most picturesque of all the mission Indians' hiding places."[63] Tucked away in nooks and crannies were eight to ten Indian houses of adobe or tule reeds surrounded by fields of corn, barley, potatoes, and hay.

The Jacksons sailed to Oregon from San Francisco in June. Because Will Jackson could only spare two weeks from his business, the couple made a hasty trip to Victoria and Puget Sound. However, this was sufficient time for his wife to write the two Oregon articles she promised the *Atlantic*. On July 3 they sailed for San Francisco where Helen Jackson had arranged to work in The Bancroft Library, finishing up the research for her *Century* articles on the missions.[64] The large private library was owned by Hubert Howe Bancroft, businessman and historian who had begun collecting western Americana in the 1860s.

In addition to her research, she took time to write Antonio Coronel for any legal documents or deeds defining the Temecula Indians' right to their land. She needed this additional information for a special description of the Temecula settlement, to be included in her *Century* article on the Mission Indians.[65]

In San Francisco she learned from Commissioner Price of her appointment to visit the Mission Indians. As a special agent, she would offer recommendations to the Indian Office but would not have the full duties or powers of a Mission Indian agent. Nonetheless, she wrote him that "nothing would give . . . [her] greater pleasure than to aid . . . in securing homes for the Mission Indians in Southern California."[66]

Jackson had requested that Kinney be allowed to accompany her. Teller agreed. In a September 16 letter informing the secretary that Kinney would be pleased to serve, she noted she now had "more courage to undertake" the task because of his assistance. She described the young man as "clear-headed, well informed, and indefatigable in going to the bottom of everything he undertakes." He affectionately called her General. She believed they could write a report which would result in the passage of a bill which Teller could frame "so to cover the ground once for all, and leave that fragment of the Indian race safe for all time from the avarice of white men."[67]

Jackson also informed the secretary that it would take at least three to four months to look over the land, visit villages, and examine land titles. She estimated her personal living expenses to be approximately $1,200. Her time "in easy literary work" was worth on the average of $200 a month, however, she was willing to forgo that "If . . . [she could] be of any real service in getting permanent provisions made for these poor creatures."[68] She intended to even visit those villages that Agent S. S. Lawson had not yet seen.

Teller in mid-October informed her that he had a small civilization fund and would provide for her expenses. Two days later Commissioner Price reaffirmed reimbursement for expenses incurred by both her and Kinney. A sense of justice demanded that unprincipled white men should not be allowed to deprive the Indians of "the fruits of their labor," Price noted.[69] He also informed Jackson that Congress had repeatedly been told the condition of these Indians but had so far not acted in their behalf.

During the fall of 1882, Jackson remained in Colorado Springs writing her *Century* articles.[70] Apparently, several created some concern. In an October 28 letter, she mentioned her mission articles were historical and "are not & from the nature of the case could not be, in the least sensational nor in any way calculated to raise 'hair on end.'" She earnestly believed that these "articles have far more real value & substance than anything merely 'descriptive' I have ever done."[71]

In addition to reworking her *Century* articles, Jackson had given her appointment to investigate the condition of the Mission Indians great thought. Writing to Commissioner Price, she outlined what she understood to be the "scope and interest" of their investigation. She listed four matters to examine: the number and location of Mission Indians, what government lands were available for reservations, what other lands could be purchased, and how the Indians felt about moving onto reservations. She believed, from what she had learned during her prior visits to the villages, that they would "rather die than be removed." If her ideas met with his approval, she requested that he put them into a "letter of specific instructions" giving her full authority with all land offices in the various counties in Southern California. She also requested that Kinney receive a separate letter of authorization, guaranteeing his expenses.[72]

In his response, Price concurred that her four points covered her duties. He also agreed that many of the Indians would prefer to continue in their settlements, working as day laborers. He cautioned that she was not to feel obligated to visit every village and ranch and take an official census but to instead use the services of the Indian agent and others.

Price also accepted the additional expense of the interpreter she had requested. To save money, however, he suggested that at times they use the agency interpreter, provided Agent Lawson could spare him. Further, he requested she take accurate and minute descriptions of any recommended lands to be set aside or purchased. He reaffirmed payment of her expenses and those of Kinney but recommended that accurate records of all expenditures be kept. She would not be able to get an advance unless she furnished a bond.[73]

The same October day she wrote to Price, she penned a letter to Warner. Bedridden because of her chronic bronchitis, she mentioned her appointment as an agent for the Indian Office to report on the condition of the Mission Indians. Rejoicing in the opportunity to do this work, she informed him she had faith that she would write a report that would reach the hearts of the congressmen. "There is not in all the Century of Dishonor, so black a chapter as the history of these Mission Indians," she wrote. "Peaceable farmers for a hundred years—driven off their lands like foxes & wolves—driven *out* of good adobe homes & the white men who had driven them out, sitting down calm & comfortable in the houses!" Her *A Century of*

Dishonor had not sold, she told him, but it had stirred things up and various publications were beginning to appear on the subject. "I'm no saner on the Indian question than I was,"[74] she concluded.

Once she had her appointment confirmed, she wrote Henry Chandler Bowen of the *Independent* about her upcoming visit to the Indian villages and wondered if he might be interested in a series of articles describing what she saw. She had received $1,250 for the five papers accepted by the *Century* but was only asking $250 from him for the six suggested articles.[75]

The high altitude in Colorado Springs and the approaching winter months always brought a fear of a recurring bout of chronic bronchitis. Therefore, Jackson's thoughts at that time of the year always turned to her annual trip east. By the end of October, she was bedridden. On November 15 she boarded the train for New York, intending to stay several weeks before heading for Boston. Her husband would spend a month with her in December, and when he returned to Colorado Springs, she would return to Southern California to undertake her investigative duties among the Mission Indians.

4

Helen Hunt Jackson:
Official Agent to the
California Mission Indians

Writing on January 15, 1883, from her hotel room in New York City, Jackson thanked Commissioner Price for the copy of her appointment as special agent to the Mission Indians. She had accepted his stipulation that the total expenditure would not exceed $2,100 and planned to start west in February, but a severe case of influenza kept her shut up in her rooms.[1] At mid-month she informed Bowen of the *Independent* that she intended to take detailed notes and would write the articles for him during the summer. She requested he put a notice in the paper concerning her assignment to report on the Mission Indians for the Interior Department. She also wrote Aldrich of the *Atlantic Monthly* and inquired if he might be interested in any narratives of her journey.[2]

By February 22, after four nights on the train, she was somewhere in Kansas. Her health had improved sufficiently that five days later, from Los Angeles, she wrote Aldrich that Southern California took "the palm for all the world for climate."[3]

In good spirits and with renewed health, she wasted no time in beginning her government assignment. She first visited the Land Office to learn what lands had been patented to homesteaders and what remained available for Indian use. Next she met with Henry T. Lee, a United States Court commissioner and learned that the initial step in protecting Indian land rights was to order a survey, locating their lands in relation to those held by white claimants. Finally, she wrote Secretary Teller, requesting a survey of the San Ysidro Indian lands which had recently been filed on.[4]

The San Ysidro were former Mission Indians from San Luis who for generations had lived in the San Ysidro Canyon, a few miles from

Warner's Ranch. Under the Homestead Act, on January 18, 1883, Armon Cloos had filed on land at the lower end of the canyon—land including the village itself. A decade earlier, Chatham Helm had purchased sections adjoining the village at the upper end of the canyon. Helm had not only moved his fences several times, incorporating Indian fields, but also once murdered an Indian. He then filed a homestead claim. Hemmed in by these two men, the San Ysidro Indians had only the water that Helm permitted to enter the canyon. One Indian child had already died of starvation. The desperate Indians appealed to Agent Lawson but met with no success.[5]

The survey requested by Jackson was to show what village lands had been lost by the replacement of the fences and what lands remained to be defended. Teller's letter was directed to Commissioner Price who notified Jackson there were no funds for such surveys. Apparently, these lands had already been surveyed. He suggested she check the files of the land office in Los Angeles.[6]

Based on this new information, Court Commissioner Lee saw only two alternatives. An executive order could be issued setting aside the land as a reservation, or the Indians could apply for the land under the 1875 Indian Homestead Act.[7] The latter course of action, Lee noted, required that the Indians sever tribal relations—an act he assumed they were unwilling to do. They could contest Cloos' entry on the grounds of their prior settlement only if they followed this latter course.

Lee also suggested that Jackson and Kinney employ an attorney because the unscrupulous settlers holding Indian lands had their own attorneys. In answer to her question of whether an Indian living on public lands could contest the homestead entry of a legally qualified settler and still maintain his tribal affiliation, he replied in the negative. The Indian had no standing in the courts, and if he pleaded equity before the court, he would be asked why he did not sever tribal relations and enter the land under the Indian Homestead Act.[8]

Searching through the files as Price had suggested, Jackson discovered a letter from the General Land Office in Washington dated May 16, 1877, ordering the tract known as the San Ysidro ranchería to be withdrawn from public sale or entry until an executive order could be issued. In a hurried letter to Commissioner Price, she expressed hope there was yet time to save this village.[9]

On April 2, Jackson and Kinney met with Pablo, the captain of the San Ysidro ranchería. Accompanied by two companions, one lame, the captain had walked ninety miles from the village to confer with Commissioner Lee. Jackson described the Indian as possessing a noble countenance with a direct and open glance and a face so "furrowed by the lines of privation and suffering" that it reminded her of Abraham Lincoln's "grief-stamped face."[10] She never really forgot her first glimpse of Pablo as he walked toward her that day in the Los Angeles Plaza.

Aided by an interpreter, Jackson suggested the Indians claim their land under the Indian Homestead Act. Pablo refused. If his people owned land like the whites, they would have to pay taxes, and because they were so poor, they would lose the land.[11] Confronted with this strong stand, Lee instead encouraged the Indians to sign an affidavit to be forwarded to the Washington Land Office in an effort to stop Cloos. At Jackson's suggestion, a copy was privately sent to Secretary Teller.

In this affidavit, Pablo stated he was a former San Luis Rey Mission Indian, baptized fifty years earlier as a child. Captain at San Ysidro for more than thirty years, he still represented the seventy-seven members of his village. He explained how Cloos had fenced in the land occupied and cultivated by the villagers—lands upon which corn, beans, wheat, melons, barley, and pumpkins had been raised for years. One resident had already been killed by Helm, and the rest feared what Cloos might do if they encroached upon what he claimed was his property.[12]

Acting upon Jackson's letter of late February to Teller and one to Price dated March 10, Commissioner N. C. McFarland of the General Land Office informed Secretary Teller that Cloos' entry upon Indian land was suspended until Agent Lawson could initiate a contest against the illegal entry. In turn, Price informed Jackson of the cancellation. Furthermore, steps were being taken through the Department of Justice to have Helm's patent set aside on the grounds that his land was not subject to the Homestead Act.[13]

In mid-April Lawson informed Jackson of the cancellation of Cloos' entry and the action to set aside Helm's claim. "Glory halleleyah! Just what I told them in my last letter on the subject, might, and should be done," he jubilantly wrote. He would take special pleasure watching the old reprobate Helm "take up his bed and walk" out of the Indian village.[14] There was good reason for his elation. Lawson had initially written the Indian Office about the San Ysidro case way back in December, 1881, and again the following January and February.[15]

Although Jackson was interested in the struggle to aid the San Ysidro Indians, she was much more emotionally and personally involved with the Saboba Indians whom she just learned were ordered to move.[16] Her devotion to their cause was much like her devotion to the Ponca. To Ward she wrote that the Indians of Saboba had been farming that land for a hundred years and had good adobe houses, irrigation ditches, and fenced fields. She realized that the two hundreds acres that encompassed the village was worth at least $30,000— Byrnes' asking price—and the government would not spend that much money.[17]

Enraged by this latest action against the Saboba, Jackson wrote Mary Sheriff several times in March. Informing the teacher of her appointment by the Interior Department, Jackson expressed hope that her final report would be strong enough to prevent the future issuance of patents until an initial inquiry was made into the whereabouts of Indian villages. She also suggested that Sheriff again question the Estudillo heirs about the presence of a protective clause supposedly included in the original land grant issued in 1842—the clause which allowed the Indians use of their cultivated lands. Earlier, Sheriff had informed Jackson that the Indians had been "promised" that they would not be disturbed on their land. But Jackson, after inquiring of the General Land Office in San Francisco and finding that the surveyor general could find no such clause or "promise" in the original Mexican grant, asked Mary to again question Mr. Estudillo.[18]

In mid-March, Jackson asked Ephraim W. Morse to search the records of the San Diego Land Office for the patent of the San Jacinto Nuevo Colony. She hoped he might find in the original Mexican grant a clause protecting the Indians in their possession of cultivated lands.[19] She also informed him that Byrnes, the current owner of the land, had requested the government remove the Indians.

Morse, like Sheriff, was pleased that Jackson had not forgotten the Mission Indians. "I am ashamed of my government when I think of the heartless cruelty with which their [the Indians'] kindness to the whites has been treated," he wrote Jackson.[20] He believed the Mission Indians deserved much better treatment.

Sympathetically supported by Sheriff and Morse and having done everything possible in behalf of the Saboba that could be done from Los Angeles, in mid-March Jackson and Kinney journeyed to the village to confer with the schoolteacher about the removal. From Saboba they headed for San Jacinto and finally to San Bernardino to meet with Agent Lawson on March 17.[21]

While Jackson was in conference with Lawson, a letter relating the murder of Juan Diego by Sam Temple arrived from Mrs. M. J. Ticknor, the government schoolteacher in the nearby Cahuilla village. Diego, a Cahuilla Indian, had ridden into the San Jacinto Valley from his home in one of the spurs of the San Jacinto Mountains to inquire why he had not been invited to participate in the annual sheep shearing. When he returned home that evening, he was not riding his own horse. Known to be absent-minded, his wife feared he might be falsely accused of stealing the horse. But before the animal could be returned, its owner, Sam Temple, arrived at the Diego home and shot Juan. Temple, claiming self-defense, turned himself in. He was tried before a jury of six local white citizens who ruled the shooting justifiable homicide.

Weeks after the murder, when Jackson and her party were driving over the San Jacinto Mountains, someone brought up the incident. Their driver so strongly defended Temple that it set her wondering about the type of people living there. Returning to San Diego, she met with the district attorney who, after hearing the circumstances of the murder, explained that there was no use in reopening the case because no jury would convict a white man for murdering an Indian. Later, in an article written for the *Independent* Jackson remarked that it was "easy to see that killing of Indians is not a very dangerous thing to do in San Diego County."[22] This murder remained so firmly etched in her mind that, when writing *Ramona*, she used it to characterize the death of Alessandro, Ramona's husband.

Back in Los Angeles by March 20, Jackson continued writing to Sheriff in behalf of the Saboba. In early April, Jackson and Kinney, joined by artist Sandham and a driver, set out in a two-horse double-seated carriage for a long tour of Indian villages. When the terrain became difficult they were forced to proceed on horseback. While Jackson took notes and recorded names for her later publications, Kinney acted as interpreter and intimidated squatters whenever possible.

After a visit to San Juan Capistrano,[23] they headed for Pala and neighboring villages of Pauma and Rincon and then on to Temecula. At Pachanga Canyon, Jackson noticed considerable improvements. In the time between her visits, the tract had been set aside by executive order, and the Indians, with a renewed sense of security, had planted more crops and orchards and built more corrals.[24] Jackson was less pleased with government teacher Arthur Golsh. She questioned his moral character and recommended that in the future female teachers be employed in Indian schools.[25]

Some thirty to forty miles south of Saboba, high up in the San Jacinto Mountains, lived some 150 to 200 Cahuillas whose village was reached only by a steep and perilous road. Jackson described them not only as the strongest and most intellectual of all she had seen in Southern California but the most individual and independent. They were poor but industrious; men worked either as stock raisers, sheep shearers, or harvesters while the women made baskets and lace. In addition, they raised wheat, barley, corn, squash, and watermelon on their sixteen fields.

The progress of the forty to fifty Cahuilla schoolchildren pleased Jackson, but she found the absolute desolation of the reservation appalling. She was impressed by the fortitude of the widowed teacher, Ticknor, who lived alone with her ten-year-old daughter. "I honestly do not believe there is one woman in a million that could endure life in that Cahuilla village," she wrote to Sheriff. "It is lonely enough where you are—but it is a metropolis compared with that Cahuilla wilderness."[26] The nearest white person was ten miles away.

Arriving at the Cahuilla village about noon, the party drove immediately to the schoolhouse. Once classes were over, Jackson and Ticknor visited while the children brought bunches of wild flowers for the unexpected visitors and their mothers brought milk and meat. That afternoon the men of the village met with Jackson and Kinney and requested that they be shown the exact lines of their reservation and be supplied with a wagon, harness, ten plows, and some spades and hoes. A dance was held for the guests in the evening.

The following morning, the murder of Juan Diego was again brought to Jackson's attention when she noticed a mere skeleton of a dog crouching near Ticknor's door. A week after the murder, the dog, who had belonged to Juan Diego, crawled to the teacher's home. Tended by her and her little daughter, it soon gained strength, but Jackson could hardly bear to look at the poor animal, seeing in its "despairing expression . . . all the woes which had fallen on the heads of those whom he had loved."[27]

From Cahuilla they journeyed in mid-April to the Warner's Ranch Indians. This large ranch was formally confirmed in patent to Jonathan Trumbull Warner (also known as Juan José Warner) on January 16, 1880, and to Silvestre de la Portilla on January 10, 1880. As of April, 1880, it was owned entirely by former governor Downey of Los Angeles. On January 17, 1880, immediately following the patenting, the executive order which had set aside the area as a reservation was cancelled.

Jackson found the ranch, with its water and woods, to be beautiful. Within its boundaries were five Indian villages. The village residents had been well-treated by Downey who employed them at sheep shearing time. However, well aware of other nearby removals, the Indians began to fear they might someday also face removal from their lands.[28]

During the Jackson and Kinney visit, the captain of nearby San José, one of the smaller villages on the ranch, came for help. A roving sheepherder, hired by an Italian living some twenty miles away, had deliberately torn down his fence. The sheep had subsequently destroyed fifty acres of wheat. Kinney immediately rode to the village, saw the damage, located the herder, and learned the act had been deliberate. The final damage estimates were only a fraction of the crop's total worth. Jackson later received a letter from the Indian indicating he had settled, but no specific amount of money was recorded. Jackson firmly believed that the only reason the Indian received any money was because she and Kinney took immediate action.[29]

Leaving the Warner's Ranch, the party headed for nearby San Ysidro where they discovered that Cloos had sold his homestead to a poor, old widow who was surprised to learn that her claim was questionable. A few days later Jackson was pleased to learn that Cloos' original filing was held by the government for cancellation.[30]

After their arrival at San Ysidro, one of Helm's brothers, fully armed, and described by Jackson as a swaggering ruffian with an evil face, rode to the Indian village to intimidate them. He stayed only a short time, then dashed off. When Jackson and Kinney visited the man's house, they found to their surprise that it was quite comfortable. His wife, whom Jackson described as coarse and shrewish, answered their knock. She boasted of helping the Indians last winter, but Jackson had difficulty restraining her indignation at the thieves' "boasts of kindness . . . to the poor creatures they themselves had robbed of the means of livelihood."[31]

Located on the Santa Ysabel Ranch, the Santa Ysabel village, with a population of 171 residents, was the next stop. This well-wooded and well-watered area adjoining Warner's Ranch had been confirmed to José Ortego and the heirs of Edward Stokes on March 17, 1858. The government patent had been issued on May 14, 1872. The current owner, Captain Wilcox, had so far protected the Indians in their use of the lands. Jackson and Kinney were met by the young man in charge who reported he had eight villages under his authority. These Indians, unlike those at nearby Agua Caliente, had no school. They did not even own a wagon to carry their surplus wheat to the local store to sell.

On the second day of their stay at Santa Ysabel, the commissioners met with four of the local captains from Puerta San Felipe, San José, Anaha, and Laguna. Only those at Laguna were reasonably well-off, primarily because the village of eleven people could be reached only by a very steep trail. Therefore, even with a settler living among them under a lease or contract, they led a peaceful existence.[32]

Following a steep and narrow trail five miles up from the head of

San Ysidro Canyon, the party found a small valley of about eight acres, slightly more than "a pocket on a ledge." Here lived the Los Coyote Indians, described by Jackson as active, robust, and finely made people. They had substantial homes of hewn timber with yucca-thatched roofs. In addition to raising twenty-five head of cattle and a number of horses, they grew beans, corn, wheat, barley, and pumpkins. They informed the visitors they had no desire to leave their mountaintop home but they did request five more ploughs, a harness, and a chain.

Due to the inaccessibility of this valley, even Agent Lawson had not visited them. Three weeks earlier, however, Jim Fane, an acquaintance of Helm, offered to buy the land. When the Indians refused, he informed them he had already filed and was prepared to stay. When Jackson made an inquiry at the land office, she learned that Fane had indeed filed, but his papers had been returned for correction of errors.

When the commissioners arrived at the Los Coyote village, they found Fane hard at work cutting down Indian timber and building a corral. Informed of the Interior Department's action against Cloos, Fane agreed to take $75 for his improvements but later changed his mind and vowed to stay. The Jackson/Kinney report reflected that it was up to Lawson to protect the Indians' rights in this case.[33]

The village of Mesa Grande, high above the Santa Ysabel village and adjacent to the Santa Ysabel ranch, had been set off in 1876 as a reservation. But as Jackson found to be so often true during her tour, the actual village was outside the survey lines, and the reserved lands were essentially useless. Most of the agricultural lands had already been preempted by white settlers. Despite this encroachment, the Indians still were able to plant grain and a few fruit orchards.

Even Jackson found this case much too complicated to write of in great detail. Her travel notes reflected several incidents where settlers, armed with certificates of homestead from the General Land Office, had thrown Indian residents off the land. Unfortunately, the two commissioners could only inform government officials of the situation. Jackson was particularly displeased with the Protective League of Mesa Grande, established by white settlers to prevent the theft of their livestock. She described it as a mere vigilance committee.[34]

At Capitán Grande commissioners found the usual injustices. In 1853 a large band of Diegueño Indians were moved from San Diego to Capitán Grande Canyon by Colonel Magruder. A reservation was set off in 1876, but the village site was left outside the boundaries, and lands reserved to the Indians were mostly barren canyon walls. Settlers meanwhile had moved onto the arable lands.

On September 15, 1882, Dr. D. W. Strong received a patent on the lands formerly cultivated and used for pasturage by these Indians. He initially rented some lands from Ignacio Curo, the ranchería captain, for the raising of bees. A year later, Strong informed Ignacio he would not renew the lease but would instead file on the land.

Strong's intrusion, however, was not the only one. Charles Hensley had purchased a small adobe house and a crop of barley from the captain. Hensley then filed on the land through the Los Angeles Land Office and moved into the village, occupied Ignacio's home, and cultivated the land. He claimed that when he purchased the house and crop he had also purchased the land. Furthermore, James Mead also had homesteaded a portion, as did Captain Amos P. Knowles and G. S. Grant who rented lands from the Indians for beekeeping. Immediately upon obtaining the Indian signatures on the rental agreement, they filed, claiming it was government land. But all these lands were obviously well within the limits of the old ranchería.

To defend the Indians' claim, Jackson included a copy of Magruder's orders and affidavits by the captain of the village and Ubach, the priest in San Diego, along with her letter to Price. These affidavits all testified to long-time Indian occupancy of the area. During the summer of 1881 Lawson had presented much the same information to government officials in an attempt to defend the rights of these Capitán Grande Indians but had been unsuccessful.[35]

About twenty miles from San Diego, Jackson and Kinney visited the Sequan Indians, members of the Diegueño group. Numbering less than fifty, they were wretchedly poor and totally demoralized. Their cultivated lands had diminished with the encroachment of settlers. They could no longer pasture any cattle. Jackson suggested it would be best to move them to Capitán Grande, once it had been cleared of illegal settlers.[36]

The two commissioners were unable to visit all reservations. The Conejos, members of the Diegueño tribe, lived in an inaccessible spot, reached only by a nine-mile trip on horseback. Although Jackson personally met with the Conejo captain in San Diego, she also gathered information from Mrs. Mariette Gregory who had spent eleven summers among them and was sufficiently respected that they often sought her counsel. The eighty hard-working members of the village planted wheat, corn, squash, and beans. The captain requested ploughs and harnesses from Jackson as well as clothing for older village members.[37]

Also unable to visit the 60,000-acre desert reservation of Agua Caliente, (not to be confused with the village of the same name on Warner's Ranch) Jackson relied upon Captain J. G. A. Stanley, former Southern California agent, to report upon the 560 Desert Indians, mostly Cahuilla, living in the Cabezon Valley under old Chief Cabezon. Stanley's report to Jackson, dated May 28, 1883, was accompanied by a cover letter explaining he had written his observations as clearly as possible. He had made no promises to the Indians but hoped something could be done for them immediately.

Though unable to visit all the eight rancherías or villages himself, Stanley sent runners to invite the Indians to a council at Walter's Station. Before an audience of over a hundred, including old Cabezon and the captains of all the rancherías, Stanley explained that ill health prevented Jackson from visiting them personally. Learning that the Indians would be willing to live in one village if a suitable site could be found, he urged that steps be taken immediately to establish their reservation.

Stanley, as a former special agent, had been cordially received by the Indians. They expressed their displeasure with the current mission agent, Lawson, who not only did not visit them but also appeared to take no interest in their well-being. They were also dissatisfied with his interpreter, Juan Morongo, who had arranged a contract with a merchant in San Bernardino to cut wood for the railroad. Morongo then took several hundred dollars belonging to the Indians. Stanley cautioned Jackson that this incident might be exaggerated, but it was evident that no one was watching over the Indians' best interest.[38]

A month after he reported to Jackson, Stanley, at the request of the Cabezon Indians, wrote Secretary Teller. He informed Teller that their eight Indian villages were located along the base of the mountains where water could be found near the surface. And while the Southern Pacific line ran alongside the eastern side of the valley, it did not interfere with the reservation. Stanley suggested that the mesquite found in the valley could become a source of income if the Indians only had wagons and harnesses. He excused himself for taking the liberty of writing, but he was concerned for their well-being.[39]

Stanley had also informed Lawson, whose agency handled not only the Cahuillas but also the Serranos, San Luis Rey Indians, and several Diegueño groups, of his visit to the Cabezon Indians. Lawson expressed surprise that Jackson had delegated an outside party for such a visit. He felt she should take the time to personally look into their condition. The "bane" of his agency was the visit to his Indians of various government-sponsored commissions which made "promises of this, that & the other thing which . . . [they were] without authority & without the power to fulfill." He concluded that the Jackson/Kinney commission would have the same result as others, ending up in nothing but a report and a large expenditure for the government.[40] Fortunately, he was wrong, and although nothing immediately resulted from the Jackson/Kinney report, Congress did eventually pass legislation to protect Mission Indian landholdings.

Jackson had received Stanley's report and a short time later a note enclosing Lawson's letter. She expressed surprise that the agent was annoyed. After all, she had the authority to delegate others to make investigations for her, and furthermore, government officials had never expected her to visit every single village. She had been quite ill and unable to make the trip anyway.[41]

Jackson had the innate ability to anger officials when she enthusiastically undertook research or tours. Before, she had battled with Secretary Schurz and Editor Byers. Now she was engaged in a similar situation with agent Lawson. For several months, letters flew back and forth between them. Both attempted to enlist Commissioner Price as an ally.

There was a similarity between the incidents with Schurz and Lawson. Both officials, in their own way, had tried to help the Indians. Schurz, for example, had not been responsible for the original removal order for the Ponca. He was merely carrying out his predecessor's orders. When faced with the angry Jackson, he naturally defended himself. Lawson had repeatedly written government officials, pleading for help in improving the conditions at El Potrero, San Jacinto, Agua Caliente, Santa Ysabel, and among the Cahuilla Indians, to no avail. Therefore, in retrospect, Jackson's attack of him may have been unwarranted. Unaware of his previous letters in behalf of these Indians, she believed he was ineffective, and when he confronted her, her stubbornness surfaced.

The initial contact between Jackson and the Mission Indian agent was through the mails. In a March 2, 1883, answer to her letter of February 26, Lawson expressed surprise at her appointment—no one had informed him of it. He was currently busy trying to defend the Saboba Indians from losing their land and had just been ordered by government officials to remove them. He appeared visibly shaken when he wrote Jackson: "In the name of justice and humanity they ought not to be removed from their present homes."[42]

The information she requested of him he felt could better be communicated verbally. Therefore, he suggested either they meet in Los Angeles or she should come to the agency when she was ready to go into the field. He agreed to lend his interpreter, but the man was temporarily in San Francisco aiding in the prosecution of individuals selling liquor to the Indians.

Within a short time, Lawson personally complained to Commissioner Price about Jackson's interference. She was busy stirring up discontent and bad feelings among the San Luis Rey Indians. Although she had come "ostensibly, to 'inquire into the condition of the Indians,' she assumed the prerogative of the Agent," he complained. The last time he visited Pachanga, the Indians had called a council to decide whose orders they should obey. Furthermore, she had ordered him to request a Temecula Day School teacher to resign or she would report the teacher herself. Lawson described Jackson as driven by "mere sentiment," having no knowledge of Indian character. She had done more harm for his agency than good, and he hoped in the future to be delivered from female commissioners.[43]

By the end of June he had backed off on his criticism and explained to Price that it had just come to his attention that the real author of all the mischief among the Indians was the interpreter Jesús López. Because Lawson had prosecuted some of López's friends for selling liquor to the Indians, López decided to get even. Apparently, in Jackson's absence and without her knowledge, the interpreter assured the Indians he was speaking in her behalf.[44]

Although Lawson may have backed down on criticizing Jackson about misleading the Indians, he would not forget the controversial firing of Temecula Day School teacher Golsh. During their investigation, Jackson and Kinney had learned that Golsh fathered a child by a Pala woman and seduced an Indian girl at Pauma. They informed Lawson of these charges. Furthermore, they learned Golsh had driven four families off their lands in Pala and then patented the land. Because they respected Golsh's sister, Flora, who taught at Agua Caliente, they chose not to make a report to Commissioner Price. Instead they wanted Lawson, if he thought it advisable, to request a resignation. The agent could forward Jackson's letter as a reason for the request.[45]

Apparently, five years earlier Golsh had rented part of the Pala ranchería from Louis Ardillo for a three-month period at five dollars a month. He then claimed Ardillo's land and that of three others, ordering them to leave. On one occasion he threatened Patricio Soberano with a gun. Golsh had then filed on the land which included four homes and twenty-nine people and enclosed fields and an irrigation ditch. In December 1882 Lawson, reluctantly, informed the Indians that if they did not leave voluntarily, the sheriff would remove them.[46]

After five years at the agency Lawson expressed no surprise in hearing complaints about the character of personnel connected with the "Indian Service." There had even been rumors charging him with various crimes. His long experiences with the lying, thieving, slanderous people in the mountain districts had made a skeptic of him. Consequently, he requested the source of Jackson's information. Because of Golsh's German nobility background, Lawson had difficulty believing what Jackson and Kinney reported.[47]

Jackson, on the other hand, believed that the evidence they had accumulated was very strong. The information about Pauma came from the captain of the ranchería and at Pala from the Indian bringing up his child. Without waiting for Lawson's answer, Jackson and Kinney forwarded an affidavit relative to Golsh and the four Indians he had driven off their lands to Commissioner Price.[48]

After the initial reading of Jackson's evidence, Lawson agreed it was reliable and dismissed the teacher. But he made a point of informing Jackson that the incident on the land deal at Pala had taken place before he assumed office. After hearing Golsh personally deny both charges, however, Lawson abruptly changed his mind and defended him. Golsh also informed the agent that he was unable to drive off the Indian girls when they came to his classroom after hours. Furthermore, the teacher accused Jackson of listening to notorious gossips and only his enemies. In his reply to Jackson, Lawson also placed part of the blame on her interpreter Jesús López who had a reputation as a horse thief as well as a liar. A better knowledge of the Indian character, before she set out on her mission, he believed, would have been of "incalculable value."[49]

Upon learning that Golsh intended to sue both of them for defamation of character and damages, Jackson regretted the shape the affair had taken but would say nothing further until called into court. "We did what we thought was right and in the line of our official duty—we tried to do it in the kindest way," she wrote to Lawson.[50] She also reminded the agent that he had previously praised the interpreter whom he was now maligning. Apparently, no suit was filed because Jackson never referred to it again.

Lawson accompanied Golsh's replacement to Pachanga on June 5. The villagers would sorely miss the former teacher for he had not only befriended them but lent money. Furthermore, the school had made excellent progress. Lawson sincerely regretted the removal but did it because of an earlier situation, fearing the consequences that multiple scandals in his agency might have on his own reputation. Finally, he simply dismissed the land-taking at Pala by declaring that scores of others did the same thing.

Following his return from Pachanga, Lawson continued the verbal debate through the mails with Jackson. He argued over whether the witnesses in Golsh's case were honest and whether she had authority to become involved in the conduct of the agency. The character of Jesús López had nothing to do with his ability as an interpreter or driver/guide he remarked. López did in fact have a reputation as a horse thief but had so far evaded detection.[51]

As usual, Jackson was fully capable of defending her position. She explained to Lawson that several statements in his letter of June 6 reflected his misunderstanding of the facts. No threat was ever intended in the case of Golsh, and she disclaimed any authority to interfere in agency affairs. Furthermore, she would never have hired the interpreter had she known beforehand that he was a liar. Both she and Kinney were dependent upon Lawson's recommendation. She emphatically denied his accusation that they had given commissions as captains or generals to any Pachanga Indians. They did, however, give papers to the captains to be used to show to white trespassers in the hopes of protecting Indian lands.[52]

Lawson's accusations continued to haunt Jackson. When writing Commissioner Price from her home in Colorado Springs in July, she enclosed a clipping from the *San Bernardino Times*. The editor wrote that Jackson had demanded the removal of the teacher, that she had given an Indian a commission as a chief, and that the Indian Office did not take any stock in "this female policy of the Secretary." Denying every accusation presented in the editorial, she hoped that the recent news that Lawson had resigned was true. "If so, it would be idle to take up your valuable time, with this contemptible newspaper rubbish."[53]

Returning to Los Angeles in early May, after almost a month of visiting eighteen Indian villages, Jackson immediately engaged in a furious exchange of letters. To Aldrich of the *Atlantic Monthly* she had remarked before undertaking the tour that she expected to return "wrung dry of sympathy by the sign of so much patient suffering. The gentleness and meekness of these people are enough to break your heart." Upon her return she sadly wrote that her opinion of human nature had decreased by one hundred percent. "Such heart sickening fraud, violence, [and] cruelty as we have unearthed here—I did not believe could exist in civilized communities."[54]

A week later she informed Mary Sheriff that the law firm of Brunson and Wells had been hired to protect Indian rights. It was their opinion that the Indians had a legal right to remain on the land. Mexican law stated that land occupied by Indians could not be conveyed away, and it had been a consistent policy of the United States to respect property legally recognized by prior sovereigns. Jackson impressed upon Mary that the Saboba Indians were not to breathe a word to anyone about the lawyers, or the landowners might attempt to drive them off. If the Indians were served papers of any sort, they were to take them immediately to the law firm. "I cannot too strongly impress on you the necessity for their keeping all this *secret*," she implored.[55] She had guaranteed the legal fees when services were rendered even if the government did not authorize the firm.

Jackson did not wish to wait until the official government report was completed to make requests and recommendations. Therefore, immediately upon her return to Los Angeles in early May, she penned numerous letters to government officials. On May 5 she wrote Price that if the Interior Department could turn "out the robbers" in Capitán Grande Canyon and reclaim it, rout "those cruel Austrians the Golshes" in Pala, and reinstate the San Ysidro Indians of their lands a "most salutary impression will be made on the Californian mind." If Helm and Cloos could be driven out of San Ysidro, it would be best to create a reservation rather than encourage the Indians, who were much too poor and broken spirited, to take up land individually under the Indian Homestead Act. To remedy the situation of the Indian lands in Capitán Grande and Pala, she included numerous affidavits, hoping the Interior Department would be as successful with them as they were in the case of San Ysidro Canyon. Unfortunately, the average settler looked upon the presence of an Indian community on lands they wanted as little more of an obstacle than a fox or a coyote. She thanked Price for his energetic and prompt responses to the matters she brought before him.[56]

Commissioner Price forwarded the affidavits and her letter to Teller, recommending that the entries of Mead, Hensley, and Knowles at Capitán Grande be held for cancellation. If approved, an executive order would be issued adding the lands to the reservation. The situation at Pala, however, was hopeless because the land involved had been patented for a long period.[57]

Two days later Jackson wrote Price of Stephano Domo, an old Indian who lived alone with his grandson at Mesa Grande. He had farmed a small plot of land for twenty-three years, raising corn and wheat as well as cultivating a vineyard. He was in danger of losing the land because of encroaching settlers, and she requested his land be protected by an executive order.[58]

While visiting Saboba, the commissioners had discovered Indian Canyon, home of half a dozen families, who with the available water and arable land grew an excellent crop of wheat. On May 9 Jackson requested the area be set aside immediately by executive order. If the Saboba Indians were ejected from their village, some might be able to take up residence here.[59] At the end of May, Price recommended that Secretary Teller prepare an executive order for President Arthur's signature. Arthur complied, thus formally setting Indian Canyon aside as a reservation.[60]

Desperate for a final solution to the Saboba case, Jackson wrote Secretary Teller that she had located a lawyer willing to take up their case. Twelve years ago, this same lawyer, a Mr. B. D. Wilson, had forced the registration of two Indian voters to prove that they were citizens under both the Treaty of Guadalupe Hidalgo and the fourteenth amendment. She asked Teller to withdraw his order to Lawson to remove the Indians, thus allowing Byrnes to bring a suit of ejectment which Wilson could contest.[61]

In a mid-May letter to Teller, Jackson asked that Wilson be replaced by the Los Angeles firm of Brunson and Wells as special United States attorney in all cases concerning the Indians. Apparently, Jackson felt that Wilson spent too much time away from his office, tending his bee ranches. Furthermore, Wells believed that Saboba might be saved without the need of a lawsuit because the initial survey had not included the Indian village, and the current owners might prefer to settle out of court. If no compromise could be reached, then Wells would defend the Indians against a suit of ejectment. This action promised to affect the cases of other villages by setting legal precedent. Jackson sincerely believed that it was terribly wrong for the government to fail to "protect a whole village of industrious peaceable farming people, like these Saboba Indians from being driven off lands they have tilled for over one hundred years."[62]

By June, Jackson was home in Colorado Springs working on the final draft of the official report. Receiving a copy of the June 1 *San Diego Union* "containing a scurrilous paragraph in regards" to her work as an Indian commissioner, Jackson immediately wrote Morse on June 13 asking if he could quietly find out who wrote the letter that had been quoted. She was appalled that any decent newspaper would print such "an indecent paragraph." She added that she "should also have supposed that a woman of . . . [her] age, and reputation, would have been sheltered from just that kind of attack." But she realized when undertaking her commission that she would be subject to hostility and antagonism.[63] No reply to her letter has yet surfaced.

In the meantime, the flurry of letters to government officials did not abate. In early June she informed Secretary Teller that Kinney was on his way to Washington to speak to government officials about various matters they did not want to send through the mail.

She hoped Teller would appoint the thirty-one-year-old man to the position of Indian commissioner for California. He had been much more than a mere assistant. His knowledge of land matters and discretion in dealing with people had allowed them to get to the very bottom of the situation.

If she and Kinney accomplished nothing more than the saving of San Ysidro and the Los Coyotes, she felt rewarded; but she was expecting much more from the final report. She informed Teller that her third article for the *Century* on the conditions of the Mission Indians was due out in August and hoped it would generate popular sentiment and make Congress more receptive to the bill that would surely result from the publication of the official report.[64]

In late June, Jackson informed Price she had received a letter from Father Ubach, who had recently returned from a visit to Capitán Grande. The priest expressed his uneasiness about the situation. Dr. Strong, described by Jackson as "just as wicked a thief and robber as Helm," was awaiting the arrival of a special Indian commissioner from Washington. Ubach feared Strong would mislead this commissioner with false information, thereby jeopardizing efforts to improve the Indians' condition. "I have seen so much roguery and thievery in these matters," he concluded.[65]

Jackson reminded Price that the entire Capitán Grande Canyon had initially belonged to the Indians and was formally assigned them in 1853 by Colonel Magruder. She described this as one of the worst "steals" that she and Kinney had uncovered. It was unfortunate that Strong's patent could not be treated in the same way as that of Helm's in San Ysidro. Jackson apologized for her emotionalism but noted it was "impossible . . . [for her] to speak in moderate terms of this class of men."[66] Once the commissioner read her report, Jackson assured him, he would feel as deeply indignant.

Jackson continued writing Sheriff. Although a Mr. Foster had rented the Saboba tract, Jackson reminded the schoolteacher that if he drove off the Indian stock it could still be pastured in Indian Canyon which was being set aside by executive order. She urged Sheriff to continue encouraging the Indians and to remind them to keep the employment of Brunson and Wells secret.

On August 23, Sheriff informed Jackson that her salary had been reduced by one hundred dollars but that of the teachers both at Cahuilla and Warner's Ranch remained unchanged. She was reluctant to blame Lawson. "If Lawson did it, it is because he thinks you a friend of mine," wrote Jackson and offered to replace the lost salary.[67]

In early August Jackson wrote Secretary Teller about Sheriff's salary reduction. She was particularly upset because the Saboba schoolteacher was not only better educated than the other two teachers but also maintained a closer and more affectionate relationship with her pupils. Furthermore, Sheriff possessed the "most exquisite gentleness and refinement of character." If the department had to save a hundred dollars somewhere, there should be other places they could cut. Jackson noted that not "one out of ten thousand could be hired for any sum, to lead such a dreary, desolate life, and endure such deprivations."[68]

Following Teller's suggestion, Jackson wrote Commissioner Price of the salary dispute. To elicit his support, she explained that, unlike the other two teachers who lived in rooms built onto the school, Sheriff had to board and drive the five miles to the school daily in a rented horse and buggy. In addition, because of the poverty of the Indians, the schoolteacher always spent a considerable portion of her salary on them. Jackson believed the loss of this money would "cripple her sorely."[69] Apparently, as Jackson had initially believed, the salary had been reduced only because Sheriff's daily attendance was less than that of the other teachers and not because of any interference from Lawson. The salary was restored.

Jackson completed the official government report the first week in July. Months earlier she had written to Joseph B. Gilder, former city editor of the *New York Herald* and co-founder of the *Critic*, that she had intended to make the report so "strong" that it would aid Secretary Teller in pushing through a bill for monies to buy land for the Indians.[70] She informed Warner that she thought the commission had done some good.[71]

The final report numbered fifty-six pages and dealt mostly with the Mission Indians in the three southernmost counties of California. Well over half was documentary evidence including the legal brief of Brunson and Wells, letters, and affidavits gathered during the three months stay in California. Eleven specific recommendations were detailed, including: (1) resurveying and marking existing reservations; (2) removal of all white settlers from reservations; (3) removal of the Indians or the upholding and defending of their claims; and (4) the patenting, with a twenty-five-year trust period, of both old and new reservations to Indian residents.

In addition, the commissioners recommended (5) the establishment of more schools, one immediately at Rincon and a second at Santa Ysabel. Following an earlier recommendation by Jackson, it was suggested that only female teachers be employed in isolated villages. In addition, religious as well as industrial training should be included. (This latter suggestion was more than likely a reflection of the current trend in Indian reform.) (6) Proper supervision of the reservations was to include two inspections a year for each village or settlement. (7) A law firm in Los Angeles was to be hired to serve as special attorneys in cases relating to the Mission Indians.[72] Jackson and Kinney also recommended both (8) a judicious distribution of farm equipment and (9) a fund for the purchase of food and clothing for the aged and the sick. (10) The purchase of two tracts of land was suggested: the Pauma Ranch, located between Rincon and Pala and owned by Francis Mora, Bishop of Los Angeles, and the Santa Ysabel Ranch.[73] Finally, the two commissioners concluded that (11) the San Carlos group in Monterey and other small bands north of the mission agency boundary be included under its jurisdiction.

When discussing the surveying of Indian reservations after 1876, Jackson had noted that the lines had been "laid off by guess" on an imperfect county map by the San Diego surveyor. These areas were then reported by the Indian commissioner and set aside by executive order. Therefore, when the actual survey was made, in many cases the Indian villages were outside reservation lines. This particular comment interested Commissioner Price, and in a November 19 letter, he requested she send him without delay the proper descriptions of such tracts upon which the Indians were living so this error could be corrected and the land added to the reservations.[74]

During a furious snow storm, Jackson contracted a severe bronchitis attack that disabled her, delaying her reply to the commissioner. When finally able to write, she noted she had deliberately used the expression "laid off by guess." The surveyor in question, a Mr. Wheeler, who currently worked in the General Land Office in San Francisco, personally showed her the reservation plats that he had laid out on a map. He had come "as near as he could guess to the tracts in which the Indian villages were."[75] She knew of no way in which the Indian Office could gain additional information except by use of those plats.

In a private letter written the same day, Jackson gave Price more details. She explained that had it been the plan originally to avoid giving the Indians good lands and to leave their villages outside the reservation boundaries they could not have done a better job. While the Capitán Grande Reservation was being laid off, both Wheeler and the agent, who was a clergyman, were living in the home of Strong, the very man who first rented those lands and then stole the best part. If new reservation lines were to be surveyed, she suggested that Major Horatio N. Rust, whom both she and Kinney recommended to replace Lawson, should supervise. Rust and Kinney were the only men in Southern California that Jackson absolutely trusted.[76]

In his annual report for 1883, Commissioner Price agreed to submit a draft of legislation necessary to implement most of the recommendations in the Jackson/Kinney report. "With the measures already taken and with these herein recommended," he wrote in his report, "it is believed that these poor and persecuted people may be protected from further encroachments, and enjoy . . . the prosperity to which their peaceful conduct under all their wrongs entitles them."[77]

With her report completed, Jackson began rewriting the six papers promised to the *Independent*. She requested that Ward publish them in the order they were numbered and in six successive weeks to double their effectiveness.[78] They were all published but not as Jackson had suggested.

When her government reimbursement failed to arrive, Jackson spent the fall busily writing Price and Teller requesting her money. Because she was about to undertake a trip east, she informed the secretary that she needed money as soon as possible. The draft finally arrived on November 4, and in thanking Price, she inquired when the report would be printed in pamphlet form. He had promised her as many copies as she wanted. She requested two hundred, fifty of which were intended for various newspapers.[79]

The Indian Office agreed to mail one hundred if she supplied the names and addresses. The remainder would be forwarded. Jackson decided to wait until the bill for the Mission Indians was likely to come up in Congress and then put the report in the papers so more pressure could be brought to bear on Congress.[80] Her list included prominent ministers, senators, businessmen, and judges, mostly in New York City, Boston, various cities in Southern California, and Philadelphia. Several prominent members of the Women's National Indian Association were also included.[81]

On January 10, 1884, the draft of the bill along with a printed copy of the Jackson/Kinney report was submitted by Commissioner Price to Secretary Teller in a long, detailed explanatory letter. A day later it was sent to President Arthur who on January 14 submitted it to Congress.[82]

The bill passed the Senate on July 3, 1884, but failed in the House. A Senate subcommittee in the fall of 1884 visited the Mission Indians and reported their sad neglect by the government. Lengthening the trust period to thirty years, Commissioner John D. C. Atkins, in a letter of November 30, 1885, resubmitted the draft of the Mission Indian bill along with the Jackson/Kinney report to Secretary Lucius Q. C. Lamar. Lamar in turn sent the bill and a letter to President Grover Cleveland on December 15. Four days before Christmas, 1885,

Cleveland submitted the bill to Congress.[83] Again it failed to pass both houses.

The WNIA, the IRA, and other reformers carried on the fight in Jackson's behalf following her death. Through their efforts, the Indian Office persistently presented this bill yearly until January 12, 1891,[84] when the "Act for the Relief of the Mission Indians in the State of California" finally passed both houses. Although Jackson had been dead for six years, Albert K. Smiley, a member of the Board of Indian Commissioners and founder of the Lake Mohonk Conference, noted the bill was based on her recommendations with only a few modifications.[85]

The bill, For the Relief of the Mission Indians in the State of California, included many of the specific Jackson/Kinney recommendations. For instance, it called for the appointment of three commissioners authorized to select reservations for each band or village. These reservations, whenever possible, would include lands already occupied by Indian villages. Once selected, each reservation was to be patented by the government. In addition, heads of households or single adult Indians were eligible upon request for an allotment in severalty of 160 or 80 acres with a protective twenty-five-year period of trust. Finally, the government agreed to defend Indian land rights formerly protected by Mexican land grants and to spend $2,000 on food and clothing for the aged and destitute.

Even before her death, however, Jackson had successfully accomplished her original goal. Numerous magazine and newspaper articles had been published on California, its missions, and the Mission Indians, and an authoritative government report had been written with the help of Abbot Kinney and accepted by government officials. Also, now at least some of the Indians of California had permanent reservations. But her work in behalf of the Mission Indians was not yet completed. One more task remained—the writing of a novel based on the numerous incidents she had uncovered during her various tours of the Indian villages. Ramona would remain the most lasting legacy of her Indian reforming activities.

5

Ramona, Its Successes and Failures

By November 1883, with the report and her *Independent* articles completed, Jackson could reflect upon a job well done. She and Kinney had saved several tracts of land and had removed what they believed to be an immoral teacher. In addition, much to Jackson's pleasure, Lawson had resigned as agent. Her critical exchange of letters to government officials may well have been one of the reasons for his leaving government service.

Lawson's replacement, J. G. McCallum, took office on October 1, 1883. Unfortunately, not only was he inefficient but time would prove him dishonest as well. In December, while Jackson was busy writing her Indian novel *Ramona*, McCallum traveled nearly three hundred miles to visit at Temecula, Cahuilla, and Agua Caliente and to see about building schools at Rincon and Santa Ysabel, as recommended by the Jackson/Kinney report. He found Santa Ysabel to be a beautifully located village with 159 Indians, 80 of whom were children. Because it was too late in the season to build an adobe school, he decided on a frame building instead. The Indians agreed to haul the necessary lumber.

Away from his office a week, McCallum had no time to visit the village of Rincon but did meet with the captain, who had to consult with his villagers before committing them to building the school. A month later McCallum wrote Commissioner Price requesting authority to rent a suitable house for the Rincon school and employ a female teacher. The school at Rincon was finally established on April 1, 1884.

Leaving the village and school of Agua Caliente, located within the grant belonging to Downey, McCallum unexpectedly met him the following day. Downey informed the agent that he fully intended to have the Indians removed within the next year. Returning to his agency, McCallum visited the offices of the United States surveyor general to look at Downey's grant. He found it to contain the usual protective clause favoring the Indians. The agent was also well aware that Byrnes, the claimant at Saboba, had hired a lawyer and begun proceedings to eject the Indians from their village.[1]

As McCallum began his visit to the various Mission reservations, Jackson pondered what more she could do for their inhabitants. Perhaps a novel—one that presented the true picture of the Indian— as Jackson viewed it. In 1881 *Ploughed Under* by William Justin Harsha had been written with that purpose in mind. Jackson had not only seen the manuscript but had helped Thomas Henry Tibbles make corrections. She remarked to Joseph B. Gilder that it was a pity the first novel on the Indian question was such a bad one.[2] Gilder immediately suggested she write one, but Jackson reluctantly replied that she lacked the local color necessary to do the job adequately.[3] Now she realized she had more than enough background material.

After completing the month-long tour with Kinney in May 1883, she had written Thomas Bailey Aldrich about the fraud and cruelty they had unearthed. "If I could write a story that would do for the Indian a thousandth part that Uncle Tom's Cabin did for the negro, I would be thankful the rest of my life,"[4] she wistfully commented. Following the publication of *Ramona*, she wrote Aldrich that she only hoped the novel would make his heart ache. She wanted to create such a winning and alluring picture through her characterization that the reader "would have swallowed a big dose of information on the Indian question without knowing it."[5]

Now in November 1883, home again in Colorado Springs, her thoughts again turned to creating a novel. She asked Ephraim W. Morse of San Diego for additional information on the Temecula removal as well as the theft of a large number of sheep from the Pala or San Luis Rey Indians by Major Cave J. Couts. She wanted to write a story set in Southern California that would influence public sentiment in behalf of the Indians, something *A Century of Dishonor* had not accomplished. Only her intimate literary friends would be privy to this project, and she urged him to keep it secret.

In her ending postscript to Morse she mentioned Lawson's resignation and an editorial from the *San Luis Rey Star* that contained "slurring and contemptuous references to . . . [her] in connection with this charge." "It is plain that the Indians have some bitter ene-mies in San Luis Rey," she concluded.[6] In his editorial column, Francis H. Whaley of the *Star* had called for Jackson's removal. De-scribing her as a "busy body" and a "meddlesome feminine pet of the Hon. Secretary," he concluded that "no woman should occupy the position of Indian Commissioner; it is no place for any member of the feminine gender."[7]

Writing to the Coronels, she remarked that her government report had been favorably received and the recommendations were to be in-cluded in a bill coming up before Congress in winter. Realizing that most people would be more apt to read a fictionalized account, how-ever, she was currently writing a novel setting "forth some Indian experiences in a way to move people's hearts."[8] She was especially interested in everything Mr. Coronel could remember of the Te-mecula village while he was marking off the Indian boundaries. She lamented not writing a novel while in Los Angeles, but now, with the report finished, she felt able to undertake such a task.

A letter to Mary Sheriff requested information about the murder of Juan Diego by Sam Temple. Jackson had written a detailed ac-count in her *Independent* article, "Justifiable Homicide in Southern California." Now she wanted information about the jury, the pro-ceedings, and the judge. In reply to Sheriff's letter, Jackson remarked that cities all over the country were organizing branches of the In-dian Rights Association, so work on behalf of the Indian was pro-gressing. The captain at Saboba may not see an improvement, but his children would.[9]

Her annual bout of bronchitis forced her to move to New York in late November where she settled in at the Berkeley Hotel. Shortly thereafter, she informed Aldrich she was going to write a long story which would take three to four months. She inquired if anybody had ever written a book entitled "In the Name of the Law." The story was all planned—so well thought out that it was practically half done.[10]

As the new year dawned, Jackson was still busily working on *Ramona*, while her hand-picked lawyers, Brunson and Wells, worked equally hard defending Indian land titles. In the case of the Indians of Capitán Grande, the lawyers had found that the homestead entries of Mead, Hensley, and Strong were valid while that of Knowles was fraudulent. The attorneys recommended to Commissioner Price that the improvements and interests of the three legal entries be pur-chased by the government. They agreed to await instructions as to whether or not the government would prosecute Knowles.[11]

Three weeks later Commissioner Price informed Brunson and

Wells that the entries of Mead and Hensley had been cancelled by the General Land Office on January 8 because the Indians had resided on the land for thirty-one years. Although Colonel Magruder had not legally created a reservation, he had determined the Indian occupancy, therefore removing the tract from jurisdiction of land laws. Knowles' entry was cancelled because of fraud while that of Strong had already passed to the patent stage, and no action had been taken. Furthermore, the commissioner believed that these cancellations would be sustained.[12] However, not until November 3, 1886, almost three years later, did Secretary of the Interior Lucius Q. C. Lamar write the new commissioner, John D. C. Atkins, that the Interior department had authorized the "immediate and summary removal" of Hensley, Mead, and Knowles from the Capitán Grande Reservation.[13]

In the meantime, Jackson was busy on her novel. After completing twenty chapters, she wrote to Kinney, asking if it would be improper to rearrange events chronologically. She also informed him there was a bill of some sort prepared and placed before Congress.[14] Next, she requested a copy of this bill from Commissioner Price so she could write supporting letters to newspaper editors, much as she had done when working in behalf of the Ponca, Cheyenne, and Ute Indians.[15]

The first word of Ramona was written on December 1, 1883, in the Berkeley Hotel in New York City. The plot had flashed through her mind in less than five minutes the previous October. Frightened by the power of the story, she had rushed into her husband's room to tell it to him. Haunted ever since, she wrote two thousand to three thousand words a morning as if engaged in a struggle with an outside power. It was impossible to write fast enough. Twice stricken by a persistent cold and a case of "nervous prostration," she found being kept away from the writing was "like keeping away from a lover, whose hand . . . [she could] reach." The strain became so hard that she occasionally forced herself to stop and write a bit of verse or prose. Never before had she written half that amount in the same period of time, and it was her best work ever. Then she mused—she had turned fifty-two in October and was not "a bit steadier-headed!"[16]

Warner, a frequent visitor, observed that she seemed completely possessed and that "chapter after chapter flowed from her pen as easily as one would write a letter to a friend."[17] On the night of March 9, 1884, only about ten pages remained. And although she generally never wrote anything more than a letter in the evening, she continued working until eleven.[18] When she finished the last sentence, she put her head down on her desk and cried: "My life-blood went into it—all I had thought, felt, and suffered for *five* years on the Indian Question."[19]

Ironically, two weeks later, the *San Diego Union* carried an article about the county sheriff who had been ordered to serve notice of ejectment upon the Saboba Indians on the San Jacinto grant. The paper was sympathetic to Byrnes, who was described as having honestly purchased the land with no desire to upset the Indians. If the government wished to use the land as a home for the Indians, it should pay him. The author of the article concluded that his view, however, would hardly meet with Helen Hunt Jackson's approval. In addition, the paper accused Jackson of believing that the government had the right to take private property for public use without any compensation.[20] Unfortunately, no letters written by Jackson for that time period have been found, and therefore her reaction to the formal ejection of the Saboba Indians or to the newspaper article remains unknown.

About the time the *San Diego Union* published the article on the ejectment of the Saboba village, two members of the Board of Indian Commissioners were busy visiting various agencies in New Mexico, Arizona, and California. The California leg of their tour was a direct response to the Jackson/Kinney report.

Albert K. Smiley and General E. Whittlesey arrived in Los Angeles on March 19 and met first with the law firm of Brunson and Wells. They later conferred with Kinney who filled them in on the problems he and Jackson had encountered during their investigative work. Smiley and Whittlesey then met with Rust of Pasadena regarding the site for an Indian industrial school and traveled to San Bernardino to confer with Mission Agent McCallum.

Unexpected spring rains and flooding made it impossible for the two commissioners to visit many of the San Diego County Indian villages. However, after a visit to the day school in the village of El Potrero near Banning, they were convinced that the Mission Indians had been wronged. Justice demanded their lands be defended.[21]

In mid-April, the Indian Office informed Brunson and Wells of the status of the Byrnes case against the Saboba village. In reply, the two lawyers, serving as special assistants to United States Attorney S. G. Hillborn, noted that Byrnes had begun an action in the Superior Court of San Diego County in early April. They immediately wrote the United States district attorney in San Francisco, suggesting that this was the proper case to have transferred to the United States Court. On May 12 the district attorney advised Brunson and Wells that Attorney General Benjamin Harris Brewster was in agreement. Therefore, the two attorneys immediately filed a petition to have the case transferred to the federal court as a test case.[22]

The original title that Jackson had chosen for her novel was "In the Name of the Law," but for unknown reasons, she changed the name to *Ramona*. Writing to Aldrich, she vowed someday to write a long story without a purpose in mind and maybe then he would print it in the *Atlantic*. "This one, [*Ramona*] is not for *myself*."[23]

Ramona, first serialized in the *Christian Union* in May 1884, was published in book form by Roberts Brothers the following November. It was a historical novel, combining both fact and fiction. Kinney remarked that he and Jackson had met with many of the "characters whose pictures were afterwards drawn with fidelity . . . in the pages of her book."[24] Jackson herself informed Aldrich that the incidents in the book were all true. "A Cahuilla Indian was shot two years ago exactly as Alessandro is—and his wife's name was Ramona and I never knew this last fact until Ramona was half written," she confessed.[25]

But Jackson was to face yet another disappointment in public acceptance of her Indian writings. *A Century of Dishonor* and her government report did not result in the passage of reforms or awaken the public's concern for the Indians—at least during her lifetime. *Ramona* as the *Uncle Tom's Cabin* of Indian history failed partially because times and issues were different. *Uncle Tom* represented four million slaves in fifteen southern states. The issue of human bondage was so explosive that a war resulted. The Indian population at most, however, was in the low hundreds of thousands. Furthermore, the vast majority of westerners living near Indian communities were not sympathetic; they only wanted Indian land. Those few Indian supporters were eastern humanitarians who still retained a romanticized vision of the "noble savage." The Indian issue would not result in a war for their freedom and rights. Still, it was a significant issue and occupied the attention of politicians and reformers.

Although *Ramona* sold fifteen thousand copies before her death, seven thousand of those within the first three months of publication,[26] Jackson did not live long enough to see its impact. *Ramona* was in print only ten months before she died. Since its initial publication by Roberts Brothers in November 1884, however, it has gone through more than three hundred reprintings and inspired numerous stage and screen versions as well as a score of books written by authors claiming to have discovered the real Ramona, or the real Alessandro, or the real rancho where the story took place.

George Wharton James, for example, after carefully retracing Jackson's steps for his book *Through Ramona's Country,* commented that in a pigeonhole in a baggage room of a railway station in 1910 he saw a well-worn copy of *Ramona.* The book's owner informed James it was "the bulliest story [he had] ever read in [his] life." James firmly believed that the "humanizing influence" of the novel continued to be felt by readers. Thus Jackson's good work continued.[27]

Jackson would, no doubt, have been pleased to learn this for she had put her heart and soul into the writing of *Ramona,* hoping it would accomplish what her other writings had not. She had no idea it would be her last novel; the illness which she continually attributed to various other problems was in fact cancer of the stomach. To her despair, *Ramona* did not achieve her expectations of immediately awakening public interest in the condition of the Indians.

Interestingly, *Ramona's* impact has been stronger in the field of literature, as a love story, than in the Indian reform arena, as a condemnation of avaricious white settlers.[28] In *Inventing the Dream,* Kevin Starr remarked that the popular appeal of the novel as "one of America's persistent bestsellers—is not that it translates fact into fiction, but that it translates fact into romantic myth." He believed that Jackson "collapsed American Southern California back onto the Spanish past" and created an enduring myth about the Southern California experience—a myth used as late as the 1930s.[29] According to Starr, the benefit to Jackson of her Southern California experience was two-fold: in Southern California, she found both an escape from her always uncomfortable orthodox Calvinist background and a sense of belonging she had missed while moving from hotel to hotel and city to city. Her sympathy for mission Catholicism became apparent in her articles on California, and she returned to Southern California to regain her health.

While Kevin Starr saw *Ramona* as a romantic myth, a contemporary reviewer in the *Critic* called it "one of the most tender and touching [love stories] we have read for a considerable period."[30] Another referred to it as a poet's novel, "a prose Evangeline . . . a sweet and mournful poetic story."[31] A third described *Ramona* as an intensively alive novel of reform with artistic distinction, standing "as the most finished, though not the most striking, example that what American women have done notably in literature they have done nobly."[32]

Jackson failed to create a sympathetic feeling for the Indians among many of her readers, who instead saw only a tender love story. One reviewer described *Ramona* as a successful love story, "a little overweighted with misery," but totally inadequate in presenting the Indian problem.[33] Although calling *Ramona* the best California novel yet written, the reviewer in the March 1885 issue of the *Overland Monthly* noted that more poet than reformer emerged. It possessed "no burning appeal, no crushing arraignment, no such book as 'Uncle Tom's Cabin.'" It was "an idyl—sorrowful, yet never harsh."[34]

As reviews appeared, Jackson soon realized that some readers had missed her whole purpose. "I am sick of hearing that the flight of Alessandro & Ramona is an 'exquisite ideal,' & not even an allusion to the ejectment of the Temecula band from their homes," she wrote Warner. The *New York Evening Telegram* review had called it dull reading with no end. Jackson felt that only Warner and the *New York Daily Tribune* "seemed to care a straw for the Indian history in it."[35]

Even her dear friend Aldrich seemed to have missed the point. Thanking him on January 10 for his review, she remarked she only wished he had felt the "Indian side of the story" more deeply. "I care more for making one soul burn with indignation and protest against our wrongs to the Indians," she exclaimed, "than I do even for having you praise the quality of my work."[36]

Jackson wrote to another friend that she feared as a story the novel had been too interesting. She complained that critics were more impressed by its literary excellence than by its message.[37] Particularly disturbed by the unflattering review in the *Nation*, Jackson wrote Aldrich to see if there was such a thing as a review of a review. She found it strange that such prominent critics as Warner, Higginson, and others praised it so highly while a reviewer, clever enough to be on the staff of the *Nation*, should disagree. Later, when she discovered the reviewer was a woman, she no longer cared. Looking through the list of female reviewers for the *Nation*, she suspected the identity of the author and why she had written the review. Then Jackson poked fun at Aldrich's review for comparing her to the Spanish artist [Bartolomé Esteban] Murillo. The worst of it was that most Americans would not even know who the artist was.[38]

Fortunately, not every reviewer missed the reform message in her novel. Writing for the *Atlantic Monthly*, H. E. Scudder praised the novel, comparing Jackson's beautiful narrative to the work of an artist. Importantly, he felt, the story never became an open plea for the Indians. The reader, although indignant, never lost interest in the enfolding story. "The result is that the wrongs sink deeper into the mind than if they had been the subject of the most eloquent diatribe."[39] That Alessandro was portrayed as superior to the other Indians did not lessen the injustice done to all Indians by the whites.

Another positive review, by Albion W. Tourgée, appeared in the *North American Review* a year after Jackson's death. Tourgée, calling the book "unquestionably the best novel yet produced by an American woman," also recognized her plea for the American Indian. "A strain of angry, tender, hopeless protest against wrong pervades" the book, he noted, as Jackson presented "the cry of the poor and the weak borne down by the rich and the strong—the cry of the half-converted Indian ground beneath the feet of civilized saints!"[40]

Unfortunately, the failure of *Ramona* to become for the Indian what *Uncle Tom's Cabin* was for the slave was partially the result of characterization. Alessandro, the hero, was not portrayed as a typical Indian, at least not what the public perceived as the stereotype, unlike Uncle Tom. Instead, he was presented as a Christian with a position almost as high as a high-caste Mexican—his Indianism was ignored. Even Ramona did not see him as an Indian. Also Ramona, only half Indian, was more Mexican in her upbringing.[41]

According to historian Allan Nevins, Jackson erred by having the faithful cousin Felipe rescue the heroine after the death of her husband and her tragic flight from the village. Ramona, instead, should have been forced to live in misery and squalor. This happy ending ruined Jackson's effect of portraying a wronged people.[42]

Warner would not have agreed with Nevins's criticism. In a newspaper article written two years after Jackson's death, he noted that in only one point did she give in to her artistic sensibility—in the conclusion. But he agreed with her choice of an ending. "There is as much truth to life in a happy conclusion as in a tragic one," he noted.[43]

Unfortunately, not only did Jackson not live long enough to see the positive reviews, but also she was unable even to carry out her next project which was to have been a child's story on Indians for the *Youth's Companion*. She wanted to educate children "to grow up ready to be just." She had grown up with the "sole idea of the Indian derived from the accounts of massacres." "It was one of my childish terrors," she wrote, "that Indians would come in the night and kill us."[44]

Returning home from New York to Colorado Springs, she enthusiastically set about making renovations to her little house. Three weeks later on June 28, 1884, she caught her foot and fell down the stairs, severely breaking her left leg in three places.[45] Her keen sense of humor continued to be reflected in letters despite the injury and the resulting confinement. When asked by Warner if she thought of frescoing her leg cast, she replied she was going to be content to print "L.E.G." on it in pencil for the doctor. When asked if her husband was able to lift her and help her about, she exclaimed, "It took *four* men to lift me from the floor to the lounge—& all that into the bed!"[46] She now weighed 170 pounds. Her husband, Will, not only was unable to lift her but also, unfortunately, was too busy as receiver of the bankrupt Denver and Rio Grande Railroad to miss her companionship during the week. She particularly hated seeing him wandering around the house in misery on Sundays, missing their usual drives in the country.

She also missed her sojourns in the countryside. Although her bed was in the dining room and she had a view of the top of Cheyenne Mountain, it was not the same. According to her good friend Sarah Chauncey Woolsey, Jackson had a passion for nature and especially loved mountains.[47] In a poem written after Jackson's death, Woolsey noted that her dear friend gave "man the slip to seek in nature truest comradeship."[48]

Therefore, in early October when Jackson finally got out of the house for a drive, she described the experience as opening up "a new Heaven and a new earth!" The effort that it required was great. In a humorous letter to Warner she described the spectacle she made: "carriage driven up on sidewalk close to my gate—I sitting down *flat* on its floor backwards, and hoisting my 170 pounds of body in by my hands—dragging the *LEG* after me."[49] Even her dear maid Effie laughed at the sight. However, Jackson was determined to get out and drive daily.

Her confinement did not stop her from thinking about the Indians and writing letters in their behalf. In late August she informed Senator Dawes that she was glad he was coming to California to look after the Indians of Round Valley. She was sure they could not be any more deserving than the Mission Indians, whom she implored he not overlook.

By this time she probably was well aware that the Mission Indian bill, proposed by Price and accepted by Secretary Teller and the president, had not passed Congress. She explained to Dawes that the greatest disappointment of her life was that all her work and the report had accomplished nothing. She had just received word via Mr. Coronel from the captain of the Rincon ranchería who complained that the destruction of their lands continued. The new agent claimed he had no power to help them; therefore, they came to Mr. Coronel to have him write to Jackson, whom they called the Queen. They were awaiting her answer, believing it their only salvation. Her letter to Dawes reflected her depression. She would never go there again. "I am sick at heart, and discouraged," she noted. "I see nothing more I can do or write."[50] She enclosed a copy of the government report and letters of introduction to Kinney and the Coronels.

In late October she wrote a long, breezy letter to Moncure D. Conway who had recently returned to America from Europe. She informed him the relief bill had passed the Senate but lost in the House. "If I were the Lord I'd rain fire & brimstone on these United States," she commented. The treasury was full of money, wheat was piled up in Chicago, and "bands of Indians that we *promised to feed,* dying of starvation, north & south."[51] She was referring to something she had read earlier about a surplus of wheat that would result in the overstocking of the market. In the same paper an item appeared about the Piegan Indians who were dying at the rate of one a day. They were starving to death because Congress reduced the appropriations for the Indian Office. These two conditions, plenty and want, existing side by side haunted her so much that she wrote a poem about it.[52]

In November, Jackson wrote twice to Secretary of the Interior Teller. The day before she left for Los Angeles, she inquired if Ticknor, former teacher at Cahuilla, could be rehired by the department. The schoolteacher had been so worn out that she had resigned. The new agent, McCallum, regretting Ticknor's departure, informed her numerous times that she could have a position again either at Cahuilla or at the two new schools he had been authorized to establish. But when Ticknor finally wrote for a job, she was informed there were no openings.

Jackson also informed Teller that Coronel had written about the captain of the Rincon ranchería who reported the continued despoliation of their lands. The agent had explained that he had no power to set aside lands for pasture. Jackson described the agent as grossly inefficient since Brunson and Wells were authorized to look after land questions. She added, it was no wonder that the Indians distrusted all that was said to them. Disappointed that the Mission Indian relief bill had not included the recommendation of the purchase of the Pauma Ranch, she requested that such a recommendation be added, if possible. She also suggested that the government purchase the lands of the Rincon, Pala, and La Jolla Indians.[53]

Without knowing Agent McCallum, Jackson believed he was inefficient. After her death it became apparent that he was not only inefficient but more than likely involved in an attempt to defraud the Indians, using his former position to further his own finances. Before McCallum left office, a number of entries under the Desert Land Act had been cancelled. Late in 1885, once out of office and aware of these cancellations, he served as attorney for white applicants attempting to re-enter these lands, even filing most of their applications. His replacement, John S. Ward, described it as a land-grabbing scheme.[54]

Jackson's second letter to Teller from Los Angeles dealt with the Ponca. Apparently, Standing Bear and his followers in Nebraska were better off than those Ponca in Indian Territory. Several of the Indian Territory band had already traveled to Nebraska. She inquired if it would be possible for them to remain there. With sarcastic wit, she wrote that she would like to see all those contented Ponca from Indian Territory returned to Nebraska, "as a final settling of scores on one point, with that hypocrite, Carl Schurz."[55] She prayed daily he would not be given another cabinet position. Illness, confinement, and the passing of five years had not improved her opinion of the former secretary of the interior.

When the leg failed to heal properly, unable to undertake the long train journey to New York or Boston, Jackson moved instead to the warmer climate of Los Angeles in November.[56] Once settled, she again began her letter writing in behalf of the Indians. She suggested to a certain Mr. Frisbie that he read *Ramona*, which she hoped would strike "a stronger blow for the Indian cause than . . . [the] Century of Dishonor did."[57]

Believing she had contracted poisonous malaria, Jackson fled to San Francisco in mid-March.[58] Less than two weeks later she wrote to her husband to bid him goodbye while her mind was still clear. She was dying, but she was ready. Her only regret was not having accomplished more. She hoped that *Ramona* and *A Century of Dishonor* had helped the Indian cause. "They will tell in the long run," she wrote. "The thought of this is my only consolation as I look back over the last ten years."[59]

Jackson realized she had failed as a wife, although she informed her husband that she "loved him as few men are ever loved in this world." To make her point even clearer, she emphatically wrote: "*Nobody* will ever love you so well."[60] She encouraged him to marry her niece Helen, who was her beneficiary, and raise a family.

Unable to eat at all, Jackson shed some forty pounds. She seemed to improve a bit under the care of a homeopathic doctor. Her illness, however, did not force the condition of the Saboba Indians far from her mind. Writing to Brunson and Wells, she inquired about the case. G. Wiley Wells' reply was probably not too reassuring to the ailing woman. He carefully explained that the ejectment suit by Byrnes had been brought against the village. Wells had personally consulted with the United States attorney in San Francisco twice while his partner, Brunson, journeyed to San Diego to interview witnesses.

The partners decided to have the case removed to the federal court. In the meantime, they had spent their own money on expenses. When they presented their bill to government officials, it was disallowed. Despite this setback, they continued their efforts in behalf of the Indians, preparing the petition and papers necessary to have the case removed from San Diego County to the circuit court. Wells assured Jackson that he still believed the legal right to the land was vested in the resident Indians, but he was appalled that the government took such little interest in their welfare. Both lawyers intended to file the papers and assist the United States attorney in San Francisco. But they would not travel north unless reimbursed by the government.[61]

Wells' letter to Jackson in March had merely scratched the surface of problems the firm was having with the government. By June, Wells was furious. Although he and his partner had undertaken the work without any stipulated fee, leaving it up to the Department of Justice to decide compensation, they believed the Byrnes case would be a test case for all Mission Indians. Therefore, they enthusiastically began their work. The attorney general of the United States had authorized them to proceed as long as expenses did not exceed $200. When they finally sent in their bill, they were informed it was disallowed.

Personally committed and believing that the Indians had been "robbed, abused and mistreated," the two lawyers continued because they felt duty bound. The removal of the case to the federal court required the posting of a bond which the Mission Indians did not have. Therefore, Brunson and Wells located a wealthy individual willing to put up the money. By that time, the Indians had lost by default, and the two lawyers again plunged into the case, preparing papers and affidavits and a motion to set aside the recent judgment.

At this point they decided they could no longer go on unless treated with decency and civility by the government. In the meantime, the Indians continually came to them for help. Caught between their clients, who were being driven from their land like so many gophers, and the government, which was so weak and inattentive that it did nothing to prevent such outrages, Brunson & Wells felt totally powerless.[62]

Not only did Jackson have the problems facing Brunson and Wells on her mind, but also another situation, totally unrelated to the Indians, had emerged. Although bedridden by what she called malaria and an additional case of nervous prostration, her spunk in the face of criticism would not allow her to lie back and do nothing. She was angered about the publication of a biographical sketch by Alice Wellington Rollins in the April 1885 issue of the *Critic*. Rollins, who had already done a sketch on Whittier, visited the Jacksons in Colorado Springs in August 1882.

Disliking gossip about her private life, Jackson preferred not to be interviewed, but her husband, whom she called "the life & soul of the hospitality of [their] house," invited Rollins and her husband to be their guests. When the article appeared, Rollins never mentioned the presence of Will Jackson except as the man who harnessed the horses. Several times in May, Jackson wrote emotional letters to Joseph B. Gilder, of the *Critic*. "The cruel *idiotic* hurt of this picture of me & my life there without any allusion to my husband, is something which it passes my patience to bear, or my utmost thinking to understand!" she remarked.[63] She wanted to know how Rollins would like an article without recognition of her husband who made everything possible and was the center of her life. She requested that Gilder omit her biographical sketch when they were published in a single volume.

Two weeks later she again wrote Gilder. If he did not withdraw the sketch, she would personally write the author and request its withdrawal. In addition to the total absence of any mention of her husband, she was upset about the mention of her picnicking thirteen Sundays in a row. Jackson retorted that the world did not need to know she was a "champion Sabbath breaker." Already, the local people were about ready to stone her for her outings on Sunday; now mere strangers would have the same feeling. She pleaded with him to withdraw the article. Possibly to gain sympathy, she wrote she was growing steadily worse for nine weeks and was living for the last three days only on orange juice and iced champagne—how could he refuse her?[64] He finally relented and the article was omitted from the final copy of *Authors at Home* when it was published in 1888.

Inadvertently, Rollins' sketch revealed that Jackson did not regularly attend church. As a matter of fact, she did not speak of religion in her correspondence nor was she affiliated with any church. She did, however, marry her second husband in a Quaker ceremony. Still, the majority of nineteenth-century Indian reformers, both men and women, were imbued with an almost fanatical sense of evangelical Christianity which Jackson appeared not to possess.[65] Instead she was driven by something other than a strong Protestant obligation to engage in missionary activities.

In addition, most Indian reformers, including those who subse-

quently carried on in her behalf, had engaged previously in other reforms such as abolition or temperance or the foreign missionary
movement. For example, Mary Bonney, founder of the Women's National Indian Association, was also founder of the Chestnut Street
Female Seminary and an active member of the Woman's Union Missionary Society of Americans for Heathen Lands. Amelia Stone
Quinton, besides various activities in New York City, was a state or-
ganizer of the Women's Christian Temperance Union.[66] Jackson,
though, had no previous history of any humanitarian work. Somehow, her first glimpse of Standing Bear and the knowledge of the
difficult situation of his tribe had troubled her deeply. Possibly, her
failure to become involved in reform issues earlier resulted from
time spent raising two boys and catering to a husband. Maybe the
fact that she no longer had children to care for or was looking for
something more important to do with her life caused her to become
involved. And once involved, the condition of other tribes including
the Saboba kept her continually active in their behalf.

Shortly before her death, tired of confinement and needing fresh
air, Jackson wrote naturalist John Muir for assistance. She wanted to
be slowly drawn along through the woods to see trees and tumbling
brooks; she wanted to find a cool, moist area among the trees. Her
party would consist of an ambulance, two camp wagons, four ser-
vants, and a maid and a doctor. Could he suggest an itinerary?[67] His
kind and delightful letter pleased her, but he really had no suggestions. He sympathetically pointed out that her large party would
scare the squirrels and bears but nevertheless encouraged her to go
to the mountains. She wrote again asking numerous questions about
various areas.[68]

Her concern for the Indians consumed the remaining weeks of her
life. In mid-July she wrote Mary Sheriff inquiring if the copy of
Ramona had arrived. She was glad it was causing such a stir in San
Diego County. Touched by a message from the captain of Saboba,
she told Mary to inform him that over a hundred thousand had read
Ramona and many were working in the Indians' behalf. Also, the
new president and the secretary of the interior were friends to the
Indians. Further, Charles C. Painter, lobbyist for the Indian Rights
Association, had just paid her a visit, so others were now interested
in the Mission Indians.[69]

She remarked to Higginson in late July that her work was done,
and she was honestly and cheerfully ready to go. "My 'Century of
Dishonor' and 'Ramona' are the only things I have done of which I
am glad. . . . They will live, and . . . bear fruit."[70] Her only regret was

that she had not accomplished more. Four days before her death she asked President Grover Cleveland to read *A Century of Dishonor*. She informed the president she was dying happier in the belief that it would be his hand that was "destined to strike the first steady blow toward lifting this burden of infamy from our country, and righting the wrongs of the Indian race."[71]

On August 7 she wrote a poem entitled "Habeas Corpus." The last line reflected no fear of death, only the realization that there was still work for her to do—somewhere.

> Ah, well, friend Death, good friend thou art;
>   I shall be free when thou art through.
> Take all there is—take hand and heart;
>   There must be somewhere work to do.[72]

Just five days later, at four in the afternoon on August 12, 1885, Helen Hunt Jackson died of cancer. Her husband was at her side.[73] She was buried on her beloved Cheyenne Mountain. Her Amherst friend Emily Dickinson wrote: "Helen of Troy will die, but Helen of Colorado, never. Dear friend, can you walk, were the last words that I wrote her. Dear friend, I can fly—her immortal reply."[74]

Jackson's death inspired numerous poems and eulogies. Higginson in the August issue of the *Critic* described his dearly departed friend as brilliant, impetuous, and individualistic, "one whose very temperament seemed mingled of sunshine and fire."[75] She met death, he wrote, "with fearlessness . . . in the hope of immortality," because she saw "positive evidence that she had done good by her work."[76] He was, of course, referring to *A Century of Dishonor* and *Ramona*.

Flora Haines Apponyi, a frequent visitor in San Francisco, wrote a touching sketch for the September issue of the *Overland Monthly*. Although Apponyi saw the usual dignity and nobility in Jackson's blue eyes, she also saw "the gentle solemnity of a soul approaching the throne of its Maker."[77] Joaquin Miller, in his tribute, called her "the bravest of all brave women in History."[78] Jackson was someone who had taken up the cause of the weak, the despised savage, and made it her life's work. Sarah Chauncey Woolsey believed her fullness of life would be most remembered. To Woolsey, when Jackson died, "the world seems to have parted with a great piece of its vital force, its vital heat, a loss which it can ill afford to bear."[79]

Jackson's death touched many. Those in the literary world remembered her for her prose and poetry, but those in the field of Indian reform remembered her best for her crusade in behalf of the American Indian. Her influence was probably the greatest upon the upper- and middle-class members of the Women's National Indian Association. When she became a member of the organization is unknown. However, as early as April 1880 she had corresponded with Bonney.[80] At one point she visited organizational offices in Philadelphia[81] and in the WNIA's fourth annual report was listed as an honorary member, contributing fifty dollars. The same report described her as wielding a "vigorous pen" and ranked her as an effective pleader for the Indians.[82]

Quinton, long-time president of WNIA, mourned her loss, insisting that Jackson's soul was marching on, rallying, and inspiring "unselfish souls to the cause she died for."[83] The earnest and hardworking women of the WNIA kept Jackson's memory alive with the establishment of their Ramona Mission among the Cahuilla. Seven of the California branches of the national association paid for the missionary and the furnished cottage. Other missions were soon established among the Mission Indians to whom Jackson had dedicated her life.[84]

Another WNIA member stirred by Jackson's writings was Mrs. Osia Jane Joslyn Hiles of the Wisconsin Women's Indian Association. Hiles set out to preserve the remaining lands of the Mission Indians, investigated their condition first-hand, reported her findings to reformers and government officials, and appealed to the secretary of the interior in their behalf.[85]

Members of the male-dominated Indian Rights Association also took note. Their full-time lobbyist in Washington, Painter, visited Jackson several times before her death. She implored him not to forget the Indians but to give constant attention to their rights and interests.[86] He had been profoundly impressed by his June 27, 1885, visit with the dying woman who warmly welcomed him, declaring there was no one else she so wanted to see. Painter described her as possessing a "face radiant as the face of an angel with the glow of earth's sunset, and the ruddy flush of heaven's sunrise."[87] He believed that one of the comforts of her last days was her realization that the IRA was undertaking the investigation of the Indians whose story she had written in "Ramona with such moving pathos, and whose wretched and hopeless condition weighed so heavily upon her heart."[88] Painter was so strongly influenced by Jackson that he undertook several more extensive tours through the Mission country. He continually praised Jackson's efforts in every pamphlet he wrote, often quoting liberally from the Jackson/Kinney report.

Although his activities among the Mission Indians did not impress Father Ubach, the cleric who met with Painter in California, also believed that the Jackson/Kinney report would be "an eternal monument of truth, justice and fair play," receiving the admiration and applause of everyone reading it.[89]

In addition to her influence upon the WNIA, the IRA, and those they worked with, Jackson influenced various members of the Board of Indian Commissioners, the semi-official group of philanthropists created in April 1869 by Congress to share in the administration of Indian affairs. Their 1885 report included a lengthy tribute to her. Her death brought strong reactions from many board members and other reformers who regularly attended the Lake Mohonk Conference, including: Merrill E. Gates, president of Rutgers College, who was not only a member of the Board of Indian Commissioners, but also presided over the Lake Mohonk Conference; General Clinton B. Fisk, agent of the Freedmen's Bureau and founder of Fisk University; and Alice Cunningham Fletcher, noted anthropologist. Fletcher was deeply moved by Jackson's death. "I feel that the Mission Indians are the bequest of Helen Hunt Jackson," she noted, "and if we love her and honor her let us be faithful, and complete what she has left us to do." President Fisk lamented: "We cannot fathom that Providence that takes such a one from us in the strength of her powers and influence." Finally, President Gates noted: "The supreme significance of Mrs. Jackson's death was the consecration of her life."[90]

Mrs. Electa S. Dawes, the wife of Senator Dawes, also attended the 1885 Lake Mohonk Conference. In a letter to her daughter Anna, she mentioned that these tributes to Helen Hunt Jackson were sweet and touching.[91] Conference members not only paid Jackson a lasting tribute but resolved "to continue and complete the work inspired by her pen, and labored for to the end of her life."[92] They diligently worked in behalf of the Mission Indian bill first proposed after the publication of her report. In addition, Lake Mohonk members worked in behalf of the Saboba village, supporting the court case until it was successfully decided in favor of the Indians.

Jackson's death removed a diligent defender of the Mission Indians. She had achieved numerous successes. Several small parcels of Indian land had been protected, and she had forged a congenial working relationship with both the secretary of the interior, Henry Teller, and Indian Commissioner Hiram Price. Price, who was more sympathetic to the situation of the Indians than many government officials, was replaced by a Democrat in March, 1885, five months before Jackson's death.[93] The appointment of this new commissioner occurred about the time that Brunson and Wells were having difficulties with the government. Possibly, had Price remained in office longer, these special assistants to the United States attorney may have been more successful with their test case.

Jackson did not live long enough to see her beloved Saboba village saved nor to witness the passage of Dawes's Mission Indian bill based on the findings of the Jackson/Kinney report. Nevertheless, because of her inspirational writings, her legacy lived on as the Women's National Indian Association, the Indian Rights Association, and members of the Lake Mohonk Conference took up the fight where she had left off.

6

Indian Reform Organizations Carry On Jackson's Work

Helen Hunt Jackson's untimely death could have dealt a serious blow to the cause of the California Mission Indians, but dedicated reformers did not permit that to happen. Instead, they accepted anthropologist Alice Cunningham Fletcher's challenge that the Mission Indians were Jackson's bequest, and they were obligated to complete her work.

Reformers, whether personally inspired or supported by their respective Indian reform associations, took up Jackson's crusade. Amelia Stone Quinton, president of the Women's National Indian Association, toiled in behalf of the Mission Indians. She established missions, supported missionaries and teachers, encouraged association members to fund various projects, and made numerous visits to California to personally direct WNIA's work. Working independently, Osia Jane Joslyn Hiles of the Wisconsin Indian Association of the WNIA also made personal tours to Mission villages and wrote in their behalf.

Because of traditional networking among female humanitarians, it was logical that the WNIA chose to carry on Jackson's crusade. But Jackson also influenced various male reformers including Charles C. Painter, the Washington, D.C., lobbyist for the Indian Rights Association, who worked long hours in behalf of the Mission Indians. He served as a member of a government commission responsible for surveying and protecting their lands—a task which kept him from his home and family for almost a year. He was assisted by Albert K. Smiley, founder of the Lake Mohonk Conference, and Frank D. Lewis, a special agent appointed to the Mission Indians by Smiley's organization. But money was as critical as dedication, and IRA members

not only devoted their time to the Mission Indians but also gener-
ously supplied financial support.

Thus the fate of the Mission Indians of California rested in the
hands of prominent eastern humanitarians who, almost as stub-
bornly as Jackson, refused to give up until Indian lands were surveyed and officially set aside as reservations with white intruders
removed.

Less than a week after Jackson's death, attorney G. Wiley Wells
wrote Secretary of the Interior Lamar that a delegation of Mission
Indians had recently visited him. Because his partner, A. Brunson,
had just been elected judge of the Los Angeles Superior Court, Wells
was serving alone in the capacity of special assistant to the United
States attorney in cases affecting the Mission Indians. He had carefully listened as the delegation explained that their lands, set aside
by executive order, were continually overrun by settlers. Unsure
of the exact boundaries, the Indians were not able to have the trespassers removed. A sympathetic Wells, therefore, recommended that
reservation boundary lines be adequately established as the most
effective measure of protecting Indian properties.[1]

Meanwhile, the new Mission Indian agent, John S. Ward, began his
work with the aid of his son, Shirley C. Ward, an attorney.[2] The
younger Ward had been appointed in mid-January 1886 by A. H.
Garland, attorney general of the United States, as special assistant
United States district attorney for the Mission Indians in California. He replaced the firm of Brunson and Wells, originally hired by
Jackson.[3]

Ward encountered the same frustrations as Brunson and Wells.
The federal government, in particular, refused to completely reim-
burse him for legal services, only providing a compensation of $200
per year if backed by proper vouchers. But legal fees for the necessary
work promised to amount to well over $1,000. The Mission Indians
living on government land needed legal assistance, and settlers on
the Potrero Reservation near Banning had already filed over twenty
lawsuits. In addition, the Indians at San Jacinto, Santa Ysabel, and
Warner's Ranch were facing legal ejectment by the white owners.[4]

As the condition of the California Indians worsened, the Indian
Rights Association of Philadelphia, realizing the importance of adequate counsel, became actively interested in obtaining a more equi-
table salary for Ward.[5] IRA Secretary Welsh, writing to Commissioner Atkins, suggested that a solution to the salary differential
could best be accomplished by the successful passage of a Dawes-
sponsored bill for relief of the Mission Indians. One of the bill's sections provided for a special counsel to defend Indian rights secured

in original Mexican land grants. Already passed by the Senate, the legislation was then before the House's Indian Committee. Welsh offered the services of the IRA to help push for passage.[6] However, half a decade would pass before Indian reformers would see enactment of legislation to relieve the beleaguered Mission Indians.

Meanwhile, while Ward was having difficulty obtaining adequate reimbursement for his services, the case of *Byrnes v. the San Jacinto Indians* (the Saboba village case) came to trial in superior court in San Diego County during the summer of 1886. The case had been filed on April 12, 1886, and submitted to the court in June. On July 3, the court found in favor of plaintiff Byrnes, and eleven days later the judgment was filed by J. M. Dodge, the clerk of San Diego County. In August, Dodge informed Leland Stanford, then California Senator, that Byrnes wanted to be humane about the matter, preferring not to evict the Indians if some provision for their removal to another location could be made.[7]

The negative court decision did not deter Ward who, supported by Welsh and the IRA, appealed the decision. Because the Indians were not financially able to pay, Welsh sent his personal check for $3,300 to the clerk of the court for San Diego County.[8] On January 31, 1888, the California Supreme Court decided in favor of the Indians on the basis that the original Mexican land grant had included the Indians' right of occupancy—a provision that was continued in the United States patent.

On February 21, Ward notified Commissioner Atkins that the court had decided in favor of the defendants. Commissioner Atkins, who had the entire decision reprinted in his annual report, noted it confirmed the position of the Indian Office "that grants of lands to private parties are subject to the rights of the Indian occupants, and that *such occupants can not be legally ejected.*"[9]

As a result, the Indians won over 700 acres of land worth about $100,000 and were now secure in their home.[10] Jackson, who would have been most delighted with this decision, unfortunately had not lived long enough to see her beloved Saboba village saved. Now the adobe homes, fenced fields, and irrigation systems that the Saboba Indians had been farming for a hundred years were finally protected.

While Ward continued his legal work in behalf of the Mission Indians, IRA lobbyist Painter, inspired by Jackson's deathbed plea, conferred at her request with Antonio Coronel in Los Angeles and set out on a second tour of several Mission Indian villages in July 1885.[11] According to Father Ubach, Painter had asked the captain at Santa Ysabel to have the headmen of the various villages assembled. Twenty-eight captains and almost four hundred Indians gathered at Santa Ysabel only to have Painter fail to show up because the weather was too uncomfortable for his wife. Painter and his companions, including Joshua W. Davis of Boston, therefore, went only as far as Pala. Ubach was displeased; this kind of behavior was common for special delegations sent from Washington for the past two decades. The only exception had been Jackson and Kinney who did their duty "nobly and faithfully by going from one Indian Pueblo to another seeing for themselves the real condition of the poor Indians."[12]

Although his activities among the Mission Indians did not impress Father Ubach, he proved to be as persistent an advocate of the Indians as Jackson, returning several times to California and writing detailed reports of his tours.[13]

Following his attendance in mid-October 1886 at the Lake Mohonk Conference, Painter set out on October 22 for a third visit to Mission rancherías. After spending three weeks in San Francisco where he consulted with various officials, he headed for Los Angeles and San Diego. He soon found that the conditions of the local Indians had not improved since Jackson's first visit. Both the Indians at Warner's Ranch and on the Santa Ysabel grant had been notified to vacate their homes, and at the Morongo Reservation near San Gorgonio, forty white squatters had taken the best land and preempted the water. Furthermore, an order to remove white settlers from Capitán Grande had resulted in a protest by San Diego's leading men.

Painter discovered that Knowles, Hensley, and the other white men whom Jackson had found trespassing at Capitán Grande still remained. In addition to visiting the villages, Painter met with Father Ubach in San Diego and toured through the recently established industrial training and boarding school supported by the Catholic church and supervised by Ubach.[14] Throughout his journey, Painter recognized the dangers—both large and small—that perpetually plagued these Indians.

In June 1887, Painter returned to California where he joined John T. Wallace, special examiner from the Department of Justice, who was investigating violators selling liquor to the Indians. At Temecula they were met by a Mr. Bergman with a fine span of horses. A twenty-five-year resident of the area, Bergman proved an excellent guide, able to point out which Indians had been driven off or merely bought off with whisky and flour.

The party headed for Cahuilla where they met with Mrs. M. J. Ticknor, the schoolteacher so much admired by Jackson. Earlier, Painter had notified the secretary of the interior that some Cahuilla land had been inadvertently included in a section given to the Southern Pacific Railroad. Acting as mediator, he persuaded the railroad to accept a replacement section of land while restoring the original Cahuilla land to the Indian reserve.[15] Viewing this restored land for the first time, Painter was pleased with its excellent covering of grass.

His report, beside recording his pleasure with such land successes, included a description of a visit to "Ramona" at her little hut. Painter was able to retrace her path as she raced down the mountainside to the nearby Cahuilla village for help after her husband's murder. Jackson's sympathetic portrayal of her heroine remained so vividly etched in the minds of her readers that they, like Painter, assumed there really was one Indian woman who had served as model.

In actuality, Jackson's Ramona was probably a composite of several people woven skillfully together. Her fictionalized Ramona was truly lovely, able to turn the head of a priest, even octogenarian Father Salvierderra whose "blood was not too old to move quicker at the sight of this picture."[16] But a disappointed Painter found his Ramona to be "full-blooded and homely."[17] However, his newly acquired vision of reality in no way diminished his enthusiasm or dedication to Indian concerns.

After traveling twenty-five miles, the group arrived at the Agua Caliente village at Warner's Ranch where Painter met schoolteacher Flora Golsh and showed her a copy of the Jackson/Kinney report. Although pleased that she had been praised enthusiastically by Jackson, Golsh was displeased with the critical treatment of her brother.

At San Ysidro, Painter discovered that Chatham Helm, another "robber" whom Jackson had attempted to have removed, was still actively fighting a court battle for the disputed land. Painter and his party then climbed the six miles to Mesa Grande and visited the school built the previous summer by Agent Ward. Painter was unimpressed, even ashamed of the government for building such a structure.[18]

A visit to Pachanga, Pala, Pauma, La Jolla, and Rincon followed. During his visit, Painter learned that the Oceanside Land and Water Company was buying and claiming water rights in the vicinity. To forestall these hasty acquisitions, Coronel, Jackson's close friend and confidant, had called a meeting at Pala on June 28. About one hundred Indians along with photographers and newspapermen from Los Angeles and San Francisco were in attendance. Using this opportunity to address the large gathering, Painter informed all those gathered about what was being done to protect the interests of the Indians.

Painter then traveled to Capitán Grande to see if orders to remove all intruders had been carried out. To his chagrin, he not only found trespassers but also discovered several liquor saloons "in full blast" on the reservation and two operating just outside the boundaries. In addition, a San Diego water company was busily building a flume across the entire length of the reservation—a fact Agent Ward had curiously failed to report to the government.[19]

But displeasure and disappointment were at other times eased for Painter. While visiting the Saboba Indians at San Jacinto, for example, he encountered the best schoolhouse he had yet seen. The school was personally funded by Captain and Mrs. Fowler, the former Mary Sheriff, who had worked closely with Jackson in the defense of the village. It seems that when Agent McCallum had refused to request a new school from the Indian Office, the Fowlers took up the task themselves. Unfortunately, when Sheriff married, Agent Ward removed her from her position on the commonly rationalized pretext that only single women were employed as teachers. However, this ruling was in fact not a government policy.[20]

Painter faced another disappointing situation with Ward when learning that the agent, who had originally planned to accompany the party on this June 1887 tour, had changed his mind. On the day they were to set out, Ward resigned as agent, requesting by telegram to be relieved of his duties at the end of the month. Initially, Painter was displeased with this action. After interviewing friends and enemies of the Indians, he learned that Ward—although far from "a perfect Agent"—was "the most energetic and useful man who has held the position at this point."[21] Nevertheless, as Painter continued his tour throughout the various villages, he discovered numerous instances proving that Ward was not adequately protecting the interests of the Indians.

This animosity that developed between agent and reformer was continually repeated. Jackson had initiated the pattern during her bitter controversy with Mission Agent Lawson. This distrust between government officials and reformers was likewise continued by members of the WNIA. Like Jackson and Painter, WNIA President Quinton did not hesitate to criticize agents she believed were not acting in the best interests of the Indians.

Painter's short tour, however, had acquainted him with the desert terrain that was home for most of the mission groups. His most important contribution to the cause of the Mission Indians was yet to come.

Much as Painter was committed to continuing the work started by Jackson, Mrs. Osia Jane Joslyn Hiles, a member of the Wisconsin

Women's Indian Association, a WNIA auxiliary, was soon investigating the plight of the California Indians firsthand. Unlike Jackson, who came to Indian reform with no prior humanitarian experience, Hiles had been active in various women's groups. She was a member of the Women's Club of Wisconsin, founder and director of the Nurses' Training School, a director of the Wisconsin Humane Society, and in 1890 was appointed by the governor as a delegate to the National Conference of Charities and Corrections.[22]

Alarmed by an editorial proclaiming that reservations should be broken up and their populations scattered, Hiles, in the unflinching tradition of Jackson, wrote a letter to the editor of the *Milwaukee Sentinel*, a letter which began with a glowing review of Jackson's *Ramona*. Hiles called the novel "one of the tenderest pleas that has ever been made for an oppressed race." To Hiles, *Ramona* was "an impassioned prayer" imploring that the Indians be allowed to live undisturbed upon their lands. She quickly realized, however, that this plea was being answered not by grace but by deception from those who wanted to abolish reservations and quickly scatter the Indians among the rest of the population. Surrounded by settlers, the Indians would surely be civilized even "at the point of a bayonet."[23]

Hiles hoped that President Cleveland, along with the secretary of the interior and the commissioner of Indian affairs, aided by a Democratic Congress, would be able "to get the Indian problem well on its way to a final solution." To that end, she sent a copy of the *Sentinel* clipping along with a short letter to the president to express her fervent hope that the pressure brought by others would not deter him from aiding the Indians.[24] Ironically, her letter was written on the very day that Jackson died of cancer in San Francisco. Four days before Christmas, Cleveland submitted the Mission Indian bill that was based largely on the Jackson/Kinney report. Once again, the bill suffered defeat.

In 1886, Hiles set out for California to personally investigate the condition of the Mission Indians and to try to preserve their remaining lands. In October, she reported her findings to the Lake Mohonk Conference. Two examples of mistreatment caught her special attention. One dealt with the Banning Land and Water Company, which, despite a court decision favorable to the Indians, persisted in making improvements upon the land—including a hotel and an irrigation ditch—developing the land as if it were their own. The Indians, the rightful owners according to Hiles, "have been crowded to the foothills, or have wandered aimlessly into the desert [and] . . . are perishing through exposure and want."[25] The other case dealt with a Major Utt, who had patented land upon which an Indian was living. Not only had Utt obtained a decision in his own favor, but he also had driven the Indian's sheep into his own flock.

Displeased with what she had uncovered on her tour, Hiles had traveled to Washington, D.C., in May, 1886, to visit with both the secretary of the interior and the commissioner of Indian affairs. She was able to get the Banning Land and Water Company episode marked "special" so that it would be brought up for consideration by the commissioner months before its regular order. The case of Major Utt was also to be investigated.

Describing these Indians' condition as "pitiful," Hiles recommended to members of the Lake Mohonk Conference that an able attorney be employed immediately to contest the grants made of Indian lands and if necessary to carry a case before the Supreme Court.[26] Immediately, she issued an appeal to members to contribute to a fund to protect the legal rights of the Mission Indians. Lake Mohonk conferees responded and appointed a Committee on Legal Assistance to the Mission Indians with Philip C. Garrett as chairman and J. W. Davis as treasurer. Within two years the committee had raised almost $5,000.[27]

Her disquieting Lake Mohonk Conference speech, which had been reported in the press, prompted Lawson, the former Mission agent and nemesis to Jackson, to write Hiles from Colton, California, on December 2, 1886, requesting help in defending Indian lands. The former agent informed Hiles that he had been living among the Mission Indians since 1878, five of those years as their agent. An organized effort by land grabbers was underway to demand that lands reserved by executive orders for the Mission Indians be opened to white settlement because the land was not occupied by Indians.

Lawson also noted that monetary relief was not the critical issue. Instead, it was essential that lands Indians now occupied and those reserved for their use be held intact for future generations. He hoped she would respond quickly.[28] Whether or not she did is unknown—no letter has yet surfaced.

The General Allotment Act, or Dawes Act, was passed on February 8, 1887, and provided for the allotment of reservation land to individuals and families. The Lake Mohonk conferees had viewed the passage of this act as the closing of "the 'century of Dishonor.'" At the 1887 conference it was noted that the act offered "the Indians homes, the first condition of civilization; [and] proffers them the protection of the laws; opens to them the door of citizenship."[29] At that time, most Indian reformers believed that Indians could not become acculturated until they replaced their traditional practice of communal ownership with the concept of private property. The Dawes Act was supposedly to accomplish this change. Unfortunately, like so many of the reformers' ideas, the Dawes Act was misguided. It reduced the Indian land base by ninety million acres and not only failed to stimulate individual Indian farming but also actually brought about a decline, thus leaving as a consequence more Indians in a condition of poverty.[30]

Lake Mohonk conferees had realized that the Indian problem was only partly solved. It was hoped that allotment and citizenship would soon lead to the ending of the agency system and the reservations, thus freeing Indians from the guardianship that had ruled them for decades. The Dawes Act, however, only changed the legal and political status of the Indians, not their character. "The child must become a man, the Indian must become an American; the pagan must be now created a Christian," noted the final report of the business committee.[31] Education and Christianization were now even more essential, and the members of the WNIA readily accepted this difficult challenge.

The passage of the Dawes Act prompted Hiles to express to Electa S. Dawes, the senator's wife, how delighted she was that "the glorious Dawes Bill has passed!" She assured Mrs. Dawes that she could "almost fly to Washington now, to see what can be done for the Mission Indians under the provisions of this bill." Unfortunately, illness confined Hiles to her home, yet she remained confident that many others stood ready to embrace the challenge.[32]

In October 1887, Hiles again appeared before the Lake Mohonk Conference. During the afternoon session of the second day, the conference chairman introduced the topic of "Woman's Work among the Indians." Quinton spoke first; Hiles followed. She admonished the session, noting that the issue was not what women could do but what they could not do. "I do not believe there is anything that a woman can't do if she undertakes to do it."[33] This attitude definitely reflected Hiles' dedication and that of Jackson and the other WNIA members who actively worked in behalf of the Indians.

Hiles presented her report on the Mission Indians during the afternoon session of the third day. She explained that after conferring with Kinney, Jackson's companion and co-author, she had learned that the population of Indian villages located near existing white settlements had decreased while that of those farther removed from the whites increased. She thus concluded that "the vices of civilization kill the Indians." Furthermore, she noted that reservations that had been established were generally on useless land and that most of the best lands were already in the hands of white settlers. She cautioned that the newly passed Dawes General Allotment Act not be hastily administered.[34]

As a result of her presentation, Lake Mohonk conferees established a Mission Indian Committee, which determined that the work already undertaken by the IRA should be enlarged and that Painter, already scheduled for a tour of the mission villages, be delegated to locate the best legal advice possible in order to decide what cases should be instituted against white intruders.[35]

Following her attendance at Lake Mohonk, Hiles, as chair of the WNIA's Mission Indian Committee, secured an interview with Secretary of the Interior Lamar to consult with him prior to her next visit to the Mission Indians.[36] Then in November she paid a visit to Atkins, commissioner of Indian affairs,[37] and by January 1888 she had arrived in Southern California where she visited reservations and Mexican land grants during a three-month tour.

In letters written the first week of April, 1888, to both Secretary William F. Vilas, who had succeeded Lamar in January 1888, and to Commissioner Atkins, Hiles related the distressing conditions she found. She noted that previous surveys of Indian reservations were useless since they did not point out the exact boundaries. On every reservation, she witnessed the encroachment by white settlers who were not only taking from the Indians "a little piece of land that has been redeemed from desert barrenness," but diverting water, fencing Indian roads, turning their livestock loose upon Indian fields, and threatening the Indians with bodily harm.[38] She concluded that the solution must be accurate surveys and allotment of land in severalty. However, she cautioned that, prior to allotment, whites should be removed and the Indians given the best arable lands. She was wise not to forget that without adequate water this land was worthless.

Hiles was particularly concerned with the Sequan Indians living only ten miles from Capitán Grande. Their reservation consisted of approximately six hundred acres of which only forty were arable. She described the Sequan homeland as a mere "rift between the hills." Already a white settler had driven off one of the Indians, and if any Indian goats or horses strayed onto his land, he held the stock for ransom. No government agent had yet visited these Indians, who numbered only forty.[39] Little had changed since Jackson's visit. Even then the Sequans had numbered less than fifty and were wretchedly poor and totally demoralized. In the Jackson/Kinney report, Jackson had suggested their removal to Capitán Grande once it had been cleared of whites.[40]

Hiles was also concerned with the welfare of other groups. She described the San Ysidro to Commissioner Atkins as neglected, downtrodden, and even more poverty-stricken than the Sequans.[41] One of them had been shot by a white intruder who had fenced the road. The intruder was none other than Chatham Helm.

But neither the secretary of the interior nor the commissioner bothered to answer Hiles' letters. Returning to Wisconsin in May, 1888, she again wrote to Secretary Vilas, requesting a two-hour interview to bring to his attention certain points about the condition of the Mission Indians that "deeply interested" her.[42] Still not deterred by the lack of an answer to her letters, in late May, Hiles wrote to Commissioner Atkins, expressing the great loss his resignation would mean to the Indian cause. She reminded him of her earlier letter concerning the Sequan and San Ysidro Indians. The Sequans, she noted, "were completely shut in by white invaders; and the same lawlessness that shuts them in, shuts their half-starved animals out—from a portion of their pasture." Once again she requested that these reservations be surveyed and the Indians informed of the limits of their land. She concluded, "the Mission Indians need help," but the Sequan and San Ysidro "are the most hopeless of any that I saw."[43]

Nearly as persistent as Jackson in the face of official neglect, Hiles carried her crusade for the Mission Indians before the reformers at Lake Mohonk again in October 1888.[44] The following month her report on the Mission Indians was read by Sarah M. Taylor at the annual convention of the WNIA in Philadelphia and was published in the November issue of the organization's monthly magazine, the *Indian's Friend*.[45] Under the heading of the activities of the Women's Club of Wisconsin, the December issue reported that Hiles had delivered a paper on the Indian question to the gathering of more than one hundred ladies. The paper was a strong one; Hiles was earnest in her convictions. "She certainly seemed imbued with all the fire and enthusiasm of Helen Hunt Jackson in her subject," noted the editor of the *Indian's Friend*. "It was a surprise for her audience, for very few of the ladies had given much if any thought to that which should be a just and Christian dealing with the red race," concluded the editor.[46]

Hiles' Mission Indian report recounted her visit to fourteen villages and Mexican grants as well as five of the six government schools. Although not criticizing the work of the dedicated teachers, she noted that an industrial school would be better. She informed WNIA members that past surveys of Indian lands were incompetently drawn, thereby allowing white intrusion—a constant complaint of Jackson's. However, Hiles praised the efficient work of agent Colonel Joseph W. Preston, who assumed the position on August 16, 1887, and recommended the allotment of land to Mission Indians under the provisions of the Dawes Act.[47]

On November 31, 1888, she wrote to Commissioner John H. Oberly, requesting permission to establish a mission among the Mission Indians either on existing reservations or on Mexican land grants. She inquired if land could be obtained upon which to build the missionary cottages.[48] But as with other requests, silence was the official response. Eventually, however, the WNIA would sponsor numerous missions among the California Mission Indians under the auspices of their Missionary Department.

Hiles' anticipated return to California in 1889 was prevented by ill health.[49] Her concern for the California Mission Indians, however, did not end because of sickness. Like Jackson, Hiles continued her advocacy in behalf of these Indians, though more and more through written contact with government officials.

In the summer of 1890, a Cahuilla Indian named Tacho, suspected of membership in a gang of horse thieves, was arrested by the constable of Banning. Taken to San Bernardino for incarceration, he was allowed to escape. Citizens of Banning hunted him down and hanged him. Horacio Rust, who had assumed the position of Mission Indian Agent in August 1889, noted in a letter to the editor of the *Tribune* that the incident was regrettable and that he had personally done everything to encourage Tacho to present evidence that would lead to the arrest and conviction of the gang. Hiles was incensed with this murder and with the rather cavalier manner in which Agent Rust had dismissed the hanging. Believing that "the lives in his charge are held very lightly,"[50] she suggested that, instead of Rust, Frank D. Lewis, special agent for the Lake Mohonk Conference, be appointed agent of the Mission Indians.[51] Her recommendation was never acted upon.

Years earlier, the activities of Osia Hiles in behalf of the Mission Indians had led to the establishment of the Lake Mohonk Mission Indian Committee composed of Philip C. Garrett from Philadelphia, Moses Pierce from Norwich, Connecticut, Elliot F. Shepard from New York, Joshua W. Davis of the Boston Indian Citizenship Committee; and Edward L. Pierce also from Boston. This committee had authorized Frank D. Lewis in February 1888 to proceed to California to serve as a legal field agent to prepare the groundwork for legal cases and give legal assistance in any cases where the protection of the federal government was lacking.[52] Lewis would later work with others to implement the Mission Indian bill when it finally passed in 1891.

Following the annual failure of the Mission Indian bill to pass

Congress in 1887, Commissioner Atkins on March 9 authorized the removal of all intruders on the Mission reservations—with the use of military force if necessary. Seven days later, Mission Agent John S. Ward was instructed to notify all trespassers to remove themselves and their belongings. Some settlers, however, appealed to the courts for an injunction.[53]

Mission Agent Preston, who assumed the position after Ward, proceeded to carry out the eviction notice. At the Morongo Reservation near Banning he found thirty-eight trespassers, some of whom he immediately removed, while others who still had crops in the ground he allowed to remain until the crops could be harvested. Once the land was cleared of settlers, the Indians planted their own crops. At Capitán Grande, Preston found eight intruders, four of whom had married Indian women. Unable to remove the latter, he was, according to his official report, successful in removing all others.[54]

At the request of Commissioner Atkins, Preston investigated possible illegal activities of former agent McCallum on the northern Agua Caliente and Rincon reservations. He discovered that, while still in government service, McCallum had purchased 408 acres in one section. The remainder of the section ended up in the hands of W. E. Van Slack, who, probably with the cooperation of McCallum, diverted the water on the reservation by means of a flume—water that the Rincon Indians had used for more than five decades. When the Indians complained to McCallum of the water diversion, he either "declined or refused" to aid them.

Subsequently, both McCallum and Van Slack sold their rights to the Garden of Eden Company. After disposing of his portion of the section, McCallum accumulated other lands and built up a fortune estimated at $80,000. Preston informed Atkins that he would place the "onus upon" McCallum to establish a clean title to the land. Unable to uncover how McCallum actually acquired all of his property, Preston concluded his method was fraud.[55]

The government had granted odd sections of land to the Southern Pacific Railroad Company, but much of this land had no water; after settlers purchased this railroad land and moved in, to obtain water, they trespassed or demanded rights of way upon Indian reservations. One example of trespass cited by Preston was that of the Garden of Eden Company, which had applied to him for water rights for their future grand hotel and a sanitorium. To improve the Indians' condition and extend "a reasonable privilege" to the company, Preston established an agreement which gave the Indians more water than they had previously been granted.

When writing to Atkins of the hot springs on the Agua Caliente

Reservation, Preston claimed he was exercising the courage to be candid, even though he thought it might seem that he was more concerned for the rights of the whites than those of the Indians. He noted there was no earthly reason "why this valuable water should be so exclusively held, when the Indians rights can not *but* be increased— and better enjoyed by them, under this improved condition of things." Furthermore, the resident Indians had consented to its use. He continued that "nothing but a morbid sentimentality for the Indian" could result in an objection. This valuable hot spring, Preston believed, should be for the benefit of everyone, so he requested Atkins to permit the building of a bathhouse by the nearby hotel. The Indians would receive an annuity and would be permitted to use the facilities.[56]

Although Preston's motives are more than a little bit questionable and certainly profit driven, other individuals who during this time worked in behalf of the Indians were driven by a strong sense of humanitarianism and evangelical Christianity. The work of Hiles, representing the WNIA, and Painter, representing the IRA, was augmented by Smiley, of the Board of Indian Commissioners and the Lake Mohonk Conferences. Smiley, like Jackson, Hiles, and Painter before him, undertook personal tours of California Mission Indian reservations. During 1889 he made two visits, conferring with Preston, whom he described as an excellent agent.[57]

In his 1890 tour of Southern California, Smiley was joined by two more influential eastern reformers: Davis and Garrett, who, in addition to other duties, both served on the Lake Mohonk Mission Indian Committee. They were accompanied by Agent Rust.

The plight of El Potrero Mission Indians near San Gorgonio Pass was of particular interest to these men. In her report, Jackson had described the Morongo Reservation, situated between the San Bernardino and San Jacinto mountains, as a large tract composed of three townships. Included within the boundaries were the small white settlement of Banning and small Indian village of sixty Indians, called El Potrero, which traditionally had occupied one of the few springs in the vicinity. The remaining springs were in the hands of white settlers.

Although Jackson and Kinney had not visited Banning, city residents wrote to give their side of the story. They explained that many settlers had obtained patents to the land prior to the establishment of the reservation by executive order. These residents noted the aridity of the land, the failure of wells, and the dearth of land available for cultivation.[58]

The condition of the Indians at San Gorgonio had worsened since

Jackson's death. Much of the reservation land which had been set aside by an executive order in 1877 was worthless. The fertile valley between the two mountain ranges had been preempted by settlers, leaving the Indians reduced to using only a small strip of land at one of the canyon mouths, a few thousand acres of mountainous grazing land, and the less desirable lands on the valley floor—lands without access to water. Prior to the signing by President Hayes of the executive order setting aside the reservation, much of the best land had been patented to the Banning Land and Water Company or given to the Southern Pacific Railroad in alternate odd sections for twenty miles on each side of the track. White settlers had obtained water rights, planted orchards and fields of grain, built their homes, and laid out the town of Banning within what later became the Morongo Reservation.[59]

From Santa Barbara, following their tour, Garrett wrote Indian Commissioner Thomas Jefferson Morgan, expressing his opinion on several matters relative to the California agency—opinions that Agent Rust himself had acknowledged. Responding to the query about a possible location for an Indian industrial school, Garrett suggested Redlands would be a suitable location. Garrett also recommended against the removal of the agency from its present site at Colton. But the subject that most interested him was the controversy surrounding the Indians' title to the Morongo Reservation.

Garrett explained to the commissioner that the secretary of the Banning Land and Water Company had submitted a proposition to Shirley C. Ward, a proposition that to Garrett and his companions seemed worth considering. The plan was that the rich valley land be taken from the Indians, who would be granted the mountainside and some good grazing land with minor water rights. The settlers who had been ejected from those sections claimed by the Indians would be given the valley lands.[60]

To settle the controversy between Indian and railroad rights to the reservation, Shirley Ward presented the case of *John Morongo et al. v. Richard Gird and John G. North* in the United States Circuit Court for the Southern District of California. Based on the Indians' land rights under Mexican law and under the title created by the executive order, Ward hoped to prove Indian claims.[61]

On the surface, this proposal appeared detrimental to the Indians. Therefore, Garrett and his companions noted that the El Potrero Indians would have undisputed possession of some good land and would have control of a water supply probably adequate for their needs. The Indians would still have between six and ten acres per capita of good farm land.

President Hayes had, they believed, set aside this large tract with the idea that scattered bands of various Mission Indians could be eventually settled there. But since all attempts at consolidation had failed, they believed it was more reasonable to gain concessions on behalf of the Indians than to retain the entire tract for those few who remained. They concluded it was hopeless to attempt to stem the progress of Banning.[62] Government officials accepted the proposal, and the Morongo Reservation was reduced from its original 88,475 acres to 14,560, thus reverting almost 74,000 acres to the public domain.[63]

Although this plan corrected some of the injustices the Indians faced, it was not until January 12, 1891, that the Act for the Relief of the Mission Indians in the State of California, which Smiley had called "the bill of Mrs. Jackson, with some modifications,"[64] was finally passed—six years after Jackson's death.[65]

Following its passage, Secretary of the Interior John W. Noble was authorized to create a commission composed of three disinterested people to satisfactorily settle the Mission Indians upon reservations.[66] Those selected were Smiley of Redlands, California, Judge Joseph B. Moore, a lawyer from Lapeer, Michigan; and Painter of the IRA.[67] They were to assemble on February 23, 1891, in San Francisco.

In a lengthy letter of instructions detailing a brief history of the Mission Indians and mentioning the Jackson/Kinney report as the basis of the January 1891 act, Commissioner Morgan charged these men with the task of selecting a reservation for each band or village of Mission Indians within the state of California. These reservations were to include, when practical, lands and villages actually occupied by the Indians. Upon completion of this task, the commissioners were to report their findings to the secretary of the interior, who would then, if he approved of the reservations, order a patent issued to each band or village.

Morgan informed the three commissioners that although twenty reservations had already been set aside for the Mission Indians, only 1,841 of the total 3,143 Indians lived on this land.[68] Agent Rust had reported in 1890 the existence of 37 separate villages, with some 500 living on private lands, over 600 living on patented grants, and approximately 100 Indians living on government lands.

Smiley, Moore, and Painter had no easy task. Not only did they have to create reservations for over one thousand Indians and carefully check existing reservations to make sure that all the lands described in the original executive orders had been included, but also they had to appraise the value of improvements made by settlers with valid claims on Indian lands. In addition, for those Indians on private grants, the commissioners needed to find vacant public lands nearby upon which to move them. They also were given the task of dealing with lands granted by the federal government to the Southern Pacific Railroad. Some reservations and other lands occupied by the Indians fell within the grant of twenty miles of alternate sections along the roadbed.[69]

The miserly government compensation of $8 per day for each commissioner and the congressional appropriations of only $10,000 to accomplish the tremendous task of resettling the Mission Indians angered Painter. Writing Commissioner Morgan, he noted that the pay for commissioners sent to other reservations was $10 per day. He could think of no reason why they should be discriminated against.[70] The lack of proper funding was a recurrent plague for the Indian service. Attorneys Wells and Ward had suffered as well.

The work was onerous. Problems were sometimes almost insurmountable; letters requesting and giving advice flew back and forth among the three commissioners and Secretary Noble and Commissioner Morgan. At times the commissioners were accused of overstepping their authority. Finally, health problems interfered—one commissioner suffered with lumbago and the other two with what Smiley called *la grippa.*

Painter and Moore arrived in San Francisco only to find that, because of unseasonably heavy rains, the railroads were out and they were unable to travel to the southern part of the state. Once transportation lines were again reopened, the two commissioners joined Smiley in Redlands. During their first meeting on March 6, they decided to personally observe the various established reservations before beginning the work of creating new ones.[71]

In mid-March they wrote Commissioner Morgan explaining the complicated situation at the Morongo Reservation near Banning. Spending three days driving around the reservation and exploring the various sources of water and the canyons, they met with a number of reservation leaders and about eighty Mission Indians. Their first-hand observations indicated that, if individual exchanges of land were made, they could no doubt arrange the Morongo Reservation to everyone's satisfaction.[72]

Unsure that they had the authority to exchange lands not used by the Indians for other government lands, the commissioners sought advice from R. V. Belt, acting Indian commissioner of Indian affairs. Belt's reply two weeks later assured them authority to "give up lands within the reservation not occupied or needed by the Indians in order to secure within the reservation, free from incumbrance, lands which are needed for [them]."[73]

Leaving Banning, they crossed the desert to Agua Caliente and met in conference with the local village captain before heading for Rincon and another conference with the captain of that band. On their way through Los Angeles, headed for San Diego, the three commissioners met and conferred with Special Counsel Lewis and Shirley Ward. From San Diego they spent five days traveling mountainous roads, visiting various villages, including Capitán Grande and Santa Ysabel, and the Warner's Ranch Indians.[74] Now thoroughly acquainted with the terrain and the condition of these various Mission villages, before proceeding on to other villages, the commissioners decided to split into two groups.

Because Painter was already familiar with many of the other Mission villages, he set out separately to visit the Indians on the Colorado Desert; Smiley and Moore continued on a two-hundred-mile, week-long trip, visiting Saboba, San Jacinto, Cahuilla, Pauma, Rincon, La Jolla, and San Luis Rey Mission—places that Painter already knew.[75] During the second week of April, Painter left for Indio and met with thirty-six representatives from Torras, Cabezon, and various other nearby villages. He found it impossible to ascertain whether these Indians were living upon the lands actually reserved for them. He informed the secretary of the interior that a survey would be needed.[76] In late April he headed to San Jacinto to begin his survey work.[77]

The challenges these three commissioners faced were compounded by demands from their personal lives, demands which altered the course of their work. In a letter dated April 1 to Secretary Noble, Smiley explained that he had accepted his position on the Interior Department's Mission Indian Commission without having seen a copy of the bill detailing the extent of work. He had assumed it dealt only with the settlement of the Morongo Reservation. Business commitments at Lake Mohonk prevented him from working continuously on the commission. He would therefore be leaving California around the first of May; he planned to return at the end of October.

Smiley, however, felt confident that Painter and Lewis—along with a surveyor—could do a thorough survey in the summer, and then next autumn the three commissioners could again meet and write an intelligent final report. He assured Secretary Noble that, by the time of his departure, the general plans would be settled, leaving only detail work and the survey to be completed.

For much the same reasoning, Judge Moore also had to return to his Michigan home at the end of April. Although he wanted to be released completely from his position on the commission, Smiley and Painter believed his expertise was essential and encouraged the secretary to persuade Moore to return to work on the final report. Smiley requested that, as an incentive, the government pay for his trip from Michigan.[78]

The departure of both Smiley and Moore by late spring left most of the commission's actual work to be completed by Painter assisted by Lewis.[79] Lewis, the special agent for the Lake Mohonk Conference, had been sent to aid Indians homesteading on public lands and defend the land holdings of various individuals and bands. But he also worked closely with attorney Ward. For two years Lewis labored in this capacity, trying to implement the allotment of land under the Dawes Act. Unfortunately, the paucity of arable land made it impossible for the California Indians to obtain the 160 acres provided in the Allotment Act. Eventually, Lewis was appointed by the Indian commissioner as special counsel for the Mission Indians.

With Lewis gone, Painter was left to carry on alone. In early May, accompanied by a surveyor, he spent a week surveying at San Jacinto.[80] The work around the town of Indio proved difficult and the weather was exceedingly hot. With a bit of irony, Painter noted in a letter to Noble that the original developer of Indio had obviously "employed a surveyor who seems to have followed his own imagination, or the will of his employer," for the survey lines ideally suited the needs of the town.[81] Furthermore, the survey stakes of redwood, which had only recently been imported into that part of the state, were marvelously preserved although they were supposedly set thirty-five years ago. Finally, the Indians were not even living upon the lands set aside for them and preferred not to move to assigned lands.

At one point, Commissioner Morgan accused Painter of exceeding his authority in regard to surveys and making unnecessary original surveys, which were the legal responsibility of the General Land Office. The Interior Department's Mission Indian Commission, Morgan argued, was empowered only to use a surveyor to ascertain the exact location of various bands or villages. Once these lands were approved, the necessary boundaries were to be surveyed under the direction of the General Land Office. Painter, however, defended his original surveys as important to the best interests of the Indians.[82] For Painter, to select land where boundary disputes were so controversial and where water was so vital was unwise without an accurate survey. Moreover, surveys were necessary to ascertain whether Indian villages were located on railroad or government land.

By July, after considerable difficulty, the necessary surveys of the desert region had been completed. Desert temperatures soared to the low hundreds, bringing Painter much hardship and discomfort; water was scarce, and supplies hard to obtain.[83] After a particularly difficult fifty-mile journey on horseback from Indio, Painter and his companions discovered a small, old Indian settlement at Twenty-nine Palms with good water and good land. This needed to be protected.

Painter informed the secretary of the interior that for the estimated 320 desert Indians, three reservations totaling four sections of 640 acres had been set aside. In addition, he detailed various other smaller tracts of land and requested that these sections be reserved for the Indians, "pending the final action of the Commissioners."[84]

In a July 7, 1891, letter, Painter requested that the lands at Rincon, La Jolla, La Peche, and Pachanga be immediately alloted to the Indians. "The limit of progress has been about reached under a tribal tenure of land," he emphasized.[85] After all, the concept of allotment of reservation lands in severalty had been established with the passage of the Dawes Act in 1887. However, Painter's request created consternation among government officials who could not agree on the request. Finally, the issue was given to the assistant attorney general for a decision.

Commissioner Morgan emphatically believed that allotments could not be made under the Mission Indian relief bill until the three commissioners completed their task and the reservations were patented. The action of allotting lands would take the reservations so allotted out of the provisions of the relief bill that had been intended solely for the special benefit of the Mission Indians. Although Morgan believed it was not the intention of Congress to apply the provisions of the Dawes Act to Mission Indian lands, he nevertheless turned the weighty question over to the assistant attorney general of the United States.

After a thorough reading of the January 12 act, the assistant attorney general concluded that, since it prescribed the manner of reservation selection and allotments in severalty to those living on the reservation, there was no reason why the secretary of the interior had to await the final action of the commission to issue a patent if the reservations selected were approved. He had the right to determine whether lands should be allotted in severalty or not.[86]

While Morgan and the assistant attorney general were dealing with the issues of allotment, Painter was still hard at work. During late July and early August he traveled for twenty-two consecutive days, covering more than five hundred miles by wagon and horseback, sleeping, wrapped only in a blanket, for one week on the ground. During this arduous trip, he visited numerous small villages includ-

ing Saboba, San Jacinto, Cahuilla, San Ysidro, San Ignatio, Agua Caliente, Mesa Grande, and Santa Ysabel. After a trip to San Diego, he
intended to visit the villages of Rincon, Pauma, Pala, and Pachanga.[87]

For three weeks during September and October, he visited Santa
Barbara, Santa Ynez, San Luis Obispo, and San Francisco. He lamented to Welsh of the IRA that, had this work been carried out
earlier, the poor Indians would still possess some of the best land in
California.[88]

In the same letter, Painter informed Welsh that he would have the
work completed by mid-October and insisted that Smiley and Moore
return to California to pass judgment on the report and settle any
problems.[89] He had pressing work back in Washington, D.C., and
could not wait for their arrival much longer. After all, he had already
spent almost eleven and a half months away from his wife and son.
Painter's indignation at being left alone with the job and Welsh's in-
tervention succeeded in forcing both Smiley and Judge Moore to return to California. By mid-November the three men were completing their task.[90]

On December 4, 1891, Smiley, writing to a friend on the Board of
Indian Commissioners, confided that the Mission Indian report for
the Interior Department was finally completed and would be forwarded to the secretary that evening. Smiley believed that the most
difficult as well as the most important part of the commission's
work was adjusting the Southern Pacific Railroad claims and private
claims at the Morongo Reservation.[91]

On December 7, 1891, Lewis, now clerk of the Interior Department's Mission Indian Commission, sent the final report to the
commissioner of Indian affairs, who in turn sent it on to Interior
Secretary Noble. Commissioners Smiley, Painter, and Moore recommended that 26 reservations totaling approximately 136,000 acres
be set aside. These reservations were described in detail.

After an exchange of government land for railroad land, the settlement of suits resulting from unlawful evictions, and the resolution
of many other problems, the diligent work of Painter and Lewis and
the initial work of Smiley and Moore resulted in the creation of reservations for approximately 3,200 Mission Indians. New reservations for 350 Indians in the Colorado Desert were established at
Cabezon, Augustine, and Torros. The mountainous reservations of
Laguna, La Posta, Manzanita, and Cuyapipe were created as was the
reservation of Santa Rosa, home of approximately sixty Indians. The
Campo Reservation, which bordered Mexico, became the residence
of about fifty Indians, and three families were settled upon Twenty-

nine Palms. Finally, the little reservation of Ramona was established for three families who lived in a canyon with good water and valuable grazing lands three miles north of Cahuilla.

Despite threats from John G. Downey, the commissioners, reasonably sure that he would not bring a suit, advised the Indians of Warner's Ranch to leave only when the sheriff came with an eject-ment writ issued by the final court of appeals. At Pauma ranch, Bishop Mora, after negotiating with the commissioners, deeded over 250 acres to the government for the Indians.

The commission had recommended the setting aside of Temecula by executive order, the purchase of several patented claims on the Los Coyote reservation, and the extinguishment of Chatham Helm's claim at San Ysidro—the last at an estimated cost of $2,500. In addi-tion, they recommended that the 43,000-acre Tule River reservation be patented to the resident Indians. Formerly under an independent agency, Tule River had recently been consolidated under the Mis-sion Agency, and therefore, the commissioners presumed that the Indians at Tule were to be treated as Mission Indians.

The Morongo Reservation, which included Banning and the In-dian village of El Potrero, was the most difficult to settle. Not only did the commissioners' letters to government officials show frustra-tion, but also their report on Morongo was eight times longer than most other descriptions. They had discovered that the one hundred Indians living near or in the village of El Potrero had been continu-ally plagued by the encroachment of white settlers who had devel-oped most of the available water sources. Painter, Smiley, and Moore ejected some settlers including Richard Gird and John G. North, who had in turn commenced a suit to recover damages and deter-mine rights to both land and water. The commissioners were con-cerned that, should these suits be pressed, the outcome would be detrimental to the Indians.

After consultation with the secretary of the interior and the com-missioner of Indian affairs, land exchanges were made with those, including Gird and North, claiming Indian lands. However, this frag-ile arrangement would not remain in effect after January 1, 1892, so Painter urged the secretary of the interior and the president to accept these land exchanges immediately, thereby avoiding the placement of the Indians in a deplorable condition.[92]

Painter was deeply concerned about obtaining the land exchanges before the first of the year, 1892. Unfortunately, he was recently out of surgery and unable to meet personally with Commissioner Mor-gan. But because he believed so strongly in the importance of this matter, he would immediately respond to a telegram should he receive one.[93]

Painter was obviously pleased with his work. Writing to Welsh in mid-December, he remarked that he felt he had fully redeemed the promises he had made to Helen Hunt Jackson. He believed that if their work was approved by the president and the secretary of the interior, most of the Mission Indians would be able to make good homes for themselves.[94]

Thus Jackson's initial work in behalf of the Mission Indians had finally reached fruition; her plea to Painter on her deathbed had been answered. She undoubtedly would have been gratified to see Pala, Rincon, Cahuilla, El Potrero, Mesa Grande, Temecula, Capitán Grande, San Jacinto, Agua Caliente, Los Coyotes, Pauma, Santa Ysabel, Pachanga, and other familiar sites permanently set aside as reservations. The small reservation of Ramona, named in honor of her book, surely would have brought a smile.

Six years after her death, with the help of the IRA, the Lake Mohonk Conference, and the WNIA—all reform organizations she had reached through her writings—the Mission Indians were finally protected in the occupation of their lands. This protection, however, did not prevent settlers from desiring Indian lands and from encroaching upon them when possible.

At the October 1892 Lake Mohonk Conference, Lewis delivered an address on the Interior Department's Mission Indian Commission report. Noting approval by both the secretary of the interior and the president of the United States, he informed the audience that Miss Kate Foote, president of the Washington, D.C., Indian Association, an auxiliary of the WNIA, had been appointed allotting agent and was already at work dividing reservation lands in severalty.[95] But, he noted, many problems remained unresolved. The Indians living on Mexican land grants—particularly those on the Warner's Ranch, the Santa Ysabel Ranch, the San Felipe Ranch, and the San Fernando Ranch—still faced the possibility of forced removal.

Several months earlier, Lewis explained, the owners of Warner's Ranch commenced an action against the two hundred Indians living in the village of Agua Caliente; a similar action was brought by the owners of San Felipe Ranch. Lewis assured the delegates that the Mission Indian Legal Assistance Committee established by the Mohonk Conference in 1886 would use its funds to fight such suits. He suggested that Shirley C. Ward, who had successfully defended the Saboba Indians, be employed. Finally, he reminded his audience that the destructiveness of the Temecula and other Indian ejectments that had been so well portrayed in the writings of Helen Hunt Jackson had to be avoided.[96]

The allotment of Mission Indian land, which Lewis had referred to, was carefully recorded by Agent Francisco Estudillo, who recently had replaced Rust. In his first report in August 1893, Estudillo noted that 51 allotments totaling 2,000 acres were made by Kate Foote at Rincon; at the same time, J. F. Carrere supervised 156 allotments at Potrero (including La Jolla and La Peche and a branch of the Rincon Indians) and 13 at Pala.[97] During 1894 Pachanga and Sequan were allotted; the following year Capitán Grande joined the allotment list, to be followed in November 1897 by Temecula.[98]

Despite the passage of the Dawes Act and the allotment of Mission Indian lands, reformers realized that their work in California was by no means completed. As money was being donated by the various friends of the Indians in order to hire lawyers, the members of the WNIA began establishing missions to educate and Christianize the American Indians, including those of California.

7

The WNIA at Cahuilla, El Potrero, and Saboba

C harles C. Painter and Osia Hiles, personally driven to carry on Helen Hunt Jackson's work in behalf of the Mission Indians of Southern California, had in part been supported in their work by nationwide reform organizations, the Indian Rights Association and the Women's National Indian Association. The latter group, dedicated to improving the condition of Indian women and children, chose education and evangelism to carry out these goals. Sponsoring teachers and ministers, they soon began work at Cahuilla, El Potrero, and Saboba—Indian villages dear to Helen Hunt Jackson's heart.

On January 27, 1881, the WNIA's second annual petition, bearing 50,000 signatures, had been presented to the United States Senate by Senator Dawes. The previous day, Jackson had presented a copy of *A Century of Dishonor*, bound in blood-red cloth, to every congressman. Accompanied by Amelia Stone Quinton, who along with Mary Bonney had recently founded the WNIA, Jackson listened to the senators' speeches on the bill and heard references to her book.[1]

Since only one letter between Jackson and Quinton has been found, whether or not the two women developed a strong friendship is impossible to detail. Obviously, Jackson's death in 1885 precluded a very lengthy one. But somehow, Jackson's deep concern for the California Mission Indians became a dominant concern of Quinton's as well. Not only would Quinton make various trips to the California Mission Indian villages, but also she would closely direct the Moravian ministers and other association-sponsored workers at WNIA missions among these Indians.

The WNIA had proposed missionary work among American Indians as early as October 1882. Missionary stations, intended to be

temporary, were to be established where no missionary currently resided. As soon as a station became well established, it was turned
over to a missionary society willing to accept it on a permanent
basis.

Through the missions under the auspices of the WNIA, these dedicated female humanitarians planned to take on one of the traditional nineteenth-century woman's roles, that of caring for women
and children. Association-sponsored missionaries were to educate
the Indians in the English language and various aspects of domesticity, including the maintenance of a comfortable home. With these
goals in mind, the WNIA built missionary cottages and lent money
to Indians to construct their own homes. But above all, since WNIA
members and those they sponsored were imbued with evangelical
Christianity, Indians were to be converted to practical Christianity.[2]

Initially, the WNIA was unable to find an acceptable missionary
field. Not until May 1884 were two WNIA-sponsored missionaries
sent among the Ponca, Oto, and Pawnee living in Indian Territory.
The following year, at the suggestion of Senator Dawes, the first association mission station was established in California at Round
Valley.[3] Much of the sponsorship for Round Valley came from the
Massachusetts Women's Indian Association, which, with its thirteen branches, raised $1,000 for the annual salaries of the two asso-
ciation-sponsored missionaries. Other state associations aided in
this support. Two years later the mission was placed in the care of
the Women's Baptist Home Mission Society.

Helen Hunt Jackson had been well aware of Dawes' efforts in behalf of the Indians at Round Valley and had informed the senator in
late August 1884 how pleased she was that he was coming to California to look after the Round Valley Indians. She implored him not
to overlook the Mission Indians whom she believed were equally as
deserving.[4] Although Dawes did not directly work with the Mission
Indians, the WNIA eventually chose to do so.

The problems facing the California Mission Indians had been initially presented to the public by Jackson. And Osia Jane Joslyn Hiles
had continued to inform members of their condition. It was therefore only natural that the national association would eventually
undertake missionary work among the mission bands. In 1888, the
newly formed WNIA associate in Atlantic City, New Jersey, encouraged the establishment of a station among the California Mission
Indians and raised $300 for that new endeavor.[5] Other auxiliaries
and branches soon contributed to the proposed mission; before long
$2,500 had been collected.

WNIA national President Quinton corresponded with Commis-

sioner John H. Oberly in February 1889, requesting permission to begin work among the Cahuilla. She asked that he "resign" the unused
reservation school building, which was comfortable enough to serve
as lodging for either two women or a husband and wife team, to the
WNIA for missionary and educational work. Various WNIA branches
would pay for facility improvements. From Cahuilla, her organization hoped to reach other Mission Indian bands.[6] Commissioner
Oberly complied with Quinton's request and granted five acres on
the Cahuilla Reservation to the WNIA. In thanking Oberly, she
noted, "we shall now move forward in work at that place as rapidly
as practicable."[7]

The WNIA affiliate in Bethlehem, Pennsylvania, had also expressed considerable interest in this new missionary field. Quinton
therefore consulted with the bishop of the Moravian Church in
Pennsylvania, who recommended Reverend William H. Weinland
and his wife as potential missionaries. Both the Weinlands had prior
experience serving in Alaska. On June 19, 1889, the couple, joined
by the reverend's sister, reached San Jacinto in San Diego County,
where they settled into rented quarters. The WNIA Missionary Committee began referring to this activity as the Ramona Mission.[8]

In writing to Weinland, Quinton suggested that he inform the
Cahuilla Indians "that Mrs. Jackson who was their friend, & Mrs.
Hiles & Mrs. Ticknor all begged that we would send a friend & missionary to them."[9] Weinland was also told to inform the Indians that
a great deal of money had been collected to send him as their missionary and that Quinton would try to visit them as soon as possible.

Although the first missionary station was supposed to have been
among the Cahuilla, the 1889 WNIA missionary report noted that
"adverse influences" rendered the initial project undesirable. The
"adverse influences" mentioned were those of the Catholic church.
Quinton wrote to Weinland that Catholic influence was behind all
the opposition they faced at Cahuilla. "But we will say nothing
about that at present," she noted, and instead, "we will make our
way slowly & lovingly rather than to force it."[10] So work by the
Weinlands instead began during the summer among the Saboba and
at El Potrero village on the Morongo Reservation. Religious services
were held at Cahuilla, but two years passed before the WNIA undertook missionary work among these Indians.

Numerous letters between Quinton and Weinland reflected this
anti-Catholic bias. In all WNIA missionary work in Southern California, the Catholic church and its priests were perceived as obstacles. Writing in September 1890 to Weinland, Quinton commented
that she was sad the Catholics were rampant. But, she concluded,

"we'll make the real prosperity of our missions *contrast* with those of the Catholics, if we can, & so win *all in the end.*"[11] Three years later when referring to the possible construction of a hospital for the Mission Indians, Quinton commented that the WNIA could not "build for *Catholics to inherit. . . .* We must wait till the land is allotted, the agency ended, & religious liberty is assured."[12] Helen Hunt Jackson never showed this strong anti-Catholic bias in any of her letters or her writings.

Because Catholic priests had been actively working among many Indian tribes since the beginning of European colonization, their influence remained strong. Thus, it was logical that Weinland found the Indians he worked among to be a strange mixture of "ignorance and common sense, of Catholicism and of wild heathenism." But the Moravian missionary emphatically informed his WNIA sponsors that since the Catholic church had neglected these Indians, it had forfeited any rights to the missionary field.[13] Priests had not visited Rincon or La Jolla for three years and Saboba for over a year. From the WNIA's perspective, the appearance of Weinland, a Protestant missionary, had finally brought the priests to again visit their parishioners but only to carry off a few children to their schools and to order the Indian people not to attend Protestant church services.

The fact that the Indians at Saboba, Pachanga, Rincon, and La Jolla had been under the jurisdiction of the Franciscan missions definitely made for a more challenging task for Weinland and his WNIA sponsors. But this missionary endeavor was difficult for other reasons as well. Mission Agent Preston did not appear to be sympathetic, and various Indian factions were fighting amongst themselves.

Weinland and his wife had expected to work among all of the Mission Indian villages; with this plan in mind, he set out to visit as many villages as possible. In mid-September 1889, he traveled first to Temecula, then on to Pachanga, a trip of four miles. On Saturday, finally reaching Rincon, at a distance of fifty miles southeast of San Jacinto, he met with the two Protestant schoolteachers and held a Sunday service. The next Monday he traveled eight miles to La Jolla and the following day arrived at Pauma, where he found most of the Indians to be Catholic. Although they had not had a visit from a priest recently, they would not attend the Protestant services.

Weinland also realized that even if the Indians did attend his services, the territory he had to cover was much too great; he could only reach certain remote areas once a month. Noting that since "the devil is at work at every place every day,"[14] he concluded that once a month visits were not nearly sufficient and instead decided to concentrate on the smaller area of Saboba and El Potrero.

While he attended to spiritual matters for both villages, his wife held a sewing school every Friday at Saboba in an effort to gain the confidence of her pupils and aid them in clothing their families. Quinton, in order to help the missionary couple at Saboba, wrote to Welsh of the IRA. It was "pleasant providence," she noted, that the first WNIA work would be in the same village that the IRA had made secure through their legal support. She did not hesitate to ask if Welsh would write a letter to the Saboba Indians, supporting the women's work.[15]

Saboba village was located in a well-watered, narrow strip of land about two miles from the town of San Jacinto. Although the village had been saved through the legal work of Shirley C. Ward, proper surveys had not yet been made. The Indians were still very much in doubt over reservation boundary lines, a concern that Weinland shared. To the Weinlands, the small village of Saboba was special—a feeling they shared with Helen Hunt Jackson.

When Jackson visited the Saboba village, she had strongly relied upon Sheriff, the government schoolteacher. The month before her death, Jackson learned that Sheriff was to be married. Although pleased for the young schoolteacher, Jackson nonetheless worried about the Indians and lamented to the young woman, "but who oh who will ever love the Saboba Indians as you do!"[16] Jackson's concern was unwarranted. Now married and living in nearby San Jacinto, Mary Sheriff Fowler began teaching Spanish to the Weinlands to help them better serve their Indian parishioners. But despite her continual support and her extensive knowledge of the history of Saboba, garnered since her appointment in 1880, Fowler proved unable to completely smooth the path for the Moravian couple.

Upon arrival, the Weinlands held Sunday school every week at Saboba, with a preaching service afterwards should Reverend Weinland not be traveling. Attendance averaged about forty. During one of Weinland's absences while visiting other villages, a priest came to Saboba, held services three days in a row, and prohibited the Indian people from attending the Protestant services. Some ten villagers ignored this priest and attended Mrs. Weinland's Sunday school service anyway. It soon became apparent to the Weinlands that some of the younger generation were disenchanted with Catholicism and ready to embrace Protestantism. This was the opening the couple had been looking for, and, as a result, they never really gave up on Saboba. Even after moving on to other California mission fields, Weinland continued to visit Saboba several times a year.

Learning that the approximately two hundred Indians in El Potrero village, located about two miles from Banning, were anxious to have them visit, the Weinlands seriously began thinking about moving. The El Potrero group was not Catholic, seemed more industrious, and offered land to the Weinlands for a mission. Furthermore, the missionary work would be reinforced by Sarah Morris, the government schoolteacher, who held Sunday school regularly with much success. Despite all these favorable conditions, however, the Moravian missionaries were reluctant to leave Saboba without first discussing the possible move with Agent Rust. Rust, an acquaintance of both Jackson and Kinney, had assumed the position of mission agent on August 7, 1889.

In a letter to the WNIA Missionary Committee in late September 1889, Weinland mentioned a meeting with Rust, a staunch Presbyterian, who was willing to assist them in their Christianizing work among the Indians. The mere presence of the agent resulted in a large gathering of Saboba villagers. Rust informed them that, despite the threats made by the Catholic priest, they were free to attend Protestant church services if they desired. Weinland was pleased not only with Rust's presence but also with the kind words said in his behalf.[17] Mutual respect soon developed between the Moravian missionary and the government Indian agent—a situation that was not common between government officials and humanitarian reformers.

In his first annual report to the commissioner of Indian affairs, Rust, who had carefully observed Weinland's conducting services as well as the Indians in attendance, noted that the missionary was welcomed cordially. The agent only "wished that Christianity should put such a man in every Indian village on this coast."[18] Rust's annual report of 1890 continued to reflect his confidence in the Moravian missionary, whom, he noted, was teaching the Indians such important skills as building and farming.[19] Although Weinland and Agent Rust had a mutually respectful working relationship, Quinton soon grew to distrust the agent. She undertook an attack upon his abilities much as Helen Hunt Jackson had against former Mission Agent Lawson.

Plans for WNIA missionary-sponsored work among the villagers at El Potrero became possible during the late summer of 1889 when Morris turned her Sunday school over to Weinland while she went on her summer vacation. Every Sunday following the service at Saboba, the missionary traveled the twenty-five miles to El Potrero to conduct Sunday school through his interpreter, Captain Juan Morongo. Weinland's anti-Catholic bias surfaced again when he informed the WNIA Missionary Committee that, despite his success one Sunday baptizing twenty-seven children and young people, he still feared the power of the Catholic church. He noted that two priests had visited Morris informing her that she had to give up her Sunday school or be fired. Standing her ground, she informed the priests that until they held regular services for the villagers she would continue her Sunday school. The Protestant Sunday school continued.[20]

Since no permanent mission site had yet been chosen, Weinland notified the WNIA Missionary Committee that he preferred to locate his mission residence at El Potrero, partially because it was a regular government reservation. In addition, at Saboba he hoped to obtain land from the Indians to build a structure to house an evening school, reading room, and Sunday services. He proposed to divide his time between El Potrero and Saboba, preaching alternate Sundays during the winter and every Sunday at both villages during the summer.

With the aid of Agent Rust, the WNIA had little difficulty obtaining a tract of five acres at El Potrero. But acquiring land at Saboba proved to be another matter. In July 1889, Quinton wrote Commissioner Morgan requesting five acres at Saboba. Morgan replied that the two hundred acres upon which the Saboba village was located was not government land, having originally been included within the boundaries of a Mexican land grant which had been patented, sold, and then alloted to M. R. Byrnes. In January 1888, the California Supreme Court had determined that Byrnes held fee-simple title to the land but held "it subject to the right of the Indians to occupy the same so long as they will."[21] Therefore, the Indians' consent, not that of the government, was necessary.

Quinton advised Weinland several times on the issue of building at Saboba. On July 23, she suggested that if Indian consent could be gained, the WNIA might go ahead and build and obtain permission from the government later. Two days later she again reassured the Moravian minister that they probably ran no risk in building without permission from the government. Fortunately, by the end of the month, formal "permit" had come from the Office of Indian Affairs, and Weinland was ordered to begin building as soon as Indian consent was obtained.[22]

In late August, Weinland informed the Missionary Committee that he had held a conference with the Indians to obtain permission to use part of their land for his mission. Although they were willing to do so, the Indians believed they needed permission from Preston, Rust's predecessor. To expedite matters, Weinland personally traveled to Colton to speak to the agent. Unable to accompany the missionary back to the village, Preston instead wrote a letter to the village captain, recommending that the Indians cooperate. Despite this written permission, the village captain refused to accommodate Weinland without first personally conferring with the agent. As the missionary noted in his report, the Indians desired the opportunity to express themselves to Preston.[23]

During the fall of 1889, Quinton's letters to Weinland were continually concerned with the mission at Saboba. They finally reflected pleasure at Weinland's ultimate success in obtaining land adjoining the Saboba reservation for the WNIA mission.[24] Although proper quarters at Saboba were not yet constructed, WNIA-sponsored missionary work continued. The cold, rainy winter weather forced the Christmas festivities for 1889 to be delayed until the first of January when the Weinlands, Agent Rust, and schoolteacher Mary L. Noble handed out gifts, candies, and foods sent in Christmas boxes from various WNIA branches. The young Indian students, accompanied by an organ donated by the women in Bethlehem, Pennsylvania, provided entertainment.[25]

On June 6, 1890, Fowler, supported by the New York City Indian Association (which also raised $500 for the chapel), became the WNIA missionary at Saboba. She immediately began a sewing school two afternoons a week and established a Sunday school. Attendance fluctuated between five and two dozen. Besides teaching sewing and religion, Fowler made house to house visitations, ministered to the sick, and encouraged the women in various domestic industries.

About the time Fowler took over from the Weinlands, the Catholic church delivered lumber to Saboba for a new chapel. "If you think it *best* we'll *leave* Saboba & go where the Catholics will *not* hinder us," Quinton wrote Weinland. "We are called to *peace* if there are places where we can work without war," she concluded.[26] The completion of the Catholic church in 1891 prompted Quinton and her association to realize that the Saboba mission field was no longer Protestant. Their mission effort was suspended and money transferred to more needy missionary fields. Because Fowler lived in nearby San Jacinto, she continued her Sabbath work and whatever else she could do.[27]

In the fall of 1889, Agent Rust had recommended to Indian Commissioner Morgan that land at El Potrero be given to the WNIA for missionary and educational purposes.[28] In mid-December Rust received word from Morgan that the use of five acres on the Morongo Reservation had been granted. Despite heavy winter rains and washouts, Rust and Weinland obtained the Indians' consent to the arrangement, selected the land, and arranged for the purchase of lumber for both a cottage and stable.[29]

A cottage, complete with fencing and furnishings, was constructed at the cost of approximately $500—a gift of the Western Pennsylvania Indian Association at Pittsburgh and Allegheny. The El Potrero chapel was wholly the gift of the Bethlehem, Pennsylvania, branch.[30] Various other WNIA branches, associations, and auxiliaries supplied whatever monies they could; the New York City Indian Association donated $700, the Atlantic City Indian Association sent $300, and the Pittsburgh Indian Association donated $200.[31]

Although the mission was not yet completed, a Christmas celebration was held at El Potrero on December 28. The villagers saw their first Christmas tree decorated with gifts from the people of Banning and from schoolteacher Sarah Morris' friends in Missouri.[32] The traditional Christmas boxes sent by various WNIA branches added merriment.

The missionary cottage, named the Allegheny Cottage after the Indian association that sponsored it, was completed at El Potrero on February 12, 1890. The Weinlands expressed pleasure with the comfort it provided. The scenery from the cottage, which sat about two hundred feet above the town of Banning, in full view of the San Jacinto Mountains, was inspiring. In addition, the site had a small running stream which provided water both for irrigation and household use. The new chapel, then under construction, would be twenty by thirty feet.

The El Potrero Indians, seeing all of the work on their reservation, constructed a rough, unpainted schoolhouse. With these new additions, regular Sunday services as well as Sunday school and sewing classes were conducted.[33] The El Potrero Chapel was dedicated on April 20. Immediately following the ceremony, Weinland's interpreter, Captain Juan Morongo, was baptized. The Reverend then took up a collection from the Indians to purchase a chapel bell.[34]

Now that the WNIA had fulfilled its responsibilities toward the mission, their Missionary Committee, by unanimous vote, gave the El Potrero mission, including the missionary cottage, chapel, and land, to the Missionary Board of the Moravian Church on May 15, 1890.[35] However, realizing that the one, little church would not demand all of Weinland's time, the WNIA Missionary Committee engaged him as a "traveling missionary" to supervise new stations and continue to preach at various intervals for other Mission Indian villages at an annual salary of $400.[36]

Since 1886, various eastern WNIA branches and auxiliaries had been actively working among the Indians of California. But not until 1891, the year of the passage of the Mission Indian bill, did the white middle- and upper-class women of California become involved in working among the Indians of their own state. For seven and a half months, Quinton traveled throughout the United States, addressing public meetings, organizing new branches and auxiliaries, and visiting various mission stations. As a result of her dynamic effort, seventeen WNIA branches and committees were established in 1891 in California.

Quinton began her visit in the southern part of the state on June 26, 1891. Escorted by Agent Rust, she graphically described her trip in a letter published in the October issue of the *Indian's Friend.* Arriving by train at Temecula in the afternoon, Quinton and her party drove to the Cahuilla village, where they met Mrs. N. J. Salsberry and her thirty-seven students in the prosperous school. The following day they drove the two miles to the home of "Ramona" and bought a basket supposedly made by Helen Hunt Jackson's heroine and one by her daughter. Quinton described their home as a cabin, and "the life in it was evidently not that of the heroine of the story whose character was of course purposely idealized, though the main incidents of the story were true."[37] Much like Painter, Quinton was disappointed when confronted with what she thought was the real Ramona. Jackson's characterization of this Indian girl, although probably a figment of her imagination, had been so convincing that readers continued to believe that Ramona existed.

After a trip of twenty miles to the south, the party arrived at Agua Caliente on Warner's Ranch to visit the government school taught by Mrs. Josephine Babbitt and to see the old hot sulphur springs. Quinton immediately decided that the Agua Caliente village and its hot springs would be the ideal location for an Indian hospital to serve all the twenty or twenty-five mission villages.[38]

Traveling in temperatures well over one hundred on the first day of July, the party drove twenty-five miles to Pachanga. After passing the new government schoolhouse, a mile or two down the road they met the villagers participating in a picnic and festival. Just as everyone was gathering for a photograph, a messenger brought news that the schoolhouse had just burned to the ground, destroying all of the schoolteacher's belongings. Rust quickly assured the Indians that school would continue in temporary quarters while Quinton promised a replacement schoolhouse donated by WNIA. Within the year the school had been rebuilt.

Passing the cemetery where Quinton noted that Alessandro, Ramona's husband, was buried, the party descended the three miles of hilly country into Pala, arriving at sunset. Next morning they drove the three miles to Pauma. Although Quinton described this village as one of the most beautiful she had seen, she saw the residents as "sheep having no shepherd."[39] Like Jackson before her, Quinton was enchanted with these small mountainous Indian villages.

Thirteen miles away at the home of Ora Salmons, the government teacher at Rincon, Quinton explained the WNIA's special education and building work to the women of the village. She assured the women that "it would be easy to lead them onward in the civilized home-life already begun among them."[40] While Jackson had been more interested in protecting their lands, Quinton was interested in leading these Indian women into the sphere of nineteenth-century domesticity.

The heat, the steep, bad road, and the fact that the government school of Flora Golsh at La Jolla was closed, prompted the party to return to Pala, guided only by the light of the stars. A visit to an old Catholic mission at Pala was followed by their return to Temecula and the train ride back to Colton. Quinton ended her letter by thanking God that the Christian women of WNIA were helping to "secure a beneficent and permanent governmental service for our native Indians, until they become Indian Americans, and need only such laws as govern us all."[41] During the fall conference at Lake Mohonk, Quinton briefed reformers of her trip.

Quinton, truly as determined as Jackson, had followed many of the same roads through the Mission Indian country. The major difference between the work of the two women was that Quinton had a powerful nationwide organization behind her that could, at the very least, improve the physical condition of the Indians by sending them food, clothing, and missionaries. Jackson initially had only her own writing skills to aid her. Although during her second trip through the mission area Jackson had the authorization of the Department of the Interior, it nevertheless took years for her proposals to be realized. Most times, she saw no improvements for her labors. On the other hand, the women of the WNIA often received immediate gratification as WNIA-sponsored mission cottages were constructed, able missionaries sent, and individual Indian homes sponsored by the Home Building and Loan Committee were built.

Having, like Jackson, witnessed the needs of the Mission Indians, Quinton began to organize California women in their behalf. On July 5, 1891, at the Congregational Church in Riverside she established an Indian association. Two days later an Indian committee was created in Redlands, the home of Smiley. In rapid succession other groups followed: July 13, an association at Banning; July 15, a temporary committee in Los Angeles; July 16, an association in Pasadena; July 17, an association in Whittier; July 19, an association in Pomona; and on July 24, an Indian committee in Los Angeles. In

May, 1892 these various branches organized into the Southern California Indian Association.

Quinton arrived in San Francisco on July 31, 1891. After catching up on correspondence, she addressed three ministers' conferences on August 10 and later the same day gave an address in the handsome parlors of the Occidental Hotel. At the close of this meeting, she organized the Northern California Indian Association headquartered in San Francisco. Other northern California groups included an association in both Eureka and Chico and Indian committees in Oakland, San Jose, and Sacramento.[42] Missionary endeavors of the Northern California Women's Indian Association were carried out among the northernmost tribes at Round Valley and at Hoopa. In addition, a school was built at Greenville.[43]

These newly established California branches, especially those in the south, sponsored the WNIA mission among the Cahuillas. Their support included building a cottage for Miss C. M. Fleming, who in 1890, aided by friends in Riverside, had begun work in the mountain village of Cahuilla. She had been cordially welcomed by Salsberry, the regular government teacher who had replaced Mrs. M. J. Ticknor.[44] Ticknor, highly praised by Jackson in her report, had taught for seven years. Her death on May 7, 1888, had so affected the tribe that Mission Agent Preston was forced to close the school for the remainder of the term.[45]

During her summer visit with the Cahuilla, Quinton had become impressed with the work of Miss Fleming. She also noted the cramped quarters Fleming was sharing with Salsberry. Thus Quinton decided to sponsor a "wee house," not only to ease the housing problem but also to create an environment for Fleming to teach Indian women housekeeping skills. The various new California branches, especially that at Riverside, were expected to donate money toward this cottage, which would serve as an example to the Indian women of how to achieve the proper skills of domesticity.

To legitimize her idea, Quinton immediately wrote Indian Commissioner Morgan, requesting that he appoint Fleming as an "industrial teacher" for the women and girls. Quinton informed the commissioner that her association would pay for housing and that enough land for the house and a yard had been promised by the village captain.[46] When Morgan appointed Fleming, Quinton warmly thanked him, promising to build the cottage in which she hoped both industrial work as well as religious instruction could be carried out.[47]

In requesting that Fleming be appointed as an "industrial teacher" for women and children, Quinton was involving the WNIA in the recently established, government-sponsored field matron program.

Indian reformers were convinced that trying to acculturate the men was useless work unless their wives and daughters became a part of the overall scheme. Therefore, in the early 1890s the government created the position of field matron so that Indian women "may be influenced in their home life and duties, and may have done for them in their sphere what farmers and mechanics are supposed to do for Indian men in their sphere." A matron's job was to instruct Indian women in housekeeping chores, including food preparation, sewing, laundry work, care of the sick, child rearing, and "the proper observance of the Sabbath."[48]

The field matron concept was strongly reflective of nineteenth-century attitude toward the role of women in society. Domesticity, including the caring of hearth, home, and child, was woman's "sphere," and here was another opportunity for white women to further the education of the less fortunate women of other races. The building of cottages for these field matrons became a significant addition to the program.

But building a cottage for missionaries was only part of the WNIA work. In the fall of 1884, anthropologist Alice Fletcher had suggested before a meeting at Lake Mohonk that an essential part of the civilization process was the existence on the reservations of American-style housing for the Indians. Several WNIA members agreed, and the following year a permanent Home Building and Loan Committee was established as a new WNIA department. This department lent money to Indian families for home-building purposes.[49]

While WNIA-sponsored workers were hard at work among various California Mission Indian villages, WNIA field work was continued by William H. Weinland, who, although ministering to those at El Potrero, took time to travel hundreds of miles over rough mountain roads to visit Cahuilla, Agua Caliente, Pachanga, Saboba, Rincon, and La Jolla as the association's superintendent in southern California. In addition to preaching to the Indians, he showed pictures made by a magic lantern, illustrating *Pilgrim's Progress*. During August and September 1892, he made several trips to Cahuilla on horseback to begin construction of Fleming's cottage. In April 1892, when visiting the Warner's Ranch Agua Caliente, Weinland consulted with the Indians about locating a hospital on their reservation. The Indians, although very reluctant to share their valuable sulphur springs, finally consented.

While finding success at Agua Caliente, Weinland's five visits during the winter and spring to Saboba left him deeply saddened. Even though attendance continued to be good at religious services, he found the Indians engaging in too much drinking, gambling, and other vices. Weinland was not the only one concerned about alcohol consumption at Saboba. Noble, the government schoolteacher, had written a letter to the *Indian's Friend*, pleading for temperance work at Saboba.[50]

Despite Weinland's frequent visits to Cahuilla and his continual support, Fleming found her tasks increasingly difficult. Her health was frail, so during the summer of 1892, she took a short leave to renew her strength. When it became impossible for her to continue work as government field matron, she was replaced by Dr. Anna Johnson, a Vassar graduate and former teacher at Hampton Institution who had practiced medicine for several years. Johnson was recommended by both Quinton and the WNIA Missionary Committee to the commissioner of Indian affairs, who appointed her as field matron for Cahuilla.[51]

Shortly before Johnson set out for her post, Quinton requested a grant of five acres at Cahuilla for educational and missionary purposes which would include the cottage they had already constructed. She reminded Commissioner Morgan that Reverend Weinland had located this cottage with the Indians' consent following instructions from the Indian Office.[52]

According to official WNIA publications, Dr. Johnson arrived on January 20, 1893, and immediately began to carry out both her medical and field matron responsibilities. She also started a Sunday school service and during her first 5 weeks on the reservation made 322 medical calls.

Dr. Johnson's small living room became bedroom, dining room, drug store, office, operating room, church, reading room, reception room, and sewing room. In her first letter to WNIA sponsors she asked for money to buy a sewing machine. Despite long, hard hours at work beginning at six in the morning, she ended her letter by describing the beautiful sunset she could see from her kitchen window. "The rocks, the hills and mountains are dear to me already, and the meadow lark fills me with joy and thanksgiving."[53] Her cheerfulness and enthusiasm resulted in more than a gift of a sewing machine from WNIA: Vassar College donated an organ to enhance worship services.[54]

In one letter to her sponsors, Johnson noted that "the real Ramona" was not dead but had attended a sewing class yesterday, finishing a pair of jeans for her five-year-old son. Johnson proudly explained that the woman was a neighbor and "a good friend."[55] Again, Helen Hunt Jackson's mythical Ramona lived in the hearts of the missionaries. One wonders if the Ramona of C. C. Painter, Amelia Stone Quinton, and Dr. Anna Johnson were in fact one in the same; unfortunately, no record exists to prove or disprove this speculation.

WNIA official literature presented the Cahuilla mission as successful and peaceful. It did not, however, reflect any emerging land dispute. But this convenient omission was typical of the reports appearing in the *Indian's Friend* and in the various missionary reports. However, correspondence between Quinton and Agent Rust, Weinland, and Commissioner Morgan indicated a much different picture.

Quinton learned from Weinland that Rust had rented land with an adobe house. He planned on moving the recently built WNIA cottage to this land. Not only was the rental contract with the Indians made in the name of the association, without its authorization, but also Rust had agreed that, at the end of five years, the improved existing dwelling as well as the WNIA-built cottage would revert to the Indians. Quinton was furious. While answering Weinland, she noted that the actions of Rust represented "the greatest imprudence & dishonesty I've ever heard of I think, of *any* agent."[56]

Quinton immediately wrote an angry letter to Morgan in mid-January 1893, informing him that Rust did not have any authority to move the cottage. She reminded the commissioner that the cottage had been built at WNIA expense and placed with Weinland's direction, the consent of the Indians, and the permission of the Indian Office. Quinton also learned that Rust had prohibited Dr. Johnson from beginning her work as field matron at Cahuilla. She requested that the commissioner protect the WNIA cottage and direct Johnson to begin her government work.[57]

Less than three weeks later Quinton wrote a lengthy letter to Morgan and included a diagram showing the location of the cottage twelve feet to the west of the government teacher's living quarters. Rust, she said, was accusing the association of building the cottage without either his consent or knowledge. This accusation was absurd; not only had Weinland located the placement of the cottage with the consent of the captain and village headmen, but also Salsberry, the government teacher, and Fleming, the former field matron, preferred this location. Furthermore, Rust had made no objections at any time.

Although ill and therefore unable to visit the location personally, Rust had ample opportunity to object during his next meeting with Weinland. "Not one word of protest did I hear from him, *then, or at any other* time," wrote Weinland. Quinton assumed that Rust was displeased because he had not been in charge of the matter from the beginning. In practice, WNIA never dealt directly with agents on such matters because they were too busy and their headquarters too distant. Instead, such decisions in Southern California were left up to Superintendent Weinland. Quinton closed her letter to Morgan trusting him to leave the cottage undisturbed.[58]

Quinton noted that she personally had no attachment to that particular location for the cottage. It had been placed near the schoolhouse primarily because Fleming felt more safe. Quinton only wished that the Southern California association would purchase the cottage from the national organization's Missionary Committee and be done with it.[59] Several months later the WNIA president informed Weinland that the Missionary Committee expected him to protest the land giveaway in five years. "You will do it wisely & gently I know," she admonished him, "but we hope you will not condone nor approve such a deed."[60]

The situation worsened, and Agent Rust denied all of Quinton's accusations. He informed Morgan that Quinton's statement that he "was arranging to *remove the cottage* at Cahuilla and *had forbidden* Dr. A. Johnson to go to Coahuilla [*sic*] and *occupy the same are utterly* false."[61] Instead of forbidding Dr. Johnson from going to Cahuilla on January 2, Rust escorted her from Riverside to the reservation and tried to help her begin her work. Together they had examined the WNIA missionary cottage, finding it a cheap affair unfit to teach in.[62] They both looked for a new location; she agreed with his selection. Rust then found the owner of the new parcel and made an agreement that the association could have the lot with the existing adobe house for five years. He thought he was doing everyone a favor.

Near the end of his letter he adamantly informed Morgan that there was no truth in Quinton's perception of events at Cahuilla. Furthermore, if he continued as agent, he "should heartily wish she would keep out of the state for . . . she has only made trouble from the day she began what she calls her work in So. Calif."[63] This attack was reminiscent of Agent Lawson's complaint in 1883 to Commissioner Hiram Price about Helen Hunt Jackson.

Quinton could be very combative when she believed she was right. As head of the WNIA Missionary Committee, Quinton, much like Jackson in her capacity as official mission agent, forged ahead when she saw a task that needed to be accomplished. Rust, like Lawson, probably saw his authority being challenged and reacted accordingly. Unfortunately, not enough evidence remains to assess blame on either Quinton or Rust. Both were obviously doing what they thought was best for their Indian charges, just as Lawson and Jackson had done on a previous occasion.

Although Jackson had respected Rust, Quinton found him exasperating. When she learned in March that he had resigned, she immediately wrote Hoke Smith, secretary of the interior, requesting that Weinland be appointed to the office of Mission Indian agent. She included petitions for his appointment and noted that he had served the WNIA for five years, always with the best interests of the Indians in mind. After detailing the activities of the WNIA, Quinton remarked that his appointment would aid the association's work.[64]

The land issue at Cahuilla remained problematical. In April 1893, Quinton requested that Acting Commissioner Belt grant the five acres with the adobe house selected earlier by Rust to the WNIA and its successor for educational and missionary purposes. This particular parcel of land had sufficient water and some alfalfa which would be suitable for pasturing Johnson's horse.

Quinton followed this new approach because it seemed that, without the knowledge of her WNIA sponsors, Johnson had already paid $60 to the owner of the land, thus buying out the owner's "possessory rights" and holding the land for the association. Quinton viewed this purchase of the Indians' rights as consent and therefore made the same request for five acres of Belt's replacement, the newly appointed Indian Commissioner Daniel M. Browning.[65]

Finally, Quinton suggested that instead of moving the WNIA cottage to these five acres, the government should purchase it as a home for Salsberry, the government teacher. In turn, the adobe house would be repaired and an addition added at WNIA expense.[66]

The appointment of the new Indian commissioner and mission agent did not alleviate the Cahuilla land issue. Instead, Quinton was almost immediately embroiled in yet another confrontation over the land—this time with recently appointed Mission Agent Estudillo. Quinton and others had tried unsuccessfully to prevent Estudillo's confirmation, believing him "an intemperate man." Upon learning of his confirmation, she wrote Weinland that "if he *is* in we must be all the more diligent & watchful & alert for our poor Indians."[67] Quinton, in fact, had already judged the new agent and found his actions unworthy and intolerable.

The captain of Cahuilla and several others visited Estudillo in Colton shortly after he assumed office to explain that they were not interested in giving the land to anyone. Writing to Browning, Estudillo requested that nothing be done until he had an opportunity to visit the village and make a full report.[68] Two weeks later on July 28 after visiting Cahuilla, the agent wrote that a large gathering of Indians "vigorously" protested to both him and Anna Johnson about the land issue. The Indians claimed they had been deceived about the "true nature of the paper," or deed, they had signed with Johnson. To support their position, they presented the agent with a petition signed by thirty-six of the villagers, sixteen of whom were among the twenty-five who had originally signed Dr. Johnson's petition requesting the land grant to the WNIA.

Estudillo not only translated for Johnson during the proceedings, but ordered the Indians to be obedient and respectful to her. The Indians, he informed Browning, had requested her removal on grounds she had deceived them.[69] Unfortunately, the editor of the *Indian's Friend*, in quoting from Johnson's letter, made no mention of this controversy; therefore, the doctor's side of the issue remains unknown. What is clear, however, is that the heated controversy continued.

A rapid exchange of letters between Quinton and Estudillo occurred during July and August 1893. In a superficially cordial letter, Estudillo carefully explained to Quinton that Johnson had not properly explained to the Indians about the deed they signed giving up the land. The Indians accused Johnson of deceiving them, and therefore, they no longer respected her. Estudillo recommended that she be removed as a field matron "not from any dislike to her or fault of hers other than that the Indians don't want her about them."[70] Furthermore, he recommended that the issue of the land be dropped until such time when it could be resumed in a different manner with a different piece of land involved.

Quinton was equally as cordial and solicitous. Calling Estudillo a kind, fair, and courteous Christian gentleman, Quinton was sure he could find a way out of these problems. She explained she had been "intensely" interested in the welfare of the Cahuilla ever since her friend Jackson had made her aware of their needs. She praised Johnson as a hard-working and devoted field matron. Very neatly, she laid the entire blame on Estudillo. Had he visited the village when all of the factions had been present, she rationalized, then his impression of Dr. Johnson would have been quite different. Instead, Estudillo had found a "*full* delegation of the *conservative* side, and a *small* number, if any, of the more *progressive* elements."[71] Obviously, it was the "progressive" element that was more responsive to what reformers were attempting to accomplish.

One of the major complaints expressed by the Indians was that the tract of land in question contained all the springs and the hot springs serving the village. Quinton claimed that had she been aware of the water issue, she would never have approved of the grant. She also agreed that part of the problem was the surveyor that had been hired to lay out the boundaries. All the association wanted was a simple little home with enough land for a garden and pasturage for a horse and cow.[72] This model home or cottage was designed to stimulate the Indians to imitate it, and she hoped that Estudillo would aid her in accomplishing this goal.

Learning that Johnson had told a totally different story to Quinton, Estudillo felt sure that the field matron had made other misrepresentations. He maintained that eight out of every ten Indians he spoke to wanted her removed. Furthermore, of the twenty-five progressive Indians who had signed the deed, sixteen "told her, to her face, that she had dealt falsely with them." While accusing Johnson of knowing the land in question included all of the Indian water, he excused Quinton, not expecting her to know the water situation. Since he was unaware of any practical way of solving this problem, he encouraged Quinton to let the matter rest.[73]

But Quinton was not about to let the matter rest. She had already given fourteen years of her life to helping the Indians, visiting every state and territory but three, sharing the goals of the WNIA with others. Estudillo, she believed, had misunderstood her. She was well aware that conservatives doubted the reformers and considered that that was natural, but such skepticism did not discourage the association. The goal of the WNIA was to uplift the Indians "into a better civilization and into practical *right living in every* way," and the progressives did the most towards this goal, although, she concluded, "we long to help all, & *do* so as far as is *possible.*"[74] She continued to defend Johnson whom she truly believed had not deceived the Indians. Since the association had no special preference for that particular piece of land, she hoped the agent might select another one for the model home.

Displeased with the reaction of Estudillo toward her pleas for help, in mid-August, Quinton wrote Commissioner Browning accusing the agent of misrepresenting the facts, particularly that Johnson was "under the ban of the whole tribe." Quinton explained that only the conservatives were present at Estudillo's meeting; the progressives who expressed the most confidence in the young field matron were nearly all at work. Furthermore, three men who favored her were unable to adequately defend her because they spoke no Spanish. The conservative leader of the council refused to interpret their testimony for Estudillo who did not understand the Indian language.[75]

Quinton agreed that certain mistakes over the land issue had developed but believed that no fraud was involved. She argued that the very land that Johnson had rented as pasture for her horse had been selected by Agent Rust and Attorney Lewis following an unbiased inspection. More importantly, Weinland subsequently testified that the hot spring on the land did not amount to much and had not been used by the Indians as far as he knew. The main water supply did not originate on this land, according to Weinland, who remarked, "they might as well protest against this selection on the ground of there being *a tree* growing on it." Quinton requested the privilege of continuing to work in the Cahuilla village "where there are *best elements* desiring our presence and help."[76]

Letters on this issue probably crossed in the mails. On August 14, Browning wrote Quinton, quoting part of Estudillo's July 28 report. He informed her that it was the policy of the Indian Office to grant land only with the consent of the Indians. Since Estudillo claimed that the Indians had not given their consent, the land grant to the WNIA was denied.[77]

Despite the failure to obtain the land, WNIA work continued and WNIA literature remained full of Johnson's good works. In a letter to Browning in late November, Quinton revealed another attempt to remove Dr. Johnson. Johnson, Agent Estudillo, and Weinland had all corresponded with her on this matter, and she hoped that the commissioner could stop this attempted removal until she could personally see him in early December.[78]

Johnson finally did resign, but the reason given was her mother's health. In late February 1894, Quinton informed Browning that Johnson's mother was in poor health and she might be forced to retire.[79] A year later a notice in the February issue of the *Indian's Friend* confirmed this. However, the difficulties between Johnson and the agent and certain Cahuillas make one wonder if those were the true reasons for her departure and not her mother's condition.

On February 4, 1895, Anna J. Ritter arrived as the new field matron.[80] Ritter did not stay long; an April 1896 letter from Quinton to Commissioner Browning reflected the field matron's interest to study medicine and become a medical missionary. She left when her term expired.[81]

It was reported in the association's annual report for 1896 that Ritter left because of an illness in her family. Her replacement, Mrs. C. C. Moses, a school matron from Wisconsin, was not a member of the WNIA. Nevertheless, the editor of the *Indian's Friend* encouraged association members to send her food, parcels, and gifts of money to carry out their goal and her work as a matron.[82]

In 1896 the mission at Cahuilla was transferred from the WNIA Missionary Committee to the Southern California auxiliary, headquartered at Redlands, with branches at Riverside, Pasadena, Claremont, and Banning.[83]

Despite the transfer from the national organization to the state auxiliary, Quinton remained interested and in touch. In a 1901 letter to Commissioner William A. Jones, she requested that the government purchase the WNIA cottage (costing originally $500) for $200 to be used for governmental educational purposes.[84] Upon learning how much she was asking for the cottage, Weinland suggested that since the repairs had not been that extensive, the asking price should be $100. Quinton agreed to write the commissioner immediately.[85] But even at this bargain rate, the government declined to purchase the Cahuilla cottage since it was built on government land and they could claim it anyhow. Quinton regretted the WNIA would not be reimbursed for any of its expenses.[86]

Although Quinton failed to obtain reimbursement for the Cahuilla cottage, she could still reflect on a decade of WNIA achievement in Cahuilla, El Potrero, and Saboba. A substantial amount of money had been raised by various branches, associations, and auxiliaries to build a chapel and missionary cottages to serve as models of civilization for the Indians to imitate. In addition, Quinton had convinced California women to become intimately involved in the condition of the Indians of their state. Finally, the government's field matron program had been aided, and the health care of the Cahuilla Indians had been improved through the hard work of Johnson.

Although Quinton obviously would not admit it or maybe did not see it, WNIA work had its negative aspects. Many Indians were caught in the struggle between the evangelical Protestants and the Protestants' anti-Catholic bias. This was particularly true of those descendents of former Catholic mission converts. Furthermore, for example, the land issue at Cahuilla divided the villagers, and WNIA appeared to be a threat to Indian land. How ironic that the WNIA thought it was carrying out Helen Hunt Jackson's legacy to defend and protect Indian land.

The failures or successes at Saboba, El Potrero, and Cahuilla aside, more work remained for the women of the WNIA. Quinton's dream of a hospital at Agua Caliente had not yet been achieved, and new missionary fields awaited opening, especially among the Desert Indians of Riverside County.

8

The WNIA at Agua Caliente and Martínez

During the summer of 1889, the Women's National Indian Association had undertaken missionary and educational work among the Mission Indians of California. The following May of 1890, they turned over their successful El Potrero mission to the Moravian Church, and six years later their Cahuilla mission was transferred to the Southern California auxiliary. The relative success of these two missionary fields, however, was overshadowed by the failure of Protestant efforts to overcome Catholic traditions left by the Franciscan missionaries at Saboba.

Earlier successes and failures aside, the WNIA's California activity, directed by Amelia S. Quinton, was not yet completed. Her dream of building a hospital at Agua Caliente on Warner's Ranch faced numerous obstacles. But undaunted and with the aid of Reverend William Weinland, she pursued her dream of a medical facility to serve the various mission villages and looked for new missionary fields to be founded.

The village of Agua Caliente was one of five villages on the Warner's Ranch tract owned by former California governor John G. Downey. According to old local residents, the original boundaries of the grant did not take in the hot springs, but over the years different surveys progressively moved the line until the springs were included. As official agents to the Mission Indians, both Jackson and Abbot Kinney had visited this village, and like Saboba and Cahuilla, Jackson had included it in her writings as a way to save it. The ejectment proceedings that had threatened Agua Caliente during Jackson's visit continued to hang over the village.[1]

Following her successful tour of the mission villages in late sum-

mer of 1891, Quinton wrote Commissioner Morgan of the value
of a small hospital at Agua Caliente. She informed him of her acquaintance with two women likely to be sent there, one as a government field matron and the other as a physician. The WNIA agreed to
sponsor the latter if Morgan would make the appointment as field
matron.[2]

Several months later Quinton again wrote to Morgan requesting
a grant of land near the hot springs so water might be brought into
the enclosed WNIA building without loss of heat. In addition, she
wanted the government to appoint the field matron and pay her salary. The association would provide all other expenses for the enter-
prise.[3] Unfortunately, the pending ejectment suit against the Agua
Caliente village complicated the formal acquisition of land for Quinton's hospital.

Then in early January 1892, she conceived an idea to circumvent
the legal question of the land. If the Indians were made to understand
the WNIA plans for the hospital, they might then set apart land on
which the association could build. The property, of course, would
remain Indian. She asked Morgan if the WNIA could try this "exper-
iment" with his approval. Simultaneously, she continued to press
for a government-appointed field matron. With the commissioner's
approval and cooperation, Quinton believed, the WNIA would be
willing to undertake the funding of a medical missionary.[4]

Early in January 1892, Morgan informed Quinton that Albert K.
Smiley also approved of the hospital. Because the title to the reservation was in question and the government could not put up a building, Morgan informed Quinton that, if she received permission from
the Indians, the Indian Office would have no objection to the association building a hospital. The government would gladly provide a
field matron to assist.

Two weeks later the commissioner inquired when the hospital
would be ready and when the services of the field matron would be
needed. To insure the monies for a matron at Agua Caliente, he was
withholding a part of the year's appropriations for all field matrons.[5]
Quinton replied that, as soon as they learned from Josephine Babbitt, the government teacher, that the Indians at Agua Caliente were
willing to accept their offer, living quarters for both women would
be constructed. The hospital, however, would not be built until the
physician and field matron were in residence.[6]

In late February 1892, Quinton wrote a hurried letter to Commissioner Morgan explaining that Babbitt had written of the Indians'
pleasure with the prospect of a hospital but were hesitant to make a
formal agreement because their agent had instructed them to do

nothing without government approval. Quinton requested that Morgan write Agent Rust and Babbitt of his consent. The schoolteacher could then pass notice on to the Indians. Letters were sent from the Indian Office on March 5 to both the agent and Babbitt.[7]

During April, Quinton corresponded numerous times with Reverend Weinland about the proposed Agua Caliente hospital. The association wanted the hospital to be next to the hot springs to take advantage of a free supply of the hot water, but for no stated reason, Agent Rust wanted the building constructed some distance away, while Attorney Frank D. Lewis wanted it as much as a half mile away. A frustrated Quinton informed Weinland that she thought both men were more interested in helping local whites get hold of the hot springs. She encouraged him to visit the village and do his best in selecting the site, imploring him not to let Rust take advantage of the Indians if possible. She informed him that there was no reason for building a hospital at Agua Caliente unless the WNIA could take advantage of the benefits of the springs.[8]

In mid-May, a very upset Quinton wrote Weinland that the subsequent reluctance of the Indians to donate land to the project might have been caused by a Catholic priest. "Don't let us breathe that fear to any one," she wrote, "but if the priest *has* interfered please tell me."[9] But Quinton soon shifted the blame from the Catholics to Agent Rust, whom she accused of wanting non-reformers to build the facility for the benefit of white residents, not the Indians. She hoped his "machinations" could be circumvented. She believed he was not sympathetic to the Indians and did not want to give them a hospital.[10] "Our being there for *their* good alone will keep out *selfish* men," she wrote the minister in another letter. "We would defend them & the Spring." She encouraged Weinland to explain to the village captain that the association was only interested in protecting them. "Poor souls," she noted, "how they are ground & robbed of favors even by the machinations of the selfish & compassionless." Already, $900 had been pledged for construction costs and the women were anxious to begin building. She mused in conclusion, "if H. H. [Helen Hunt Jackson] were alive she would say 'be *sure* & let the Ass'n build the hospital.'"[11]

Temporarily setting aside her anger, Quinton wrote Rust a conciliatory letter asking him to visit the villagers and persuade them to agree to the project. Describing him as a friend to the association's work, she noted that her members naturally felt he really favored their project.[12] Not depending totally upon her written persuasive powers, Quinton personally met with Commissioner Morgan and

Babbitt who had traveled to the East to obtain help in moving the project along.[13]

WNIA literature reported the Agua Caliente villagers were receptive to the idea of medical assistance and only awaited the arrival of their agent to formalize proceedings. But months passed, Rust did not visit the village, and then Downey, backed by the Bank of California and anxious to obtain the sulphur springs for personal financial gain, announced he would institute an ejectment suit. The August 1892 issue of the *Indian's Friend* indicated that the organization decided not to fund a hospital until this issue could be resolved. Both the October and November issues were more optimistic.

The first ejectment suit was initiated in the autumn of 1892, and Attorney Lewis acquainted reformers at the Lake Mohonk Conference with the details of the case. Fraud was considered a strong motive because survey lines had continually been changed.[14] The Indians won the decision in the initial suit, but Downey's heirs appealed to a higher court. To help defray costs for the new litigation, during the annual meeting in December 1892 in Brooklyn, New York, members of the WNIA passed a resolution urging Congress to make appropriations for legal expenses to defend the Agua Caliente villagers from the ejectment suit.[15]

About the time of the first suit, Agent Horatio Rust finally visited the village and rented by the month a two-room house to be used for the proposed WNIA work. Quinton was displeased with this arrangement. Because failure to pay rent to the owner of the house would be grounds to turn the association out, she found the situation all too risky. She informed Weinland that the agent was again blocking their work for the Indians.[16] Morgan was also concerned over the arrangement and would not permit the association to rent from Rust.[17]

Finally, the Indians gave their consent, and on November 22 the WNIA took over the lease of the cottage, although they were forced to pay rent to Rust dating from September 1. Quinton characterized this arrangement of three month's extra rent as a fraud.[18] Two days later she reported the rental of the house to Commissioner Morgan and requested that he formally appoint Julia M. French of San Francisco as the field matron. The WNIA Missionary Committee had already appointed Quinton's friend, Dr. Rebecca C. Hallowell, as their medical missionary. As soon as the land question was settled, the hospital would be constructed.[19]

Hallowell, formerly of Philadelphia, and French, newly appointed field matron, were driven to Agua Caliente by Weinland in mid-

January 1893. The two women moved into the rented quarters and immediately began to take care of the medical and missionary needs of the community.

Quinton and her Missionary Committee did not view the rented quarters as a hospital. They initially planned for the doctor to minister to patients in their own homes, win them over, and then, once the lawsuit had been settled and a plot of land was obtained, build a hospital. When Quinton learned that Hallowell was willing to take patients into her own living quarters, she was displeased with the idea of the two women living in the same rooms with sick men. "We have not engaged Dr. H. to have a 'hospital' in her own two *private rooms!*" she wrote to Weinland.[20] Furthermore, at that time the association did not have enough money to provide Hallowell with a temporary hospital; they could, instead, provide her with a tent and cots if she wanted to take in one or two patients.[21]

While Quinton and her Missionary Board had come to depend upon the hard work of the various field matrons and physicians such as Hallowell, they depended even more so upon Reverend Weinland for both his spiritual leadership and his physical labor. Among other activities, he made all the necessary repairs on the rented house at Agua Caliente. Unfortunately, his official obligations for the Moravian Church increased considerably during the summer of 1893, and after five years of working with WNIA, he stepped down as superintendent of missions, although WNIA literature still referred to him as their superintendent. While his replacement, Mr. Helmich, another Moravian clergyman, took over his duties, Weinland continued to make monthly visits to Cahuilla and Agua Caliente and an occasional stop at Saboba. He also began conducting services at an Indian village at Palm Springs.[22]

Quinton's confidence in Weinland was not conferred on his replacement. From the beginning she complained about Helmich's work. She described the new replacement as "unwise," "hopeless," "easily disheartened," and not possessing the *"tact requisite"* for the California missionary field. She wished for Weinland's return to his former position until things became more settled. Obviously not as strong a personality as his predecessor, Helmich allowed the Catholic priest to intimidate him. It was his opinion "that the 'Catholics had all the power' and that 'nothing more could be done at present.'"[23]

Quinton's dislike of Helmich was exacerbated by the continual concern of adequately funding WNIA work. Although the various California branches sponsored the Cahuilla mission field, several eastern WNIA affiliates lent financial support for the new undertaking at Agua Caliente. The Jamaica Plain, Massachusetts, association donated $900 for use in building a hospital; the New York City auxiliary donated money to furnish the hospital; the Washington, D.C., auxiliary, after an address by Painter, donated money to build the cottage and pay for the physician's salary; and the Western Pennsylvania association provided the salary for the first nurse in the ward,[24] an expense which did not materialize since the hospital was never constructed.

While these association branches supported the medical activities of Hallowell, other branches supported the work of Field Matron French, who continually wrote letters to the *Indian's Friend* requesting various items and describing her work. These letters, read by WNIA members all over the country, elicited widespread help from women of the various affiliates.

French first wrote to her sponsors that she was busy convincing the Indians to lay wooden floors in their homes and install windows. She was also trying to encourage Indian women to adapt their basketry-making skills to making stools. Her sewing classes were well attended, and she requested that sponsors supply her with sewing items, as well as knitting needles and wools.[25]

While the government field matron was busy with her official duties, Hallowell tended to the health needs of the village. In December 1893, she received forty calls at her home and made twenty-one visits on the reservation. The following month she made thirty-five office calls and thirteen home visits. In addition to caring for broken bones and various diseases, she also performed general dentistry.[26]

Hallowell was especially troubled by drunkenness among the Indians, a concern shared by the government. Government schoolteachers and field matrons were strongly encouraged to engage in temperance work at their assigned posts. These efforts were backed by the WNIA, especially President Quinton, who had become a member of the Women's Christian Temperance Union (WCTU) in 1874.

Unlike many women's reform groups, the WNIA remained a one-issue organization, interested primarily in the reform of Indian policy. Since alcoholism on the reservations threatened their work, however, a WNIA Committee on Temperance Appeals was established in 1893. It was ably headed by Hannah J. Bailey of Maine, who had been a member of the WCTU since 1883. Her committee served as a clearinghouse for temperance literature sent annually to agents, missionaries, teachers, and field matrons.[27]

But alcohol abuse was only one of the many problems plaguing the Agua Caliente project. WNIA missionary and educational work at Agua Caliente went no more smoothly than work at Cahuilla. While Quinton and Agent Estudillo were sparring over the five acres for Johnson's pony at Cahuilla, they were simultaneously engaged in a confrontation at Agua Caliente. In late summer of 1893, Quinton received a telegram from Hallowell and French saying: "Ordered out. Send Protection. Indians deny Agent's power. Reply by letter."[28] This incident prompted Quinton to consult with government officials.

In late August she informed Commissioner Browning that Estudillo, while visiting Agua Caliente, learned that French's watch had been stolen by an Indian boy. When the agent threatened to have the child punished, the villagers became angry, complaining that the incident occurred only because the two women invited the children into their house. The women were given thirty days to leave the reservation. Estudillo agreed to see to their safety until their departure. Quinton requested protection for French and Hallowell, assuring the commissioner that the entire situation was a plan to drive out Protestants. She intensified her remarks by noting that "threats of this sort have from time to time come to us."[29]

After receiving a letter from Commissioner Browning questioning the theft, Estudillo wrote Quinton on August 29, 1893, informing her that the Indian Office had inquired about a disturbance at Agua Caliente—a disturbance that allegedly endangered the lives of the field matron and the missionary. He claimed to be unaware of such a disturbance. Furthermore, he informed the commissioner that the field matron had not mentioned any trouble when corresponding with him. The report, he concluded, was "without foundation in fact or truth."[30]

Quinton responded quickly, informing Estudillo that she had learned enough from the two women to believe there was "considerable 'foundation' for the report." However, she believed the entire matter would blow over if he showed his disapproval to the Indians.[31]

The WNIA missionary report for 1894 and issues of the *Indian's Friend* did not mention this incident. It was, of course, common for official WNIA literature to highlight only the positive aspects of the association's missionary work. Therefore, the membership was rarely made aware of the various petty, day-by-day problems that Quinton handled either in person or by letter through Weinland, agents, and government officials. Obviously, the situation was defused because French and Hallowell remained at their mission post.

Preferring to handle WNIA business personally when possible, during the spring of 1895 Quinton made another visit to California.

Her activities were reported in a letter published in the May issue of the *Indian's Friend*. Arriving in Redlands, she set out for a two-week drive among the various Indian villages and WNIA missions in the southern part of the state. She was accompanied by Smiley, Reverend Weinland, and Louise Hoppock, president of the Redlands Indian Association.

Traveling on many of the same roads that Jackson had traversed in the early 1880s, on Wednesday, April 3, Quinton and her small party arrived at "the Temecula of H. H.'s Ramona," and then to Pala, the Pauma Ranch, and Rincon where they visited with Ora Salmons, the government schoolteacher. The following day they followed a steep mountain road to visit La Jolla and spent some time with the government schoolteacher, Flora Golsh, who had served for nine years in that small village.

Friday morning the group headed down the steep incline to Warner's Ranch, arriving at Agua Caliente to a greeting by WNIA-sponsored missionary Hallowell, government field matron French, and Babbitt, the government schoolteacher. They visited the schoolhouse and attended a Sunday service conducted in the school by Weinland, who also performed a marriage ceremony for a young Indian couple. Quinton rejoiced over the occasion, believing it would "exercise a deep influence where long effort and teaching have prepared the way for new ideas of home life, citizenship and Christian living."[32] Quinton was especially pleased with the cottage built at Agua Caliente through WNIA sponsorship. She found it pleasantly snug and hoped to duplicate it elsewhere.

Quinton's second letter published in the *Indian's Friend* began with an April 8 departure from Agua Caliente and the picturesque eight-mile journey to San Ysidro, then to Santa Ysabel and Mesa Grande, and finally to Cahuilla over a sixteen-mile road that alternated between mountainous and desert stretches. At Cahuilla, they met with Johnson's replacement, Anna J. Ritter. Quinton's letters reflected her pleasure with the progress made by the association at Cahuilla. Nevertheless, she noticed that the missionary cottage was in need of whitewashing and that a shelter for a horse, a carriage, and hay were lacking. Within a month these improvements were made.[33]

Leaving Cahuilla, they headed back into the mountains, arriving at Banning late on Saturday. On Sunday they traveled the four miles to, as Quinton described it, "our dear little Indian church . . . at Potraro [sic]." She immediately noticed the change that had come over the community. Nearing the mission, they saw a small, tidy farm with clean orchards, promising grain fields, and a small red-roofed cottage surrounded by oriental fruit trees and a green hedge.[34] This particular cottage had been built with funds provided by the WNIA Home Building and Loan Committee. An Easter service was held at the former WNIA Indian church at El Potrero, now in the capable hands of the Moravian ministry. Quinton noted that all Christian hearts should rejoice at the work done here.

Her third letter described their railroad trip into the desert from Banning to Cabezon, Palm Springs, and Indio. Little did she know that she would soon be soliciting money from WNIA membership for a new mission among these people. Accompanied by an interpreter from El Potrero, the party ventured five miles into the desert to the village of Martínez to acquaint the residents with the work of the WNIA among other Indian groups. These Martínez villagers spoke to Quinton of their need for water. They explained that Painter had promised them help in the development of adequate water sources, but nothing had been done so far. Acting immediately, Quinton encouraged the Indians to sign a petition, which was endorsed by the WNIA, requesting that the government develop water for their needs.

During her visit to these Desert Indians of Riverside County, Quinton learned that, although they were willing to have Reverend Weinland preach to them, they were more anxious to have their own mission. She informed those gathered that her association currently had as many missions as it could operate, but if the Moravian Mission Board was willing to supply a missionary and salary, the WNIA would probably build a chapel.[35]

Both the development of adequate water and the establishment of a mission became a reality. The April 1896 issue of the *Indian's Friend* included news that plans for a new desert mission were making progress and that the petition sent by the Indians a year ago had been successful; the government had appropriated money to pipe water to the village of Torres, not too far from Palm Springs.[36] Besides traveling through the various mission villages, Quinton, as she did during her 1891 visit, met with the various WNIA affiliates in both Northern and Southern California. In the southern part of the state she formed two new branches, one at Claremont and a second at Banning. All California branches were expected to aid WNIA missions in California.[37]

Quinton delivered a positive report on her California trip before the conferees at Lake Mohonk, especially praising the work of Weinland, which had resulted in the Desert Indians requesting a missionary to live among them. She also commented on the new homes, built by association loans. The houses at Agua Caliente had glass windows and plank floors, and a mill for grinding acorns had been added by French. Now Indian women did not have to spend long back-breaking hours over a grinding stone to produce acorn flour.[38] Thus, the living standards of the Indians at Agua Caliente had changed substantially since the April 1883 visit of Helen Hunt Jackson and Abbot Kinney. Jackson, no doubt, would have been pleased with the results.

What successes Quinton and the WNIA enjoyed in Southern California were due to the capable work of Reverend William H. Weinland. Letters between the WNIA president and the cleric reflected cordiality and complete confidence. Quinton grew to depend heavily on Weinland, even for personal matters. When she purchased some retirement property at Val Verde in Southern California, she turned to him to hire builders or handle other minor situations.[39]

While the government field matrons and the WNIA female missionaries at Agua Caliente and Cahuilla seemed to have insurmountable problems with agents and the Indians, Weinland seldom encountered problems with either. He ably divided his time between his various duties, continuing to hold Sunday school and services regularly at the Moravian mission at El Potrero, while traveling the rest of the week to visit mission reservations in San Diego and Riverside counties.[40]

To implement Quinton's 1895 promise of missionary help to the Desert Indians, in September 1896 Weinland, accompanied by Rev. David J. Woosley (the new missionary for the Desert Mission) and interpreter Juan Morongo boarded a train for Banning to join Agent Estudillo. The party then headed out to Martínez where they found the Indians eagerly gathered in the schoolhouse. First to speak was Estudillo, who informed the Indians of the Christian work of the WNIA and their desire to establish a mission in the desert.

Reverend Woosley spoke next and was warmly greeted. Then Chief Alimo reminded everyone of Quinton's recent visit and their request to her of a mission and a resident missionary. Following the chief's speech, those assembled consented to the use of five acres for missionary purposes. After everyone had an opportunity to speak to the issue, an agreement was drawn up. Each Indian came forward, touching the tip of the penholder to signify that his name had been written with his knowledge and consent.

The missionary cottage for the Desert Indians at Martínez was paid for by the Brooklyn association and its Bay Ridge branches while the Redlands association provided the furniture. The Pennsylvania branches at Bethlehem, Allentown, and Lancaster along with the New Orleans association supplied money to complete the building. Through letters to Weinland, Quinton personally supervised the construction. She recommended that rooms not be cramped and that only one window in the living room for a desert climate was unreasonable. She agreed to personally see that money for an additional window was found.[41]

Once the construction costs were subscribed to, other branches at Bethlehem and Allentown provided the $600 in support for the minister and his wife. The $500 to build a chapel, with a cement floor and a double roof to keep out the desert heat, was donated to the Moravian Missionary Board by J. T. Morton of London. The first Sunday school service was held on November 15, and following the official dedication of the chapel on December 13, 1896, services were held sometimes as often as three times on Sunday and once nearly every week night. Mrs. Woosley immediately organized the young girls into a sewing class.[42]

During the summer of 1897, Woosley kept busy conducting Sunday school, preaching a service in the morning, and giving readings in the evening. In addition to his pastoral duties, he built fences and did whatever physical labor was necessary to make the mission comfortable.[43]

The Desert Mission at Martínez was turned over to the Moravian Church of the United States on November 19, 1897, although Quinton had begun negotiations for the transfer as early as the summer.[44] From the beginning it had been her intention for the Moravian Church to run this mission. As early as December 1895, she had informed Weinland that she wanted a Moravian couple for the mission field and asked that he help his board find the right couple.[45] The Woosleys had been chosen.

Reverend Woosley eventually moved to the village of Rincon, visiting nearby La Jolla and Pachanga as his other preaching places. In late 1903 he requested government permission for land for the Moravian church to build a chapel at Rincon. In March 1904, permission was granted by Ethan A. Hitchcock, secretary of the interior.[46]

While Weinland and Woosley continued their work among the Indians and aided in the establishment of the new WNIA mission at Martínez, important changes were taking place at Agua Caliente. Glass windows and wooden floors were added to many homes. Families who had formerly lived in crude grass huts now called comfortable whitewashed adobes home. Trees were planted along the street and gardens were more numerous. Families who had previously sat on the floor to eat were now sitting at a table. Part of the success at Agua Caliente was due to the diligent work of the six branches of the New York City association which had raised $1,655.85 for the medical missionary at Agua Caliente.[47] Hallowell, aided by her friend French, had been successful in carrying out government orders to bring Indian women into the nineteenth-century sphere of domesticity.

Despite all of the physical improvements at Agua Caliente, legally the Indians' land was still very much in peril. The initial ejectment case had been filed against the Indians on August 22, 1892, by former governor Downey, basing his claim on a patent issued to previous owners by the federal government on January 16, 1880. Upon his death, his heirs pursued the case. The IRA lent legal assistance, and new evidence was obtained for the case in 1893. On December 29, 1896, Judge Pierce of the State Superior Court decided against the Indians. Three days after the verdict was in, the judge resigned and became a counsel for the plaintiffs.

Attorneys Lewis and Ward believed that the Indians at Agua Caliente morally and legally owned the land. Because the Indians faced ejectment from their village on July 15, 1897, the IRA, assured by the two attorneys that this case was much like that at Saboba, raised $6,100 as an indemnity bond and appealed to a higher court in the Indians' behalf. With little time to raise individual subscriptions, the IRA deposited $4,000 of its own monies. The difference was made up by personal guarantees of two individuals interested in aiding the Indians.

Because of a backlog of cases, the California Supreme Court did not hear arguments until April 19, 1899. The court finally rendered its decision in October 1899 against the Indians. An application for a rehearing was turned down.

Father Ubach, Helen Hunt Jackson's friend and escort on her first tour of the missions, denounced the decision of the State Supreme Court as robbery. "According to the original deed for Warner's Ranch, which I translated myself," he noted, "there is no court in the United States that can oust them from the ranch."[48] Unfortunately for the Indians, the priest was wrong. Obviously, the IRA shared Father Ubach's feelings; they brought the case to the attention of the Indian Office.[49] Eventually, the attorney general took it to the United States Supreme Court, which on May 13, 1901, upheld the decision of the lower state court. Members of the IRA were keenly disappointed in this adverse decision and suggested that the friends of the Indians petition their congressmen in behalf of these needy people.[50] Now that the land was no longer legally in their possession, the Warner's Ranch Indians faced removal.

With the aid of sympathetic individuals, the government formed a special commission to locate a new reservation for these Indians.

The commission agreed to a tract of 3,500 acres in the Pala Valley, forty miles from Warner's Ranch, and the first group of Warner's Ranch Indians were relocated in May 1903.[51]

Despite the on-going land dispute, Hallowell and French continued working at Agua Caliente.[52] But during the summer of 1898 several letters between Quinton and Weinland reflected a problem. The Indians wanted both Hallowell and French to leave. In a letter to Weinland, Quinton noted that both women had been imprudent lately, but she failed to elaborate, and WNIA literature did not mention any problem.[53] In late January, Quinton alluded to an altercation between French and the agency physician as the main problem. But again, she did not provide any details, only noting that it would be best if both women left without tarnishing their six years of hard work. Quinton explained she would "rejoice to know that they are safely off the field & done with all friction there."[54] Babbitt, the government schoolteacher, was not affected by this removal and remained at her post.

In January 1899 the New York City auxiliary closed its Agua Caliente mission, transferring it to the Moravian Church though continuing to furnish the salary of the medical missionary.[55] To partially justify this action, Quinton informed Weinland that the mission at Agua Caliente had been maintained by the WNIA twice as long as any others and that New York had pledged work among the Navajos and could not afford both the Agua Caliente and the Navajo projects.[56]

Although WNIA support was removed from Agua Caliente, the Southern California association and branches of Eastern Pennsylvania continued their support of Reverend Weinland, who in turn continued his work at Saboba and Cahuilla.[57] His letters appeared in the Indian's Friend in 1900 as did letters from the various government teachers at the mission villages.

The WNIA role among the Mission Indians was nearing an end. The missions had been dutifully handed over to missionary societies to run, although through the pages of the Indian's Friend, the WNIA membership kept up with activities at their former missions and continued to send food, money, and other gifts for the Indians.

As the head of the WNIA Missionary Committee, Quinton returned to California whenever she was able. During the spring of 1898 she visited the state and returned again in the spring of 1902.[58] During the latter trip she visited the Desert Mission and met the new missionary, Reverend Robert Stavely. Following an introduction by her good friend Reverend Weinland, she spoke before a council of the Indians. The biggest concern they expressed was a lack of adequate water—a problem eventually solved by 1911 with the digging of twenty-five artesian wells on the reservation.[59]

At Agua Caliente, Quinton found notable change from her first visit in 1891. Many homes had windows, and a new school building with comfortable living quarters for Mrs. Babbitt had recently been constructed. Indians spoke to Quinton about their concern with the recent court decision. They did not want to leave their homes.[60]

After eight years as general secretary and seventeen years as president, Quinton retired from the presidency of the organization in 1903, although she remained chair of the Missionary Committee. Other changes for the organization included a new name, the National Indian Association, and the moving of association headquarters from Philadelphia to New York.[61] Despite her retirement, Quinton continued to work in behalf of the National Indian Association. At ninety years of age in 1921, with forty-two years of her life devoted to the Indian cause, she was still giving speeches at annual conventions.[62]

Although by the turn of the century the WNIA no longer had working missions among the Mission Indians, at least one of their members visited these Indians and, like both Helen Hunt Jackson and Osia J. Hiles before her, wrote of their condition. Constance Goddard DuBois, a member of the Connecticut auxiliary as well as a member of the IRA, spent six summers among the Indians in California buying native made baskets and trying to encourage a native lace industry.[63] Her report for the IRA and her pamphlet, "The Condition of the Mission Indians of Southern California," made reference to the work of Helen Hunt Jackson. For almost twenty years the legacy of Jackson had remained strong and reformers still answered her call.

Continually referring to the Jackson/Kinney report, DuBois detailed the history of the various Mission Indians since 1883. No Indians remained at the village of Santa Ysabel when she visited in the summer of 1901. Less than twenty years earlier when Jackson first visited the Santa Ysabel Ranch, she had found a beautiful, well-wooded and well-watered county with eight small villages. The main village of Santa Ysabel had a population of one hundred and seventy. Although they were poor and their homes were only of brush, they were industrious workers raising wheat.[64] In 1901, according to DuBois, these Indians had been driven up the side of Vulcan Mountain, an extinct volcano. Ninety-seven of them were "left face to face with starvation on land where only goats could find a living."[65]

By the advent of the twentieth century, other villages were in similar perilous conditions. While visiting Los Conejos, Jackson had written that the Indians asked for plows; DuBois noted years later they were still making the same request. DuBois also discovered that Jackson's recommendation to purchase the Pauma Ranch was not heeded.

The aridity of the land, according to DuBois, made it devastatingly cruel "to require of the Indians that which would be an impossible task for a white man with all his superior advantages." To expect an Indian without tools or water and with miserable soil "to support a family and rise to the refinements of civilization . . . [was] a pitiless irony."[66] Jackson would, no doubt, have shared this conclusion.

During the summer of 1901, Quinton inquired if Weinland had heard about plans to buy a reservation to be allotted to the Mission Indians. Apparently, DuBois and her friends were attempting to purchase the Santa Ysabel Ranch near Pasadena at the cost of $30,000. In addition, this group hoped to turn the hotel at Santa Ysabel into a school for Mission Indian teachers and establish a mission at Mesa Grande. Quinton believed this activity was premature, informing Weinland that she felt the land question should be settled before any new missions were established.[67]

DuBois, although listed as a member of the WNIA, was apparently unfamiliar with the work of the association in California and therefore assumed that little was being done for these Indians. Amelia Quinton took exception to this conclusion and informed DuBois of the past decade of work by Weinland in the California Mission field. Subsequently, both women agreed to combine their efforts to help the Mission Indians. "I plan to see the Ind. Rights Ass'n & us on one plea to get land & water for the Mission Indians!" Quinton informed Weinland. "Such a movement would win, now, I believe."[68]

But change was slow in coming; painfully little was done in behalf of these California Mission Indians. Then in 1906 and again in 1911, the Northern California Indian Association, an affiliate of the WNIA, published reports that included the condition of the Mission Indians; the second report by Cornelia Taber, corresponding secretary of the association, was purely informational. The 1906 report, although only half the size of the Jackson/Kinney report, reflected the pitiful condition of the Mission Indians and made a number of recommendations to the commissioner of Indian affairs, only a few of which were acted upon.

Under a congressional act of June 30, 1905, which set aside $100,000 for the purchase of water rights and land for California Indians, C. E. Kelsey, general secretary of the Northern California Women's Indian Association, was appointed as a special agent to report to Congress on the condition of California Indians.

Kelsey's report revealed a number of interesting facts. For example, the 1887 Dawes Allotment Act was too late to be of much good in California. Only 2,058 Indian allotments were made. According to the August 1898 report of the Mission-Tule River consolidated agency only 361 allotments had been made at Rincon, El Potrero, Pala, Temecula, Sequan, and Capitán Grande.[69] Over 300 allotments were located in a total desert environment while an additional 600 more were located in the Sierra Nevada Mountains on rocky land. Noting that over three quarters of the allotments were not fit for human habitation, Kelsey did not find it strange that the Indians had failed to make a living on them.[70] Kelsey, like others, soon realized that the concept of allotment was not the solution that reformers had hoped it would be.

Furthermore, the allottee in California had no protection. Anyone could move onto an Indian allotment. In addition, Indian water rights had not been secured. Numerous cases were reported to Kelsey in which white settlers merely diverted the water from the Indian's land. He therefore recommended additional legislation to protect these allotments.

Kelsey also criticized the reservation system. "The day has gone by in California when it is wise to herd the Indians away from civilization," he noted, "or to subject them to the stunting influences of reservation life."[71] Although he was critical of the reservation system, at least it afforded a home for the Indians. The failure to adequately mark off reservation boundaries was a serious problem he found everywhere—a concern he shared with Jackson, Kinney, and Painter, who spent the better part of a year surveying mission reservation boundaries. Obviously, the hard work and concern of Jackson, Kinney, and Painter in this matter had failed.

Kelsey saw nearly all of the reservations in Southern California, including those visited twenty years earlier by Helen Hunt Jackson. At Pala he discovered good land and plenty of water with about five hundred acres under cultivation—he considered this the best reservation in the southern part of the state. Although the former residents of Warner's Ranch probably would have preferred their old home, they had adjusted well at Pala.

In a rather humorous aside, Kelsey noted that, since adobe bricks would take too much time to make and rough lumber houses were also considered not desirable, fifty portable houses were ordered from New York by telegraph to be set up at Pala. Six months and four thousand miles in distance later, the former Warner's Ranch Indians got their new houses—double the cost of a wooden cabin built on the spot and about four times that of an adobe house. These portable houses proved to be unlivable, hot in the summer and cold in the winter. Moreover, the hot sun warped the thin three-quarter-inch boards.

Kelsey found the Pachanga Reservation to be one of the poorest, with less than three hundred arable acres and no water supply, not even for domestic purposes. Jackson would have been truly disappointed at this observation. During her second visit in May of 1883 she had been pleased to find new corrals, fruit orchards, and more grain planted. She had found the "whole expression of the place had changed" between her two visits.[72] At San Pascual, Kelsey discovered that an error had been made in setting aside land and none of the Indians had ever lived on the reserved section. As years passed, this land was taken up by white settlers. Thus, no reservation actually existed for them. To alleviate this predicament, he recommended that a small tract of land be purchased. And at Rincon he discovered that a syndicate was preparing to construct a large dam across the San Luis Rey River above the Indian village. He suggested that steps be undertaken to protect the Indians' right to their water.

Finally, Kelsey recommended an increase in the number of Indian day schools, a request that Jackson had made years earlier. To his dismay, he discovered that many of Jackson's recommendations had not been adequately addressed by government officials.

On the positive side, Kelsey's report prompted the commissioner of Indian affairs to purchase several small tracts of land, including 160 acres in San Ysidro Canyon and 235 acres at Pachanga. Certain tracts of government land adjoining several reservations, including Capitán Grande and Palm Springs, were withdrawn from settlement and annexed to the neighboring reservations. In addition, pipes, cement, and tools were purchased to aid in building reservoirs or digging wells at Pachanga, Pauma, Cabezon, Morongo, and Cahuilla. The total spent in the southern part of the state in behalf of the Indians was $30,425.[73]

Ironically, the reform of the Mission Indians had, by the first decade of the twentieth century, come almost full circle from the Jackson/Kinney report to the C. E. Kelsey report, both written by special agents appointed to report directly to the government. Over thirty years had elapsed since Jackson's first visit to California in 1873 and almost a quarter of a century since her report on the condition of the Mission Indians. Unfortunately, during that span of time, the conditions of the Indians did not improve appreciably; many were actually much worse off. The problems that Jackson had detailed continued despite the personal efforts of Osia J. Hiles, Amelia S.

Quinton, Charles C. Painter, Albert K. Smiley, Frank D. Lewis, and others, as well as the organizational efforts of the Women's National Indian Association, the Indian Rights Association, and those who met annually at Lake Mohonk. While Kelsey was at least able to see improvements, they regrettably were too little too late.[74]

9

Retrospective

Helen Hunt Jackson wrote *Ramona* to dramatize the condition of California Indians in the same sympathetic way that Harriet Beecher Stowe had portrayed the slave in *Uncle Tom's Cabin*. Jackson's letters showed her preoccupation with following Stowe's path. "I do not dare to think I have written a second Uncle Tom's Cabin—but I do think I have written a story which will be a good stroke for the Indian cause," she noted to Amelia Stone Quinton.[1] Jackson hoped her book would bring change, particularly protection of the Indians' land base. Unfortunately, American society at that time did not view the situation of the Indians and the slaves as similar. As a result, the impact of *Ramona* was different from that of *Uncle Tom's Cabin*. The latter became an important abolitionist tract while *Ramona* was seen primarily as a romantic love story.

In broad, stereotypical, but nevertheless prevalent views, Anglo-Americans portrayed Indians as frontier pillagers who murdered innocent citizens for no reason. Yet from the Indian perspective, these attacks were designed to maintain lands and a traditional way of life threatened by the onslaught of westward-migrating frontiersmen. From the point of view of the white American settler, this Indian/white conflict resulted in the widely held attitude that the only good Indian was a dead one. On the other hand, black slaves were often viewed as passive victims suffering undue torment at the hands of evil slave owners. Thus the defense of these slaves was required out of decency and humanity. Moreover, 4,000,000 slaves had lived and worked under bondage on plantations, whereas the Indian population, mostly living on reservations, was comparatively small, about 300,000 in Jackson's era. A civil war ended slavery, but the Indian question was never satisfactorily resolved.

Helen Hunt Jackson, in her own way, attempted to help the American Indian. When she realized that she was dying, she accepted her fate, but she also possessed a very strong sense of her historical importance. Six months before her death, she wrote to her husband, Will, that she would have liked to write a few more books. "If Ramona & the Cent. of Dishonor have not helped—one more would have made little odds—But they will tell in the long run—The thought of this is my only consolation as I look back over the last ten years."[2] Several months later she wrote to Thomas Wentworth Higginson that her *Century of Dishonor* and *Ramona* were the only writings she was truly pleased with. "They will live, and . . . bear fruit."[3] How right she was, though the fruit was not the abundant harvest that she so passionately longed for.

Death took Jackson before the legacy of her writing became apparent to her. *Ramona* has gone through numerous editions and is currently in print, along with *A Century of Dishonor* and several books of her poetry. *Ramona* was first staged as a play in Los Angeles in 1905 and has since been made into several movie versions. In 1910, Mary Pickford starred in D. W. Griffith's film, shot on location. Eighteen years later Dolores Del Rio portrayed Ramona with Warner Baxter as Alessandro. This movie also featured the 1927 hit song, "Ramona." The last adaptation of Jackson's novel was the 1936 movie with Loretta Young and Don Ameche in starring roles. In addition to these movies, the Ramona pageant has been presented annually for years in the town of Hemet.

The name Ramona has proven to be as durable as the novel. It graces or has graced a town, an expressway, a San Francisco hotel, a development in the San Gabriel Valley, an Indian reservation, an Indian mission, a chapter of the Native Sons of the Golden West,[4] and no doubt countless numbers of little girls growing up in the late nineteenth and early twentieth centuries. Unfortunately, this particular legacy is more important to California tourism than to the Indians.

Ramona may not have been another *Uncle Tom's Cabin*, but it served, along with Jackson's other writings on the Mission Indians of California, as a catalyst for other reformers. Jackson's writings, continually mentioned in the literature of the Women's National Indian Association, the Indian Rights Association, and the Lake Mohonk Conference, spurred reformers to demand protection of Mission Indian land rights. For nearly a quarter of a century, others diligently and as aggressively carried on the campaign in the state.

It was logical that Jackson's heritage was continued by nineteenth-century women who had been, like Jackson, confined to "woman's sphere." She fought to protect Indian lands and—like other reformers—favored allotment, but whether or not Jackson would have applauded the WNIA's attempt to turn Indian women into models of Victorian womanhood is unclear. Jackson herself did not fit this role—she was not confined to the house, nor did she rear her children to adulthood, and above all, she was not passive or driven by evangelical Christianity. Obviously, the death of her first husband and both children precluded her from acting out this role. But Jackson, even had her first family lived and prospered, was much too strong to be locked into the sphere of "true womanhood" or domesticity.

Neither did the women who took up Jackson's crusade strictly adhere to the role of domesticity defined by society, but curiously enough, they nevertheless forced this role upon Indian women. Amelia Stone Quinton, although married, spent over forty years giving her time and energy to the WNIA. Her annual travels were arduous exercises of independence, stamina, and foresight, leaving her little time to enact the role of typical Victorian housewife.

Indian reformers sought to attain for the American Indian what white American society as a whole desired for the American people. The Americanization process forced on the Indian was much like that forced on the newly arrived immigrant. Citizenship, Americanization, Christianization, and voting rights were goals that all should attain, even the American Indian. And the WNIA believed its destiny was to bring education, Christianity, and domesticity to Indian women and children.

Ironically, no one bothered to ask the Indians if they wanted these changes in their lives. Without doubt, the California Indian reformers inspired by Jackson and those Indian reformers elsewhere in the country contributed to the Indians' physical well-being. They sponsored teachers and missionaries and sent gifts of clothing, food, and medicine. Yet while extending their gifts, they—despite all good intentions and most probably quite unaware of the subtle destructive consequences of their deeds—continually undermined Indian tradition and religion in the hopes of replacing it with the dominant American culture. Thomas Jefferson's yeoman farmer role was the prototype for Indian men while the home life of the Victorian woman awaited their wives.

Most reformers of the day believed that Indian culture was inferior and not worth preserving. After all, a "saved" Indian was one who was Christianized, educated, civilized, and above all a self-sufficient farmer. Ironically, for centuries before Europeans arrived on American soil, Indians had farmed their land. In the long run, of course, the destruction of certain aspects of Indian culture was inevitable given the pressure of the westward movement, just as immigrant customs gave way in the face of the more pervasive American society.

Indians in the eastern United States temporarily escaped destruction by moving to lands west of the Mississippi. Yet once settlers, gold miners, cattlemen, and others went west, removal was no longer possible. For the Indians only destruction of the environmental basis of their cultures, dispossession, and—ultimately—death remained.

The women of WNIA were ready to offer something to these beleaguered Indians, maybe only a new house built by the WNIA Home Building and Loan Committee or Christmas boxes sent by various auxiliaries or education from a government teacher or the sponsorship of a field matron or a medical missionary. These women worked alongside the compassionate Christian men of the Indian Rights Association, like Charles C. Painter or Lake Mohonk founder, Albert K. Smiley. One may with more than a little justification speculate that these humanitarian reformers might not have taken up the crusade for the California Indian had Jackson not preceded them and described their condition in such a compelling manner.

Helen Hunt Jackson cared deeply for the Indians of California. She cared enough to undermine her health while devoting the last few years of her life to bettering their lives. Her enduring writings, therefore, provided a legacy to other reformers, who cherished her work enough to carry on her struggle and at least try to improve the lives of America's first inhabitants. The greatest success of these reformers was the passage in 1891 of the Act for the Relief of the Mission Indians in the State of California, based on the recommendations Jackson and Abbot Kinney proposed in their fifty-six-page government report.

But regrettably, Jackson had come to the aid of the California Indian too late—both their population and land base had declined drastically. Had she lived longer, would she have been more successful than those who carried on in her behalf? Probably not. Anglo-American settlers' demand for land in California, as elsewhere in the country, was too strong. Would she have been more successful had she begun her crusade during the early years of American domination in California? No, she was successful in the 1880s because the time was right; the rise of the humanitarian reform movement was essential to her success. Her legacy was that, as a single woman, she undertook the tremendous task of alerting the public to the condition of the Mission Indians—a task she succeeded at eloquently.

Notes

Introduction

1. Helen Jackson (H. H.), *A Century of Dishonor: A Sketch of the United States Government's Dealings with Some of the Indian Tribes*, p. 339.

2. Jackson, *Century of Dishonor*, p. 31.

1. Indian Policy, Christian Reformers, and the California Mission Indians

1. Francis Paul Prucha, ed., *Documents of United States Indian Policy*, p. 103. See also Francis Paul Prucha, *The Great Father: The United States Government and the American Indians*, I:485–488; Francis Paul Prucha, *American Indian Policy in Crisis: Christian Reformers and the Indian, 1865–1900*, pp. 14–16; Robert Winston Mardock, *The Reformers and the American Indian*, pp. 20–22; and Henry E. Fritz, *The Movement for Indian Assimilation, 1860–1890*, pp. 29–30.

2. Gregory Coyne Thompson, "The Origins and Implementation of the American Indian Reform Movement: 1867–1911" (Ph.D. dissertation, University of Utah, 1981), pp. 108–111, 120–121. See also Fritz, *Movement for Indian Assimilation*, pp. 62–63; and Mardock, *Reformers and the American Indian*, pp. 21–22.

3. Felix Cohen, *Handbook of Federal Indian Law*, p. 16. For additional information on the Indian policy of Thomas Jefferson see Bernard W. Sheehan, *Seeds of Extinction: Jeffersonian Philanthropy and the American Indian*, and for Andrew Jackson see Michael Paul Rogin, *Fathers and Children: Andrew Jackson and the Subjugation of the American Indian*, and Ronald N. Satz, *American Indian Policy in the Jacksonian Era*.

4. For the development of the reservation policy see Robert A. Trennert,

Jr., *Alternative to Extinction: Federal Indian Policy and the Beginnings of the Reservation System, 1846−51,* and Prucha, *Policy in Crisis,* pp. 103−131.

5. For more on the Peace Commission see Prucha, *Great Father,* I: 488−492; Prucha, *Policy in Crisis,* pp. 18−22; Mardock, *Reformers and the American Indian,* pp. 25−27; Thompson, "Origins and Implementation," pp. 78−80; and Fritz, *Movement for Indian Assimilation,* pp. 62−70.

6. For extensive discussions of the policy see Prucha, *Great Father,* I: 479−606; Prucha, *Policy in Crisis,* pp. 30−102; Robert M. Utley, "The Celebrated Peace Policy of General Grant," *American Indian Past and Present,* ed. Roger L. Nichols and George R. Adams, pp. 183−198; Robert M. Utley, *Frontier Regulars: The United States Army and the Indian, 1866−1891,* pp. 188−218. See also Clyde A. Milner II, *With Good Intentions: Quaker Work Among the Pawnees, Otos, and Omaha in the 1870s,* pp. 1−26; and Fritz, *Movement for Indian Assimilation,* pp. 56−86. For a view of the westerners' opinion of the policy, see Fritz, pp. 109−119; for the military's position see pp. 120−134; and for an evaluation of the policy in general, see pp. 135−167.

See also Mardock, *Reformers and the American Indian,* pp. 47−66; Larry Y. Burgess, "The Lake Mohonk Conferences on the Indian, 1883−1916" (Ph.D. dissertation, Claremont Graduate School, 1972), pp. 10−14; and Frederick E. Hoxie, "Beyond Savagery: The Campaign to Assimilate the American Indians, 1880−1920" (Ph.D. dissertation, Brandeis University, 1977), pp. 5−6 (published as Hoxie, *A Final Promise: The Campaign to Assimilate the Indians, 1880−1920*). For an excellent short general article on nineteenth-century reformers see Frederick E. Hoxie, "The Curious Story of Reformers and the American Indians," in *Indians in American History,* ed. Frederick E. Hoxie, pp. 205−228.

7. For an interesting contrast with colonial Indian policies of the English and the French see James Axtell, *The Invasion Within: The Contest of Cultures in Colonial North America.* For a brief discussion of the church/state relationship in Indian affairs prior to Grant's presidency see Robert H. Keller, Jr., *American Protestantism and United States Indian Policy, 1869−82,* pp. 3−8.

8. For a detailed discussion of the transfer issue see Loring Benson Priest, *Uncle Sam's Stepchildren: The Reformation of United States Indian Policy, 1865−1887,* pp. 15−27.

9. Keller, *American Protestantism,* p. 28. For a discussion of agency apportionment, maps, and reservation conditions faced by agents see ibid., pp. 106−148. See also Prucha, *Great Father,* I: 512−527, and Fritz, *Movement for Indian Assimilation,* pp. 77−79, 87−108. For a detailed study of the Quakers see Milner, *With Good Intentions.*

10. The original board resigned in 1874, but not until 1934 was the Board of Indian Commissioners discontinued. For additional information on them see Keller, *American Protestantism,* pp. 20−22, 29−89; Thompson, "Origins and Implementation," pp. 62−66, 80−81, 87−90; Prucha, *Great Father,* I: 501−512; Prucha, *Policy in Crisis,* pp. 26−28, 33−46; Francis Paul Prucha, "The Board of Indian Commissioners and the Delegates of the Five Tribes,"

in *Indian Policy in the United States: Historical Essays*, pp. 198–213; and Henry E. Fritz, "The Last Hurrah of Christian Humanitarian Indian Reform: The Board of Indian Commissioners, 1909–1918," *Western Historical Quarterly* 16 (April 1985): 147–162. See also Priest, *Uncle Sam's Stepchildren*, pp. 42–53; Mardock, *Reformers and the American Indian*, pp. 33–46; and Helen Marie Bannan, "Reformers and the 'Indian Problem' 1878–1887 and 1922–1934" (Ph.D. dissertation, Syracuse University, 1976), pp. 118–119.

11. For a discussion on the military challenge to the peace policy, see Prucha, *Policy in Crisis*, pp. 72–102; and for contemporary opinions of the policy, see Keller, *American Protestantism*, pp. 98–105.

12. Keller, *American Protestantism*, p. 205.

13. For a discussion of the Ponca, their removal, the court case, and its outcome, see Jackson, *Century of Dishonor*, pp. 186–217; Robert W. Mardock, "Standing Bear and the Reformers," in *Indian Leaders: Oklahoma's First Statesmen*, ed. H. Glenn Jordan and Thomas M. Holm, pp. 101–113; Mardock, *Reformers and the American Indian*, pp. 168–191, 197–198; Priest, *Uncle Sam's Stepchildren*, pp. 76–80; Prucha, *Great Father*, II: 567–571; Prucha, *Policy in Crisis*, pp. 113–119; Fritz, *Movement for Indian Assimilation*, pp. 186–197; Hoxie, "Beyond Savagery," pp. 6–11, 14–16, 21–26; Bannan, "Reformers and the 'Indian Problem,'" pp. 12–80; and Thompson, "Origins and Implementation," pp. 131–139.

14. Circuit Court Judge Elmer S. Dundy declared an Indian a legal "person" with the right to sue for a writ of habeas corpus. For a complete discussion, see Thomas Henry Tibbles, *The Ponca Chiefs: An Account of the Trial of Standing Bear*, ed. Kay Graber. Hoxie, "Beyond Savagery," pp. 8–14, gives an interesting discussion of army officers' view of the Indian. Crook, like other officers, believed the Indian should be brought into American society as quickly as possible. According to Hoxie, it was Crook who, by bringing Standing Bear to the attention of Tibbles, popularized the idea of Indian citizenship. Assimilation was attractive to officers because they believed it would end expensive guerrilla warfare.

15. Beginning with the Ponca controversy, a small group of dedicated Christian reformers became active. For a brief study, see Prucha, *Great Father*, II: 611–630; Prucha, "Indian Policy Reform and American Protestantism, 1880–1900," in *Indian Policy in the United States*, pp. 229–251; and Francis Paul Prucha, ed., *Americanizing the American Indians: Writings by the "Friends of the Indian" 1880–1900*, pp. 1–10. For an excellent general study of the reformers' legacy from 1830–1860, see Thompson, "Origins and Implementation," pp. 9–28.

16. For information on Jackson, see Allan Nevins, "Helen Hunt Jackson, Sentimentalist v. Realist," *American Scholar* 10 (Summer 1941): 269–285; and for her activities in behalf of the Indians in California, see Valerie Sherer Mathes, "Helen Hunt Jackson: Official Agent to the California Mission Indians," *Southern California Quarterly* 63 (Spring 1981): 63–82; and Valerie Sherer Mathes, "Helen Hunt Jackson: A Legacy of Indian Reform," *Essays and Monographs in Colorado History*, no. 4 (1986): 25–58. See also Thompson, "Origins and Implementation," pp. 30–31, 130–131, 135–144.

17. Helen Hunt Jackson to Charles Dudley Warner, 21 December 1879, Charles Dudley Warner Collection, Watkinson Library, Trinity College, Hartford, Connecticut.

18. For a complete history of the WNIA, see Helen M. Wanken, "Woman's Sphere and Indian Reform: The Women's National Indian Association 1879–1901" (Ph.D. dissertation, Marquette University, 1981) and Amelia Stone Quinton, "The Indian," in *The Literature of Philanthropy*, ed. Frances Goodale, pp. 116–140. See also Prucha, *Policy in Crisis*, pp. 134–138; Thompson, "Origins and Implementation," pp. 31–44, 158–173, 192–198; Bannan, "Reformers and the 'Indian Problem,'" pp. 90–97; and Priest, *Uncle Sam's Stepchildren*, pp. 81–83.

19. Indian Rights Association (IRA), *Fourth Annual Report of the Executive Committee of the Indian Rights Association for the Year Ending December 14, 1886*, inside front cover. For a detailed history of the organization, see William T. Hagan, *The Indian Rights Association: The Herbert Welsh Years 1882–1904*.

20. IRA, *Second Annual Report of the Executive Committee of the Indian Rights Association for the Year Ending December, 1884*, p. 7. See also Thompson, "Origins and Implementation," pp. 44–57, 173–205; Mardock, *Reformers and the American Indian*, pp. 200–202, 204–205, 208; Prucha, *Policy in Crisis*, pp. 138–143; and Bannan, "Reformers and the 'Indian Problem,'" pp. 94–99.

21. For a discussion of the conferences, see Burgess, "Lake Mohonk Conferences." See also Thompson, "Origins and Implementation," pp. 57–62, 205–208, 211–221; and Prucha, *Policy in Crisis*, pp. 143–145. For an interesting biographical sketch of Smiley, see Clyde A. Milner II, "Albert K. Smiley: Friend to the Friends of the Indians," in *Churchmen and the Western Indians 1820–1920*, pp. 143–175.

22. For the first quotation, see Francis Paul Prucha, "Federal Indian Policy in United States History," in *Indian Policy in the United States*, p. 31; for the second quotation, see Burgess, "Lake Mohonk Conferences," p. v. For a general discussion, see Prucha, "Policy Reform and American Protestantism," pp. 229–251.

23. Nathaniel G. Taylor (served as commissioner 1867–1869), a Methodist Episcopal; Edward Parmelee Smith (1873–1875), a Congregationalist; and Thomas Jefferson Morgan (1889–1893), a Baptist.

24. William G. McLoughlin, ed. *The American Evangelicals, 1800–1900: An Anthology*, p. 1.

25. Russell Blaine Nye, *Society and Culture in America, 1830–1860*, p. 292.

26. Prucha, *Policy in Crisis*, p. 152.

27. Ibid., pp. 155–157; Helen M. Bannan, "The Ideal of Civilization and American Indian Policy Reformers in the 1880s," *Journal of American Culture* 1 (Winter 1978): 788–789; and Bannan, "Reformers and the 'Indian Problem,'" pp. 143–154.

28. This statement was written in 1881 (Prucha, *Americanizing the American Indians*, p. 14).

29. Prucha, *Americanizing the American Indians*, p. 43. For more on this concept, see Bannan, "Reformers and the 'Indian Problem,'" pp. 215–219.

30. William T. Hagan, "Reformers' Images of the Native Americans: The Late 19th Century," paper delivered 25 February 1981, Kent State University, Center for Native American Studies, Distinguished Lecturer series, p. 3. See also Bannan, "Reformers and the 'Indian Problem,'" pp. 138–139.

31. Barbara Welter, "The Cult of True Womanhood, 1820–1860," in *Dimity Convictions: The American Woman in the Nineteenth Century*, pp. 21–41. See also Barbara Epstein, *The Politics of Domesticity: Women, Evangelism, and Temperance in Nineteenth Century America*, pp. 2–7, 67, 75, 84–85; Helen M. Bannan, "'True Womanhood' and Indian Assimilation," in *Selected Proceedings of the Third Annual Conference on Minority Studies*, ed. George E. Carter and James R. Parker, pp. 187–189; and Glenda Riley, "The Cult of True Womanhood: Industrial and Westward Expansion, 1816–1837," in *Inventing the American Woman: A Perspective on Women's History*, pp. 63–87. See also Sandra L. Myres, *Westering Women and the Frontier Experience, 1800–1915*, p. 7. For a current critique of women's special sphere, see Linda K. Kerber, "Separate Spheres, Female Worlds, Woman's Place: The Rhetoric of Women's History," *Journal of American History* 75 (June 1988): 9–39.

This idealized role did not fit the majority of American women's lives; farm women and urban working women did not have this luxury of leisure. See Gerda Lerner, "The Lady and the Mill Girl: Changes in the Status of Women in the Age of Jackson," in *Our American Sisters: Women in American Life and Thought*, ed. Jean E. Friedman and William G. Shade, p. 191.

32. Barbara J. Berg, *The Remembered Gate: The Origins of American Feminism: The Woman and the City, 1800–1860*, p. 67. For a detailed study of domesticity, see Nancy F. Cott, *The Bonds of Womanhood: "Woman's Sphere" in New England, 1780–1835*, pp. 63–100.

33. McLoughlin, ed., *American Evangelicals*, p. 18.

34. Kathryn Kish Sklar, *Catharine Beecher: A Study in American Domesticity*, p. 158.

35. William W. Fowler, *Women on the American Frontier*, pp. 508 and 522, respectively.

36. Quotations from Fowler, *Women on the American Frontier*, p. 359. For an interesting discussion of how the western woman's attitude changed toward the Indian, see Glenda Riley, *Women and Indians on the Frontier, 1825–1915*.

37. Berg, *Remembered Gate*, p. 79. For a detailed discussion of women and religion, see Cott, *Bonds of Womanhood*, pp. 126–159; for women's impact upon religion, see Barbara Welter, "The Feminization of American Religion, 1800–1860," in *Dimity Convictions*, pp. 83–102. See also Welter, "Cult of True Womanhood," pp. 21–23.

38. Nancy F. Cott, "Religion and the Bonds of Womanhood," in *Our American Sisters*, p. 196.

39. Ann Douglas, *The Feminization of American Culture*, p. 44.

40. *Women and Religion in America: The Nineteenth Century: A Docu-*

mentary History, ed. Rosemary Radford Ruether and Rosemary Skinner Keller, I: 311.

41. Welter, "Feminization of American Religion," p. 84.

42. Cott, "Religion and the Bonds of Womanhood," p. 202.

43. Mary P. Ryan, "American Society and the Cult of Domesticity, 1830–1860" (Ph.D. dissertation, University of California, Santa Barbara, 1971), pp. 284–285.

44. For general discussions on the role of women in various reforms, see Eleanor Flexnor, *Century of Struggle: The Woman's Rights Movement in the United States;* Ruth Bordin, *Women and Temperance: The Quest for Power and Liberty, 1873–1900;* and Epstein, *Politics of Domesticity.*

45. *Memoirs of John Quincy Adams, Comprising Portions of his Diary from 1795 to 1848,* ed. Charles Francis Adams, X: 36.

46. *Indian's Friend* 9 (October 1896): 2. See also Amelia Stone Quinton, "Care of the Indian," in *Woman's Work in America,* ed. Annie Nathan Meyer, p. 377.

47. Wanken, "Woman's Sphere and Indian Reform," p. 7.

48. Ibid., pp. 9–11.

49. Mary E. Dewey, *Historical Sketch of the Formation and Achievements of the Women's National Indian Association in the United States,* p. 8. See also *Indian's Friend* 9 (April 1897): 2; and Wanken, "Woman's Sphere and Indian Reform," p. 12.

50. *Indian's Friend* 9 (October 1896): 2. See also WNIA, *Annual Meeting and Report of the Women's National Indian Association* [1883], p. 6; Dewey, *Historical Sketch,* pp. 8–9; Quinton, "Care of the Indian," p. 378; and Wanken, "Woman's Sphere and Indian Reform," pp. 16–17.

51. *Indian's Friend* 9 (October 1896): 10; and Dewey, *Historical Sketch,* p. 11. By 1882, Reformed Episcopal, Reformed Church of the United States, Lutheran, Congregational, and Unitarian members brought representation on the Central Indian Committee to ten denominations (see Wanken, "Woman's Sphere and Indian Reform," pp. 19–20).

52. Quinton, "Care of the Indian," p. 381.

53. Ibid., p. 380. See also *Indian's Friend* 9 (October 1896): 11; 9 (April, 1897): 2.

54. WNIA, *Annual Meeting and Report* [1883], p. 19.

55. *Indian's Friend* 9 (October 1896): 11.

56. Ibid.

57. *Indian's Friend* 9 (February 1897): 2; Dewey, *Historical Sketch,* p. 20; and Wanken, "Woman's Sphere and Indian Reform," pp. 29–30.

58. *Indian's Friend* 9 (October 1896): 10.

59. Dewey, *Historical Sketch,* p. 6, for all quotations.

60. *Indian's Friend* 9 (April 1897): 2; Quinton, "Care of the Indian," p. 382.

61. *Indian's Friend* 9 (April 1897): 2. For a detailed discussion of the vast organizational skill used by Quinton to get the petition signed, see Wanken, "Woman's Sphere and Indian Reform," pp. 33–35; and for a discussion of the arguments engendered by its presentation, see pp. 35–38.

62. *Indian's Friend* 9 (April 1897): 2. This is not to imply that the idea of land allotment was original to the WNIA. It appeared in early federal treaties; however, the WNIA was the first national reform group to push the idea. For additional information on allotment, see Wilcomb E. Washburn, *The Assault on Indian Tribalism: The General Allotment Law (Dawes Act) of 1887;* D. S. Otis, *The Dawes Act and the Allotment of Indian Lands,* ed. Francis Paul Prucha; and Leonard A. Carlson, *Indians, Bureaucrats, and Land: The Dawes Act and the Decline of Indian Farming.*

63. *Indian's Friend* 9 (May 1897): 2.

64. WNIA, *Annual Meeting and Report* [1883], p. 10.

65. IRA, *First Annual Report of the Executive Committee of the Indian Rights Association for the Year Ending December, 1883,* p. 5.

66. *Indian's Friend* 9 (June 1897): 12.

67. IRA. *Third Annual Report of the Executive Committee of the Indian Rights Association for the Year Ending December 14, 1885,* p. 13.

68. Amelia Stone Quinton, *Missionary Work of the Women's National Indian Association,* p. 1. The entire text of the above appears in the WNIA, *Fourth Annual Report of the Women's National Indian Association* [1884], pp. 32–38. See also WNIA, *Annual Meeting and Report* [1883], p. 10.

69. *Indian's Friend* 9 (August 1897): 2; 10 (April 1898): 2; 11 (September 1898): 12.

70. *Indian's Friend* 9 (July 1897): 11.

71. Quinton, "Care of the Indian," p. 382.

72. Quinton, *Missionary Work,* p. 1.

73. WNIA, *Fourth Annual Report* [1884], p. 52.

74. WNIA, *Annual Meeting and Report* [1883], pp. 19–20.

75. Quinton, "Care of the Indians," p. 374. No exact year is listed for when Jackson joined WNIA but in the WNIA *Fourth Annual Report* [1884], p. 63, she is listed as an honorary member contributing $50. For a brief tribute to her, see Michael T. Marsden, "A Dedication to the Memory of Helen Hunt Jackson, 1830–1885," *Arizona and the West* 21 (Summer 1979): 108–112.

76. WNIA, *Annual Report of the Women's National Indian Association* [1886], pp. 16–17, 19–20. See also *Indian's Friend* 10 (April 1898): 2, and Wanken, "Woman's Sphere and Indian Reform," p. 300.

77. For a detailed discussion of the effect of the Spanish mission system upon the Indians of California, see Sherburne F. Cook, *The Conflict between the California Indian and White Civilization,* pp. 1–194; George H. Phillips, *The Enduring Struggle: Indians in California History,* pp. 21–41; and Carey McWilliams, *Southern California: An Island on the Land,* pp. 29–48. See also Herbert E. Bolton, "The Mission as a Frontier Institution in the Spanish-American Colonies," *American Historical Review* 23 (October 17 to July 1918): 42–61.

The mission system and California's Indian policy are merely incidental to this research and will not be discussed in any great detail. For additional information, see the four-volume work by Zephyrin Engelhardt, *The Missions and Missionaries of California.*

78. David J. Weber, *The Mexican Frontier 1821–1846: The American Southwest under Mexico,* p. 60.

79. For the effect of the American invasion upon the California Indian, see Cook, *California Indian and White,* pp. 255–361.

80. Albert L. Hurtado, *Indian Survival on the California Frontier,* p. 130. For a detailed description of Indian labor, see pp. 130–168. This volume is a revised version of his "Ranchos, Gold Mines, and Rancherias: A Socioeconomic History of Indians and Whites in Northern California, 1821–1860" (Ph.D. dissertation, University of California, Santa Barbara, June 1981). See also James J. Rawls, *Indians of California: The Changing Image,* pp. 87, 93–108, and Cook, *California Indian and White,* pp. 308–328.

81. For the text of the treaty with the former San Luis Rey Mission Indians, one of the major groups that Jackson worked with, see "Treaty with the San Louis Rey, Etc. 1852," in *Irredeemable America: The Indians' Estate and Land Claims,* ed. Imre Sutton, pp. 390–392.

For information on the California Indian land claims, see Ralph L. Beals, "The Anthropologist as Expert Witness: Illustrations from the California Indian Land Claims Case," in *Irredeemable America,* pp. 139–155, and Florence C. Shipek, "Mission Indians and Indians of California Land Claims," *American Indian Quarterly* 13 (Fall 1989): 409–420.

82. For a general account of the reservation system in California, see Prucha, *Great Father,* I: 381–392. See also Rawls, *Indians of California,* pp. 139–170.

83. For a detailed discussion of Beale's Indian policy, see Gerald Thompson, *Edward F. Beale & the American West,* pp. 45–79. See Hurtado, *Indian Survival,* pp. 141–144, 150–165; and Rawls, *Indians of California,* pp. 148–152.

84. Henley established Nome Lackee in the Sacramento Valley, the Fresno Reservation in the San Joaquin Valley, the Klamath Reservation, and the Mendocino Reservation. The two Indian farms of Nome Cult, later to become the Round Valley Reservation, in Mendocino County and the Kings River farm in the San Joaquin Valley were also created. In 1863 the Tule River Reservation was established, followed the next year by the Hoopa Valley reserve. See Edward E. Hill, *The Office of Indian Affairs, 1824–1880: Historical Sketches,* pp. 19–26.

85. Michael A. Sievers, "Funding the California Indian Superintendency: A Case Study of Congressional Appropriations," *Southern California Quarterly* 59 (Spring 1977): 49–73; and Richard L. Carrico, "San Diego Indians and the Federal Government: Years of Neglect, 1850–1865," *Journal of San Diego History* 26 (Summer 1980): 165–184.

86. Board of Indian Commissioners (BIC), "Mission Indians in Southern California," *Third Annual Report of the Board of Indian Commissioners to the President of the United States* [1872], pp. 9–10.

87. BIC, *Seventh Annual Report of the Board of Indian Commissioners for the Year 1875* [1876], p. 79.

88. Keller, *American Protestantism,* pp. 188–204.

89. Rawls, *Indians of California,* p. 171. For a detailed discussion of the

decline of the California Indian population, see Cook, *California Indian and White*, pp. 3–56, 161–194, 197–233, 236–239, 267–279, 351, 357, 399–446, and Russell Thornton, *American Indian Holocaust and Survival: A Population History since 1492*, pp. 80, 83–85, 107–113, 125–126, 200–210. See also Albert Hurtado, "California Indian Demography, Sherburne F. Cook, and the Revision of American History," paper read at the Western History Association Meeting, Billings, Montana, 1986, pp. 1–33.

90. U.S. Department of the Interior, Office of Indian Affairs, *Annual Report of the Commissioner of Indian Affairs to the Secretary of the Interior for the Year 1881*, p. 13. See also Helen Jackson (H. H.), "The Present Condition of the Mission Indians in Southern California," in *Glimpses of Three Coasts*, pp. 81–82. This article originally appeared in the August 1883 issue of *Century Magazine*. The "List of Indian Villages with the Population of each by Tribe, as per last Census Return, 1880," Helen Hunt Jackson Papers (MS. 0020, Part I, Box 3, fd. 3), Charles Leaming Tutt Library, Colorado College, Colorado Springs, Colorado, cites the population of the former Southern California Mission Indians at only 2,907.

2. Early Indian Reform Work of Helen Hunt Jackson

1. Mathes, "Legacy of Indian Reform," pp. 25–58. See also Virginia McConnell, "'H. H.,' and Colorado, and the Indian Problem," *Journal of the West* 12 (April 1973): 272–280; Ruth E. Friend, "Helen Hunt Jackson: A Critical Study" (Ph.D. dissertation, Kent State University, 1985), pp. 227–243; Ruth Odell, *Helen Hunt Jackson (H. H.)*, pp. 151–170; Evelyn I. Banning, *Helen Hunt Jackson*, pp. 142–163; Antoinette May, *Helen Hunt Jackson: A Lonely Voice of Conscience*, pp. 58–69; Rosemary Whitaker, *Helen Hunt Jackson*, pp. 24–29; and George V. Fagan, "Helen of Colorado Reexamined," paper read 28 October 1977, Colorado Springs Ghost Town Club, Charles Leaming Tutt Library, Colorado College, Colorado Springs, Colorado.

2. H. H., "Standing Bear and Bright Eyes," *New York Independent*, 20 November 1879.

3. All quotes Jackson to an intimate friend, 17 January 1880, in Thomas Wentworth Higginson, "Mrs. Helen Jackson ('H. H.')," *Century Magazine* NS 31 (November 1885): 254. This letter is reprinted in Thomas Wentworth Higginson, *Contemporaries*, p. 155. Banning, *Helen Hunt Jackson*, p. 149, says the letter was written in early December 1879 to Reverend Moncure Daniel Conway; more than likely it was to Higginson. For a second reference to the Indians as a hobby, see Jackson to William A. Rideing, 28 May 1884, Helen Hunt Jackson Papers, Special Collections, Jones Library, Amherst, Massachusetts.

4. Higginson, *Contemporaries*, p. 156.

5. October 15 is commonly given as her birth date but according to Banning, *Helen Hunt Jackson*, p. 226, she was born a little before midnight on October 14.

6. Higginson, *Contemporaries*, p. 144.

7. For an interesting account, see Susan H. Dickinson, "Two Generations of Amherst Society," in *Essays on Amherst's History*, pp. 168−188. The author was the wife of Emily Dickinson's brother, Austin.

8. Sara A. Hubbard, "Helen Hunt Jackson," *Dial* 6 (September 1885): 109, for the first quotation, and Moncure Daniel Conway, *Autobiography, Memories, and Experiences of Moncure Daniel Conway*, I: 202, for the second quotation. See also "Helen Jackson," *Critic* NS 4 (August 22, 1885): 86. Odell, *Helen Hunt Jackson (H. H.)*, p. 302, noted that Higginson wrote this tribute to Jackson, although no author's name appeared on the sketch.

9. Thomas Wentworth Higginson, "To the Memory of H. H.," *Century Magazine* 32 (May 1886): 47.

10. Susan Coolidge [Sarah Chauncey Woolsey], "H. H.," Helen Hunt Jackson Collection (#7080-a), Clifton Waller Barrett Library, University of Virginia, Charlottesville, Virginia. This biographical sketch was written shortly after Jackson's death as a tribute.

11. Susan Coolidge, "H. H.," *Critic* NS 4 (3 October 1885): 164.

12. Thomas Wentworth Higginson, "Helen Jackson," *Critic* NS 4 (22 August 1885): 86.

13. Andrew F. Rolle, ed., introduction to Helen Hunt Jackson, *Century of Dishonor*, p. x, and Julia C. R. Dorr, "Emerson's Admiration of 'H. H.,'" *Critic* NS 4 (29 August 1885): 102.

14. Higginson, *Contemporaries*, p. 162. See also Thomas Wentworth Higginson, *Short Studies of American Authors*, p. 41. In a November 1885 issue of *Century* on p. 256, Higginson states that Jackson's poetry ranked "above that of any American woman, and in the opinion of many above that of any Englishwoman but Mrs. Browning." He also included several of her last poems.

15. "The Birthday Feast" *New York Daily Tribune* [hereinafter cited as *Tribune*], 4 December 1879.

16. This 19 June 1879 letter by Crook to Tibbles is quoted in "Indians and the Law: Opinion on the Proposition to Open the Court to the Indians for the Security and Protection of their Rights," *Boston Daily Advertiser* [hereinafter cited as the *Advertiser*], 29 July 1879. See also James T. King, "A Better Way: General George Crook and the Ponca Indians," *Nebraska History* 50 (Fall 1969): 239−256, and Thomas Henry Tibbles, *Buckskin and Blanket Days: Memoirs of a Friend of the Indians*, pp. 193−203.

17. For general information on the Ponca removal, court case, and tour, see the following: Jackson, *Century of Dishonor*, pp. 186−217; Thomas Henry Tibbles, *The Ponca Chiefs: An Account of the Trial of Standing Bear*; Earl W. Hayter, "The Ponca Removal," *North Dakota Historical Quarterly* 6 (July 1932): 263−275; Valerie Sherer Mathes, "Helen Hunt Jackson and the Ponca Controversy," *Montana: The Magazine of Western History* 39 (Winter 1989): 42−53; Valerie Sherer Mathes, "Helen Hunt Jackson and the Campaign for Ponca Restitution, 1880−1881," *South Dakota History* 17 (Spring 1987): 23−42; Mardock, "Standing Bear and the Reformers," pp. 101−113; Mardock, *Reformers and the American Indian*, pp. 168−191; Bannan, "Reformers and the 'Indian Problem,'" pp. 12−80;

Thompson, "Origins and Implementation," pp. 131–147; and Friend, "Critical Study," pp. 227–234. For a description by Secretary Schurz of the official point of view of the removal, see "The Trials of a Tribe: The Two Sides of the Ponca Indian Story," *Advertiser*, 23 August 1879. For a detailed description of the Indian's point of view, see "The Other Side: Statements of White Eagle and Standing Bear," same issue. See also "The Ponca Indians," *Advertiser*, 2 August 1879.

18. For a study of Susette LaFlesche, see Dorothy Clarke Wilson, *Bright Eyes: The Story of Susette LaFlesche, an Omaha Indian*; Margaret Crary, *Susette LaFlesche: Voice of the Omaha Indians*; Norma Kidd Green, "Four Sisters: Daughters of Joseph LaFlesche," *Nebraska History* 45 (June 1964): 165–176; and Norma Kidd Green, *Iron Eyes' Family: The Children of Joseph LaFlesche*, pp. 56–81, 97–121.

19. Tibbles, *Buckskin and Blanket Days*, p. 216.

20. Joaquin Miller, "The Life Work of Helen Hunt Jackson," *San Francisco Call*, 18 September 1892.

21. Helen Hunt Jackson, 6 December 1879, a letter to the editor signed H. H., "An Appeal for the Indians: Full History of the Wrongs of the Ponca Tribe—Bright Eyes on Law and Liberty," *Tribune*, 9 December 1879. The book has since been reprinted as Tibbles, *Ponca Chiefs*; see p. 2 for the Phillips dedication.

22. Jackson to Charles Dudley Warner, 18 November 1879. For another example of her persuasive letters, see Jackson to Warner, 15 January 1880, both in Warner Collection, Watkinson Library.

23. Jackson to Whitelaw Reid, 7 December 1879. See also Jackson to Reid, 9 December 1879. Papers of Whitelaw Reid (Reel No. 151, Series 3, Vol. 105, Self Ascession No. DM 14,900.2), Library of Congress, Washington, D.C.

24. Jackson to Warner, 15 January 1880, Warner Collection, Watkinson Library.

25. All quotes Jackson to Moncure D. Conway, 25 July 1880, Moncure D. Conway Papers, Butler Library, Columbia University, New York, New York.

26. All quotes Jackson to the editor, 20 November 1879, signed Justice, "Standing Bear and the Poncas: The Story of their Hardship and Sufferings Retold . . . ," *Tribune*, 24 November 1879.

27. "Arrival of the Ponca Indians," *Tribune*, 6 December 1879.

28. All quotes Jackson to Warner, 14 December 1879, Warner Collection, Watkinson Library.

29. Jackson to William Hayes Ward, 27 January 1880, Helen Hunt Jackson manuscripts (HM 13980), Huntington Library, San Marino, California; see also Jackson to Ward dated the Berkeley, 1880 (probably April or May), (HM 13991), Huntington Library, in which she stated, "I have been working every day at the Astor Lib from 9 till 4!" In Jackson to Mrs. Elizabeth Ann McNeil Benham, 30 January 1880, New Hampshire Historical Society, Concord, New Hampshire, she remarked she was at the Astor "all the forenoon but am usually in after five or half past." See also Jackson to Charles Scribner, 20 February 1880, Archives of Charles Scribner's Sons (Author Files I, Box 82), Princeton University Library, Princeton, New Jersey; and

Jackson to Edward Abbott, 20 March 1880, Abbott Memorial Collection: Edward Abbott *Literary World,* Lowell Tribute Scrapbook, Bowdoin College Library, Brunswick, Maine. (Abbott was then editor of the *Literary World*). See also Jackson to Conway, 10 June 1880, Conway Papers, Butler Library. In Jackson to Miss Clarke, 14 April 1880, Sophia Smith Collection, Women's History Archive, Smith College, Northampton, Massachusetts, she notes that "since last October, I have hardly thought for one moment of anything except the Indian question, and that I have been ever since Jan. working from five to six hours a day in this Library."

30. All quotes Jackson to the editor, 11 December 1879 signed H. H., "The Indian Problem: Questions for the American People," *Tribune,* 15 December 1879.

31. All quotes ibid.

32. All quotes Jackson to William Hayes Ward, 20 December 1879, Jackson manuscripts (HM 13977), Huntington Library.

33. Jackson to Warner, 21 December 1879, Warner Collection, Watkinson Library. See also Jackson to Reid, 20 December 1879, Papers of Whitelaw Reid, Library of Congress, in which she expressed much the same sentiment.

34. In Jackson to Warner, 2 May 1880, Warner Collection, Watkinson Library, Jackson noted the appendix of *A Century of Dishonor* would contain a few odds and ends including letters between her and Schurz on the Ponca case as well as letters between her and William N. Byers over the Sand Creek Massacre.

35. Higginson, *Contemporaries,* p. 165.

36. Jackson to Henry Wadsworth Longfellow, 2 March 1881, Henry Wadsworth Longfellow Papers, and to Oliver Wendell Holmes, 2 March 1881, Oliver Wendell Holmes Papers, Houghton Library, Harvard University, Cambridge, Massachusetts. The entire text of this letter is reprinted, with permission from the Houghton Library, in Mathes, "Campaign for Ponca Restitution," pp. 36–40.

37. U.S. Department of the Interior, Office of Indian Affairs, *Annual Report of the Commissioner of Indian Affairs to the Secretary of the Interior for the Year 1879,* "The Poncas," p. XIV.

38. BIC, *Eleventh Annual Report of the Board of Indian Commissioners for the Year 1879* [1880], p. 13.

39. "Indian Affairs: The Red Man Improving in Civilization and Generally Living a Peaceful Life . . . ," *Tribune,* 28 November 1879.

40. "Mr. Schurz on Indian Affairs: The Secretary replies to the letter of H. H., in the Tribune," *Tribune,* 19 December 1879, p. 1. For more on Schurz's point see letter dated 28 November 1879 to Edward Atkinson in *Speeches, Correspondence, and Political Papers of Carl Schurz,* ed. Frederick Bancroft, III : 485. Nevins, "Sentimentalist v. Realist," pp. 271–274, ably defends Secretary Schurz in this controversy.

41. Jackson to Ward, 20 December 1879, Jackson manuscripts (HM 13977), Huntington Library; see also Jackson to Reid [20 December 1879], Papers of Whitelaw Reid, Library of Congress. See also Jackson to the editor, 23 De-

cember 1879, signed H. H., "Wrongs of the Indians: 'H. H.' Takes up Mr. Schurz's Reply." *Tribune*, 28 December 1879.

42. H. H., "Wrongs of the Indians: 'H. H.' Takes up Mr. Schurz's Reply," p. 5.

43. "The Week," *Nation* (12 February 1880): 150.

44. Jackson to Carl Schurz, 9 January 1880, *Century of Dishonor*, pp. 359–361. For a brief discussion of the Jackson/Schurz correspondence, see Thompson, "Origins and Implementation," pp. 137–139.

45. Schurz to Jackson, 17 January 1880, *Century of Dishonor*, p. 362. This letter can also be found in Schurz, *Speeches, Correspondence* III: 496–499.

46. See first Jackson to Schurz, 22 January 1880, *Century of Dishonor*, p. 364; and Schurz to Jackson, 26 January 1880, ibid., p. 366. The latter can also be found in Schurz, *Speeches, Correspondence* III: 501–503.

47. All quotes Jackson to Ward, 27 January 1880, Jackson manuscripts (HM 13980), Huntington Library.

48. Jackson, *Century of Dishonor*, p. 368. See also "Civil Rights in Acres," *New York Times*, 21 February 1880.

49. "Civil Rights in Acres," *New York Times*, 21 February 1880.

50. Jackson to Ann Schofield Fiske Banfield, 29 February 1880, William Sharpless Jackson Family Papers (Part II, Box 3, fd. 31), Charles Leaming Tutt Library. See also Jackson to Ann Banfield, 10 January 1880, ibid.

51. Jackson to the editor, 2 January 1880, signed H. H., "The Case of the Utes: A Few More Points by 'H. H.,'" *Tribune*, 19 January 1880.

52. All quotes Jackson to the editor, 18 January 1880, signed H. H., "A Small Matter to Murder an Indian: 'H. H.' Scores Another Point," *Tribune*, 25 January 1880.

53. All quotes Jackson to the editor, 31 January 1880, signed H. H., "The Starving Utes: More Questions for the People by 'H. H.' What white men have done and are doing to Indians in Colorado," *Tribune*, 5 February 1880; reprinted in *Century of Dishonor*, pp. 343–346.

54. William N. Byers, "The Starving Utes: A Reply to Questions Asked by 'H. H.,' *Tribune*, 22 February 1880; reprinted in *Century of Dishonor*, pp. 346–350. For an unbiased account of Sand Creek, see Robert M. Utley, *Frontiersmen in Blue, 1848–1865*, pp. 290–297.

55. Jackson, *Century of Dishonor*, p. 350.

56. Jackson to the editor, 22 February 1880, signed H. H., "The Sand Creek Massacre: A Slaughter of Friendly Indians," *Tribune*, 24 February 1880; reprinted in *Century of Dishonor*, pp. 350–356.

57. All quotes Jackson to Reid, 22 February 1880, Papers of Whitelaw Reid, Library of Congress.

58. Jackson to Tibbles, 4 March 1880, Jackson Collection (#7080-b), Clifton Waller Barrett Library.

59. Byers to the editor, "The Sand Creek Massacre: A Card from William N. Byers in Reply to 'H. H.'s' Letter . . . ," *Tribune*, 27 February 1880; reprinted in *Century of Dishonor*, pp. 356–357.

60. Jackson to Reid, 29 February 1880, Papers of Whitelaw Reid, Library of Congress.

61. Jackson to the editor, 28 February 1880, signed H. H., "The Sand Creek Massacre: 'H. H.' Takes a Final Shot at . . . Byers," *Tribune*, 3 March 1880; reprinted in *Century of Dishonor*, pp. 357–358. See also Jackson to Reid, 26 February 1880, Papers of Whitelaw Reid, Library of Congress.

62. Jackson to Reid, 2 March 1880, Papers of Whitelaw Reid, Library of Congress.

63. Jackson to Reid, 3 March 1880, Papers of Whitelaw Reid, Library of Congress.

64. Jackson to Ward, 27 January 1880, Jackson manuscripts (HM 13980), Huntington Library.

65. H. H., "The Wards of the United States Government," *Scribner's Monthly* 19 (March 1880): 781–782.

66. Jackson to the editor, 21 March 1880, signed H. H., "The Indian Problem," *Tribune*, 27 March 1880. Using the annual report of 1879, Jackson emphasized that failure to enforce these eleven laws had led to bad feelings among the Indians.

67. Jackson to the editor, 4 April 1880, signed H. H., "The Massacre of the Cheyennes," *Tribune*, 11 April 1880.

68. Jackson to Ward, 1880 [probably April or May], Jackson manuscripts (HM 13992), Huntington Library. Since she left for Boston in the latter part of May and the manuscript was completed by then, this letter was written in early spring, although in the manuscript collection it followed a letter dated 30 November 1880. See also Jackson to Mr. Payne, 28 December 1880, Jackson Collection (#7080-b), Clifton Waller Barrett Library. For the exact date she completed the manuscript see Jackson to Mr. Alden, 6 May 1880, Helen Maria Fiske Hunt Jackson Collection, The Bancroft Library, University of California, Berkeley, California.

69. All quotes Jackson to Warner, 21 December 1879, Warner Collection, Watkinson Library. See also Jackson to Ward, 21 and 27 January 1880, Jackson manuscripts (HM 13979, 13980), Huntington Library.

70. All quotes from *Century of Dishonor*, pp. 339, 31.

71. Jackson to Anne Lynch Botta, 30 July 1880, Helen Hunt Jackson Papers, Jones Library, Amherst, Massachusetts.

72. Jackson to Warner, 11 November 1880, Warner Collection, Watkinson Library; Jackson to Ward, 3 November 1880, Jackson manuscripts (HM 13990), Huntington Library; Jackson to Henry B. Whipple, 22 May 1880 and 27 and 29 October 1880, Henry B. Whipple Papers (Box 14), Division of Library and Archives, Minnesota Historical Society, St. Paul, Minnesota.

73. "Condition of the Indians," *Tribune*, 22 November 1880. See also U.S. Department of the Interior, Office of Indian Affairs, *Annual Report of the Commissioner of Indian Affairs to the Secretary of the Interior for the Year 1880*, pp. XXXV–XXXVI. For Jackson's answer to the November 22 news item, see Jackson to the editor, 22 November 1880, signed H. H., "Broken Indian Treaties: A Letter from 'H. H.'" *Tribune*, 5 December 1880.

74. Jackson to Reid, 22 November 1880, Papers of Whitelaw Reid, Library of Congress.

75. Jackson to Mr. Lyman Abbott, 11 December 1880, Chapin-Kiley Manuscripts, Amherst College Library, Amherst, Massachusetts.

76. Jackson to Mr. Payne, 15 December 1880, Henry W. and Albert A. Berg Collection, New York Public Library, Astor, Lenox and Tilden Foundations, New York, New York.

77. Jackson to Reid, 1 December and 30 November 1880, Papers of Whitelaw Reid, Library of Congress.

78. *Diary and Letters of Rutherford Hayes: Nineteenth President of the United States,* ed. by Charles Richard Williams, III: 629.

79. Price to Delano A. Goddard, 31 May 1881, Henry L. Dawes Papers (Box 25, General Correspondence, 1879–1881), Library of Congress.

80. All quotes Jackson to Dawes, 10 December 1880, Dawes Papers (Box 24), Library of Congress. See also Jackson's letters of 23 and 30 December 1880 to Dawes.

81. Jackson to Warner, 12 February 1881, Warner Collection, Watkinson Library.

82. All quotes Jackson to Warner, 3 December 1880, Warner Collection, Watkinson Library.

83. Jackson to Warner, 6 December 1880, Warner Collection, Watkinson Library.

84. Jackson to Dawes, 10 December 1880, Dawes Papers (Box 24), Library of Congress.

85. Jackson to Ward, 6 January 1881, Jackson manuscripts (HM 13993), Huntington Library.

86. Jackson to Warner, 6 January 1881, Warner Collection, Watkinson Library.

87. Jackson to Ward, 23 February 1881, Jackson manuscripts (HM 13994), Huntington Library.

88. Jackson to Warner, n.d., Warner Collection, Watkinson Library. Although this undated letter was included with an envelope postmarked 19 May 1881, it probably was written around 22 February. In the letter, Jackson mentioned she was in the capitol and that a dinner in Boston was to be given for Schurz. Both events took place in mid to late February. In a February 22, 1881, letter to Warner, she dropped him a short note and enclosed a clipping of the dinner.

She was particularly unhappy about the "100 influential men" in Boston honoring Schurz with this prestigious dinner. She called this the "cleverest trick" Schurz had played yet. See Jackson to Lyman Abbott, 21 February 1881, Abbott Memorial Collection: Lyman Abbott Autograph Collection, Bowdoin College Library.

89. All quotes Jackson to Ward, 23 March 1881, Jackson manuscripts (HM 13996), Huntington Library.

90. Jackson to Warner, 6 January 1881, Warner Collection, Watkinson Library.

91. Agreement between Mrs. Helen Jackson and Harper & Brothers for the publication of "A Century of Dishonor," 21 May 1880, Harper & Brothers Papers, Butler Library, Columbia University.

92. Jackson to Scribner, n.d., Author Files I, Box 82, Archives of Charles Scribner's Sons, Princeton University Library.

93. Jackson to Warner [probably 22 February 1881], Warner Collection, Watkinson Library. For a very complimentary review, see M. Le B. Goddard, "A Century of Dishonor," *Atlantic Monthly* 47 (April 1881): 572–575. For a discussion of *Century of Dishonor*, see Friend, "Critical Study," pp. 234–243.

94. Jackson to Warner, 31 October 1882, Warner Collection, Watkinson Library.

3. Helen Hunt Jackson's First Visit to the Mission Indians

1. H. H. [Helen Hunt], *Bits of Travel*, pp. 91, 107; see also Helen Hunt Jackson, *Ah-Wah-Ne Days: A Visit to the Yosemite Valley in 1872*, pp. 20, 38; and Helen Hunt Jackson, *My Day in the Wilderness: Six California Tales*, pp. 1–19.

2. H. H., *Bits of Travel*, p. 36.

3. Jackson to Mrs. Elizabeth Benham, 26 March 1873, New Hampshire Historical Society, Concord, New Hampshire.

4. Jackson to Warner, 3 March 1881, Warner Collection, Watkinson Library. See also Jackson to Ward, 1 and 23 March 1881, Jackson manuscripts (HM 13995, HM 13996), Huntington Library; Jackson to Henry Oscar Houghton, 20 March 1881, Henry Oscar Houghton Papers, Houghton Library, Harvard University; and Jackson to Daniel Coit Gilman, 4 March [1881], Ms. 1, Daniel Coit Gilman Papers, Special Collections, Milton S. Eisenhower Library, Johns Hopkins University, Baltimore, Maryland.

5. Jackson to Warner, 13 April 1881, Warner Collection, Watkinson Library. See also Jackson to Joseph B. Gilder, 2 April 1881, Personal—Miscellaneous Papers (Helen Hunt Jackson), Rare Books and Manuscripts Division, New York Public Library, Astor, Lenox, and Tilden Foundations, New York, New York.

6. Jackson to Thomas Wentworth Higginson, 22 July 1881, and Jackson to Thomas Bailey Aldrich, 19 August 1881, Thomas Wentworth Higginson Field Book and Thomas Bailey Aldrich Papers, Houghton Library, Harvard University.

7. Jackson to J. B. Gilder, n.d., Personal—Miscellaneous (Jackson), New York Public Library.

8. These tribal designations are more modern than those used by Jackson. See "Serrano Division," "Gabrieliño," "The Juaneño," "The Luiseño," "The Cupeño and Cahuilla," "The Diegueño and Kamia," A. L. Krober, *Handbook of the Indians of California*, pp. 611–619, 620–635, 636–647, 648–688, 689–708, 709–725. See also Lowell John Bean and Charles R. Smith, "Gabrieliño"; Bean and Florence C. Shipek, "Luiseño"; Bean and Smith, "Serrano"; Bean, "Cahuilla"; Bean and Smith, "Cupeño"; Katharine Luomala, "Tipai-Ipai"; and Shipek, "History of Southern California Mission Indians," in *Handbook of North American Indians*, Vol. 8 *California*,

ed. Robert F. Heizer, pp. 538—549, 550—563, 570—574, 575—587, 588—591, 592—609, 610—618. See also George Harwood Phillips, "The Cahuilla, Luiseño and Cupeño," *Chiefs and Challengers: Indian Resistance and Cooperation in Southern California*, pp. 7—19.

Kroeber used the term Diegueño to denote more southerly divisions; modern scholars use Ipai in reference to the northernmost Diegueños. Since different spellings of village names exist, those used by Jackson will be continued for consistency. To avoid confusing the two villages of Potrero, I am calling the village near Banning El Potrero. Jackson called it "the Potrero," while the WNIA called it Potraro. Today Pachanga is spelled Pechanga and Saboba is Soboba.

9. Phillips, *Chiefs and Challengers*, p. 16 notes that in addition to the original Cupeño there were Cahuilla, Luiseño, and Diegueño living at or near Agua Caliente. Although Jackson called the villagers at Saboba members of the Serrano tribe, their exact tribal affiliation is questionable. The term Saboba is a Luiseño place name; see Kroeber, *Handbook of the Indians of California*, p. 896. The Sabobans might possibly have been Cahuillas; see Heizer, ed., *Handbook of North American Indians*, pp. 585, 612, which indicate a present-day Cahuilla population.

10. In *Southern California*, pp. 70—83, McWilliams accuses Jackson of almost single-handedly creating the romantic legend of happy, contented Mission Indians supervised by caring Franciscan friars, any mistreatment meted out not by the missionaries but by "vulgar gringos."

The 1985 recommendation by the Sacred Congregation of Rites to canonize Father Junípero Serra has brought this romantic viewpoint under strong criticism. Charges that Serra enslaved and brutalized the Indians were presented by Indian activists Rupert and Jeannette Henry Costo in *The Missions of California: A Legacy of Genocide*. For more on this same theme, see James A. Sandos, "Junipero Serra's Canonization and the Historical Record," *American Historical Review* 93 (December 1988): 1253—1269. However, Donald C. Cutter notes in his review of *Missions of California* that the book is based on interviews from which short answers were taken out of context and one-sided attacks by scholars who have not attained prominent stature in the historical profession. See Donald C. Cutter, "Books," *Californians* 6 (November/December 1988): 56. The Costo/Sandos' point of view in no way detracts from Jackson's view of the missionary period and her important work among the former California Mission Indians.

11. For a detailed study of Indian resistance, the activities of the Cupeño, Luiseño, and Cahuilla, and the roles of Cahuilla leader Juan Antonio, Cupeño chief Antonio Garra, and mixed-blood leader Manuelito Cota, see Phillips, *Chiefs and Challengers*, passim.

12. J. E. Colburn, U.S. Indian agent, 15 August 1877 annual report, U.S. Department of the Interior, Office of Indian Affairs, *Annual Report of the Commissioner of Indian Affairs to the Secretary of the Interior for the Year 1877*, p. 36.

13. The Desert Land Act passed on 3 March 1877 enabled citizens to obtain 640 acres with a small initial payment of twenty-five cents per acre. After a period of three years, if the individual could prove he had irrigated part of the land, he could purchase the entire section for an additional dollar per acre.

14. J. E. Colburn to J. Q. Smith, commissioner, 3 August 1877, Office of Indian Affairs (Record Group 75, Special Case 31—Mission Indians in California, Letters Received, #1085—1877), National Archives and Record Service, Washington, D.C. (hereinafter cited as NA, RG 75, OIA, SC 31, LR). See also S. S. Lawson to E. A. Hayt, 3 April 1879 (NA, RG 75, OIA, SC 31, LR, #348—1879).

15. Lawson to Hayt, 28 November 1878 (NA, RG 75, OIA, SC 31, LR, #826—1878).

16. Chalmers Scott to Lawson, 7 December 1878, and Lawson to Hayt, 17 December 1878 (NA, RG 75, OIA, SC 31, LR, #863—1878).

17. Lawson to Hayt, 21 April 1879 (NA, RG 75, OIA, SC 31, LR, #412—1879).

18. All quotes from Lawson to P. D. Wiggington, 21 December 1878 (NA, RG 75, OIA, SC 31, LR, #29—1878).

19. Lawson to Hayt, 8 January 1879 (NA, RG 75, OIA, SC 31, LR, #66—1879).

20. Lawson to Price, 28 December 1881 (NA, RG 75, OIA, SC 31, LR, #198—1882).

21. Lawson to Hayt, 26 March 1879 (NA, RG 75, OIA, SC 31, LR, #317—1879).

22. Bill to Provide for the Consolidation of the Mission Indians of California, HR 4067, enclosed with Hiram Price to Lawson, 7 March 1883, Jackson Papers (Part I, Box 2, fd. 7), Charles Leaming Tutt Library. See also Lawson to Hayt, 8 February 1879 (NA, RG 75, OIA, SC 31, LR, #155—1879).

23. Lawson to Hayt, 14 February 1879 (NA, RG 75, OIA, SC 31, LR, #177—1879).

24. On 17 January 1880 an executive order rescinded the Agua Caliente Indians' right to the land on Warner's Ranch. See Lawson to Roland E. Trowbridge, commissioner, 11 May 1880 (NA, RG 75, OIA, SC 31, LR, #723—1880) for the January 17 rescinding of this order.

25. Lawson to Hayt, 1 and 7 March, 22 April, and 19 December 1879 (NA, RG 75, OIA, SC 31, LR, #221, #251, #422, #1124—1879). See also "Reports of Agents in California," U.S. Department of the Interior, Office of Indian Affairs, Annual Report 1880, pp. 12–14.

26. Lawson to Hayt, 21 April 1879 (NA, RG 75, OIA, SC 31, LR, #413—1879). For an interesting report on the Cahuilla see Robert W. Frazer, ed., "Lovell's Report on the Cahuilla Indians 1854," Journal of San Diego History 22 (Winter 1976): 4–10.

27. Lawson to Trowbridge, 10 January 1881 (NA, RG 75, OIA, SC 31, LR, #4063—1881).

28. Acting commissioner to Lawson, 8 March 1881, Records of the Bureau of Indian Affairs (Record Group 75, Letters Sent—Land Division, Vol-

ume 39, LB 78, pp. 105–106), National Archives (hereinafter cited as NA, RG 75, OIA, LS).

29. Lawson to Price, 12 July 1881 (NA, RG 75, OIA, SC 31, LR, #12362–1881), and Price to Lawson, 7 March 1883, Jackson Papers (Part I, Box 2, fd. 7), Charles Leaming Tutt Library.

30. All quotes Jackson, "Present Condition," pp. 90–91.

31. Jackson to Ward, 10 April 1882, Jackson manuscripts (HM 13998), Huntington Library.

32. Jackson to Thomas Bailey Aldrich, 17 January 1882, Aldrich Papers, Houghton Library, Harvard University.

33. Jackson to Aldrich, 12 April 1882, Aldrich Papers, Houghton Library, Harvard University.

34. Helen Hunt Jackson and Abbot Kinney, "Report on the Condition and Needs of the Mission Indians of California, Made by Special Agents Helen Hunt Jackson and Abbot Kinney, to the Commissioner of Indian Affairs" [hereinafter referred to as "Report"], reprinted in *Century of Dishonor*, p. 462. See also: Helen Jackson, "Report on the condition and needs of the Mission Indians," U.S. Congress, Senate, S. Ex. Doc. 49, 48th Cong. 1st Sess., 1884, pp. 7–37; and S. Ex. Doc. 15, 49th Cong. 1st Sess., 1885, pp. 4–33; and S. Rept. 74, 50th Cong. 1st Sess., 1888, pp. 3–33. See also Helen Jackson, "Report on the condition and needs of the Mission Indians," U.S. Congress, House of Representatives, H.R. Rept. 3282, 50th Cong. 1st Sess. 1888, pp. 7–37.

For Jackson's work in California see Mathes, "Official Agent," pp. 63–82. See also Joyce C. Vickery, "Contradictory Realities: Helen Hunt Jackson's California," *California Historical Courier*, February/March 1986, p. 6.

35. Helen Jackson, "Echoes in the City of the Angels," *Century Magazine*, December 1883, p. 205. See also Odell, *Helen Hunt Jackson (H. H.)*, pp. 174–175. The Los Angeles article was the last of a series of four written for *Century*. "Father Junipero and His Work" appeared in May/June, "Present Condition" in August, and "Outdoor Industries in Southern California" in October. All were reprinted in Jackson, *Glimpses of Three Coasts*, pp. 3–128.

36. Odell, *Helen Hunt Jackson (H. H.)*, pp. 177–179. See also Jackson to Aldrich, 21 February 1882, Aldrich Papers, Houghton Library, Harvard University.

37. The *Santa Barbara Daily Press*, 14 February 1882, issue noted that Mrs. W. S. Jackson would leave the city in a few days, returning in March.

38. Odell, *Helen Hunt Jackson (H. H.)*, pp. 177–181; and Katheryn E. Marriott, "Helen Hunt Jackson in Santa Barbara," *Noticias* 28 (Winter 1982): 85–92.

39. The *San Diego Union*, 1 March 1882, listed her as arriving on the *Ancon* last night. The next issue of the *San Diego Union* stated rough weather prevented the steamer from mooring. The *San Diego Union* of March 7 noted her arrival on the last steamer; she was expected to spend two or three weeks.

40. See Richard L. Carrico, "San Diego Indians and the Federal Govern-

ment: Years of Neglect, 1850–1865," *Journal of San Diego History* 26 (Summer 1980): 165–184; and Evelyn I. Banning, "Helen Hunt Jackson in San Diego," *Journal of San Diego History* 24 (Fall 1978): 457–467.

41. For a detailed history of San Luis Rey, see Fr. Zephyrin Engelhardt, O.F.M., *San Luis Rey Mission*, and Msgr. Francis J. Weber, ed., *King of the Missions: A Documentary History of San Luis Rey de Francia.*

42. For a tour of Pala, see Charles Franklin Carter, *Some By-Ways of California*, pp. 1–23. San Antonio de Pala was restored to its original splendor during the 1950s. See Fr. J. M. Carillo, *The Story of Mission San Antonio de Pala*, pp. 6–39. Beginning as an *asistencia*, Pala eventually became a full-fledged mission.

43. Jackson, "Present Condition," p. 89. See also "Report," pp. 460–461, and Father A. D. Ubach to H. F. Coronel, 8 January 1883, Jackson Papers (Part I, Box 2, fd. 7), Charles Leaming Tutt Library.

44. Jackson, "Present Condition," pp. 84, 86, for the quotations. For more on the Pachanga Indians, see Jackson, "Report," pp. 504–506. In "Present Condition," p. 83, Jackson cited the removal date from Temecula as 1869, but in "Report," p. 505, she used 1873 as does "The Mission Indians of Southern California," U.S. Department of the Interior, Office of Indian Affairs, *Annual Report of the Commissioner of Indian Affairs to the Secretary of the Interior for the Year 1875*, p. 513.

45. Jackson, "Report," p. 505.

46. In *Pechanga Band of Mission Indians v. Kacor Realty, Inc., et al.*, filed in the District Court in Los Angeles, the Pachanga attempted to regain four hundred acres adjacent to their Riverside County reservation. John C. Christie, Jr., chief counsel for the defendants, details the merits of the case in "Indian Land Claims Involving Private Owners of Land: A Lawyer's Perspective," in *Irredeemable America: The Indians' Estate and Land Claims*, pp. 233–246.

The Indians argued that the land had been included in the 1882 executive order and that patents were fraudulent, although they had not occupied the land in question since 1882. The defendants argued that in 1893 the United States had issued a trust patent to the Indians which did not include those in dispute and that Mouren had sufficiently occupied the lands prior to the executive order. In 1980 the court decided in favor of the defendants.

47. Jackson, "Present Condition," p. 88.

48. Lawson to Hayt, 27 December 1878 (NA, RG 75, OIA, SC 31, LR, #15[19]—1878).

49. Lawson to Price, 8 February 1882 (NA, RG 75, OIA, SC 31, LR, #3256—1882). See also "Reports of Agents in California," U.S. Department of the Interior, Office of Indian Affairs, *Annual Report of the Commissioner of Indian Affairs to the Secretary of the Interior for the Year 1882*, pp. 11–12.

50. Jackson, "Present Condition," p. 93. See also pp. 93–95; Jackson, "Report," pp. 479–481; and Price to Teller, 23 June 1882, Jackson Papers (Part I, Box 2, fd. 7), Charles Leaming Tutt Library. For more on Saboba, see Van H. Garner, *The Broken Ring: The Destruction of the California Indians*, pp. 75–96.

51. For an account of Mary Sheriff's meeting with Jackson, see Odell, *Helen Hunt Jackson (H. H.)*, pp. 188–191. See also Jackson to Henry Teller, 11 June 1882 (NA, RG 75, OIA, SC 31, LR, #11701—1882).

52. Jackson to Mary Elizabeth Sheriff (Fowler), 4 May 1882, Jackson manuscripts (HM 14204), Huntington Library.

53. H. H. "A Night at Pala," *New York Independent,* 19 April 1883. See also Jackson, "Present Condition," pp. 97–98; and Jackson, "Report," pp. 502–503. She visited Pala on April 24, 1882; Jackson Papers (Part I, Box 5, fd. 3), Charles Leaming Tutt Library.

54. For information on the Potrero, see Jackson, "Present Condition," pp. 98–100.

55. For information on Pauma and Rincon, see Jackson, "Present Condition," p. 100, and Jackson, "Report," pp. 502–503. Both Pauma and Potrero were located at the Pauma Ranch. See also Phillips, *Chiefs and Challengers,* p. 48.

56. Jackson to Jeanne C. Carr, 14 March 1883, Jeanne C. (Smith) Carr Collection (CA 193), Huntington Library.

57. Kinney founded Venice, California, and served as chairman of the California State Board of Forestry and as presiding officer of the Yosemite Commission. See Kevin Starr, *Inventing the Dream: California through the Progressive Era,* pp. 78–81.

58. Jackson to Sheriff, 19 May 1882, Jackson manuscripts (HM 14205), Huntington Library. The Castillo letter was reprinted in Jackson, "Present Condition," p. 94.

59. Jackson to Teller, 11 June 1882 (NA, RG 75, OIA, SC 31, LR, #11429 [11701]—1882) for all quotations.

60. Teller to Hiram Price, 30 June 1882 (NA, RG 75, OIA, SC 31, LR, #11429[11701]—1882).

61. Copy of Price to Teller, 23 June 1882, Jackson Papers (Part I, Box 2, fd. 7), Charles Leaming Tutt Library. See also Price to Jackson, 7 July 1882 (NA, RG 75, OIA, LS, Land Division Volume 49, LB 98, pp. 434–439).

62. *Santa Barbara Daily Press,* 15 May 1882.

63. Jackson, "Present Condition," pp. 100–101. For an account of her trip to Monterey, see H. H., "A Chance Afternoon in California," *New York Independent,* 5 April 1883.

64. Jackson to Houghton, 3 July 1882, Houghton Papers, Houghton Library, Harvard University. See also Jackson to Warner, 19 October 1882, Warner Collection, Watkinson Library; and Jackson to Henry Oak, 3 October 1882, Henry Oak Correspondence and Papers, The Bancroft Library, University of California, Berkeley. Oak served as librarian for Hubert Howe Bancroft's collection of western Americana housed in a San Francisco mercantile firm. Eventually, the large collection became the nucleus of The Bancroft Library at the University of California. See also Jackson to William Alvord, 12 July 1882, William Alvord Correspondence and Papers, The Bancroft Library, University of California. Alvord was a prominent California businessman, president of the Bank of California, trustee of the College of California, and mayor of San Francisco.

65. Jackson to Coronel, 11 July 1882, Antonio F. Coronel Collection (DE 152C), Seaver Center for Western History Research, Los Angeles County Museum of Natural History, Los Angeles, California.

66. Jackson to Price, 19 July 1882 (NA, RG 75, OIA, LR, #13619—1882). See also Jackson to Price, 14 December 1882 (NA, RG 75, OIA, LR, #23457—1882); "Mission Indians in California," U.S. Department of the Interior, Office of Indian Affairs, *Annual Report of the Commissioner of Indian Affairs to the Secretary of the Interior for the Year 1883*, p. xlv; Jackson to Henry Chandler Bowen, 6 November 1882 and 13 February 1883, Jackson manuscripts (HM 13999, 14191), Huntington Library; Lawson to Jackson, 2 March 1883, and draft of Jackson to F. Crocker (President of the Southern Pacific Railroad), 18 April 1883, Jackson Papers (Part I, Box 2, fd. 4 and fd. 8), Charles Leaming Tutt Library; and Jackson to Joseph B. Gilder, 12 March 1883, Joseph Benson Gilder Papers, Rare Books and Manuscripts Division, New York Public Library.

67. All quotes Jackson to Teller, 16 September 1882 (NA, RG 75, OIA, LR, #18905—1882).

68. Ibid.

69. Teller to Jackson, 14 October 1882, and Price to Jackson, 16 October 1882, Jackson Papers (Part I, Box 2, fd. 6 and fd. 5), Charles Leaming Tutt Library.

70. In Jackson to Coronel, 16 October 1882, Antonio F. Coronel Collection (DE 152B), Seaver Center, Lós Angeles County Museum, she informed him of the five articles and that the "curious old reminiscences" she gathered from him would be included. She also wrote that there was a possibility she would be returning to Southern California next winter.

71. Jackson to Robert Johnson, 28 October 1882, Robert Underwood Johnson Papers, Butler Library, Columbia University.

72. Jackson to Price, 31 October 1882 (NA, RG 75, OIA, LR, #19910—1882). This letter has been reprinted in George Wharton James, *Through Ramona's Country*, p. 13.

73. Price to Jackson, 28 November 1882, Jackson Papers (Part I, Box 2, fd. 5), Charles Leaming Tutt Library. See her answer, Jackson to Price, 14 December 1882 (NA, RG 75, OIA, LR, #23457—1882).

74. All quotes Jackson to Warner, 31 October 1882, Warner Collection, Watkinson Library. For much the same sentiment see Jackson to J. B. Gilder, 12 March 1883, Gilder Papers, New York Public Library.

75. Jackson to Henry Chandler Bowen, 6 November 1882, Jackson manuscripts (HM 13999), Huntington Library. See also Jackson to Bowen, 14 November 1882, Jackson manuscripts (HM 14190). (Beginning in April 1883, her six articles for the *Independent* were published.)

4. Helen Hunt Jackson: Official Agent to the California Mission Indians

1. Jackson to Price, 15 January 1883 (NA, RG 75, OIA, LR, #1120—1883). See also Price to Jackson, 13 January 1883, Jackson Papers (Part I, Box 2,

fd. 5), Charles Leaming Tutt Library. In Jackson to Coronel, 22 January 1883, Coronel Collection, Seaver Center, Los Angeles County Museum, she wrote she intended to leave for California by February 20.

2. Jackson to Bowen, 13 February 1883, Bowen Collection (HM 14191), Huntington Library. Jackson to Aldrich, 13 February 1883, Aldrich Papers, Houghton Library, Harvard University.

3. Jackson to Aldrich, 22 and 27 February 1883, Aldrich Papers, Houghton Library, Harvard University.

4. Jackson to Teller, 2 March 1883 (NA, RG 75, OIA, SC 31, LR, #4638—1883). See also N. C. McFarland to Teller, 15 March 1883 (NA, RG 75, OIA, SC 31, LR, #5189—1883). She had originally written to Secretary Teller on this particular filing on 28 February 1883.

5. Jackson, "Exhibit E: The San Ysidro Indians," "Report," pp. 488–490. See also Jackson to Price, 5 May 1883 (NA, RG 75, OIA, SC 31, LR, #9103—1883); W. B. Fain to Commissioner William A. J. Sparks, 25 March 1886 (NA, RG 75, OIA, SC 31, LR, #9237—1886); and H. H., "Captain Pablo's Story," New York Independent, 25 October 1883, for a detailed discussion of the San Ysidro problem.

6. Price to Jackson, 15 March 1883, Jackson Papers (Part I, Box 2, fd. 5), Charles Leaming Tutt Library.

7. This 1875 act extended the benefits of the 1862 Homestead Act to Indians without endangering their share in tribal funds. These lands would be inalienable for five years after patented.

8. Henry T. Lee to Jackson, 6 March 1883, Jackson Papers (Part I, Box 2, fd. 6), Charles Leaming Tutt Library.

9. Jackson to Price, 10 March 1883 (NA, RG 75, OIA, SC 31, LR, #5272—1883). There is a slight contradiction on the date of Cloos' homestead entry. Jackson noted the date was January 15 while Lee, in his letter of March 6, stated it was January 18.

10. H. H., "Captain Pablo's Story," New York Independent.

11. Price to Jackson, 21 April 1883, Jackson Papers (Part I, Box 2, fd. 5), Charles Leaming Tutt Library, noted that lands patented under the Indian Homestead Act were inalienable for twenty years and not subjected to taxation.

12. Jackson to Teller, 2 April 1883, and Affidavit, 3 April 1883 (NA, RG 75, OIA, SC 31, LR, #7200—1883).

13. N. C. McFarland to Teller, 15 March 1883 (NA, RG 75, OIA, SC 31, LR, #5189—1883), and Price to Jackson, 2 April 1883, Jackson Papers (Part I, Box 2, fd. 5), Charles Leaming Tutt Library.

14. Lawson to Jackson, 16 April 1883, and also Price to Jackson, 21 April 1883, in Jackson Papers (Part I, Box 2, fd. 4 and fd. 5), Charles Leaming Tutt Library.

15. Price to Lawson, 7 March 1883, Jackson Papers (Part I, Box 2, fd. 7), Charles Leaming Tutt Library.

16. For a detailed sketch of the Saboba, see H. H. "The Fate of the Saboba," New York Independent, 13 December 1883, pp. 1–2. To gain public

support, in this article Jackson included the text of two letters written by the Saboba schoolchildren, one addressed to her and a second to the president of the United States.

17. Jackson to William Hayes Ward, 3 March 1883, Personal—Miscellaneous (Jackson), New York Public Library. See also Jackson to Aldrich, 1 April 1883, Aldrich Papers, Houghton Library, Harvard University.

18. Jackson to Sheriff, 12, 20, and 26 March 1883, Jackson manuscripts (HM 14206, 14207, 14208), Huntington Library. See also W. H. Brown, U.S. surveyor general, to Jackson, 14 March 1883, Jackson Papers (Part I, Box 2, fd. 6), Charles Leaming Tutt Library.

19. Jackson to Ephraim W. Morse, 12 March 1883, Phelan Collection, San Francisco Archives, San Francisco Public Library, San Francisco, California.

20. Morse to Jackson, 9 March 1883, Ephraim W. Morse Letter Book (January 1883–19 August 1884, pp. 82–83), Research Archives, San Diego Historical Society, Balboa Park, San Diego, California.

21. In her diary entry for Saturday, 17 March, she noted meeting with Lawson in the morning. See Jackson Papers (Part I, Box 5, fd. 3), Charles Leaming Tutt Library. She was still in San Bernardino on the 18th. See Jackson to Harriet M. Lothrop, 18 March 1883, Helen Maria (Fiske) Hunt Jackson Collection (Ms.Am.1282–8), Rare Books and Manuscripts, Boston Public Library, Boston, Massachusetts. Jackson intended to visit five Indian schools on her tour and asked if Lothrop would like to mail books for the children. In Jackson to Lothrop, San Jacinto, 9 April 1883 (Ms.Am.1282–9), she expressed thanks for the books.

22. H. H., "Justifiable Homicide in Southern California," *New York Independent,* 27 September 1883. For additional information on this murder, see Odell, *Helen Hunt Jackson (H. H.),* p. 200; and Jackson, "Report," pp. 483–484.

23. There is confusion about the dates and locations of this tour. Even Jackson's letters and her diary entries do not agree. For example, a letter to Mr. Morse, dated Warner's Ranch, 15 April 1883, can be found in the Phelan Collection, San Francisco Public Library. However, her diary entry for 12 April 1883 notes she was at the ranch. I have chosen to use the chronology of Odell, *Helen Hunt Jackson [H. H.],* pp. 200–201.

24. For more on Temecula and Pachanga, see H. H., "The Temecula Exiles," *New York Independent,* 29 November 1883.

25. Jackson, "Exhibit M: The Pachanga Indians," "Report," pp. 504–506.

26. Jackson to Sheriff, 1 December 1883, Jackson manuscripts (HM 14214), Huntington Library. For information on the Cahuilla see "Present Condition," pp. 91–93, and "Report," pp. 481–485.

27. H. H., "A Day with the Cahuillas," *New York Independent,* 11 October 1883. This long article gave a good description of the village and its people.

28. Jackson, "Exhibit D: The Warner's Ranch Indians," "Report," pp. 485–488. For a very complicated history of the Warner's ranch and its Mexican land grants, see Joseph John Hill, *The History of Warner's Ranch and Its Environs,* especially pp. 158–165, for the following. In 1901, Charles Lum-

mis and other noted Californians founded the Sequoya League to aid in the protection of the Mission Indians. Unable to arrange with owners of the Warner's Ranch for purchase of the Indians homes and fields, land was found in the Pala Valley, and in May 1903 the first group of Warner's Ranch Indians were removed to their new home.

29. Jackson, "Report," p. 488.

30. Jackson, "Exhibit E: The San Ysidro Indians," "Report," pp. 489–490.

31. H. H., "Captain Pablo's Story," *New York Independent.*

32. For information on Santa Ysabel, see Jackson, "Exhibit G: The Santa Ysabel Ranch," "Report," pp. 492–494.

33. For the Los Coyotes, see Jackson, "Exhibit F: The Los Coyotes," "Report," pp. 490–492.

34. See Jackson, "Exhibit H: Mesa Grande," "Report," pp. 494–496.

35. Jackson, "Exhibit I: Capitán Grande," "Report," pp. 496–500. The 24 April 1883 affidavit by Anthony D. Ubach, that of Ignacio Curo dated 25 April 1883, and another by J. S. Mannassee dated 26 April 1883, which appear in "Report," can also be found in Jackson Papers (Part I, Box 3, fd. 3), Charles Leaming Tutt Library. The complete set is also in Jackson to Price, 5 May 1883 (NA, RG 75, OIA, SC 31, LR, #8650—1883). See also D. M. Strong to Ubach, 9 September 1886, and Ubach to Adkins, 8 October 1886 (both in NA, RG 75, OIA, SC 31, LR, #27553—1886).

36. See Jackson, "Exhibit J: The Sequan Indians," "Report," p. 500.

37. Jackson, "Exhibit K: The Conejos," "Report," pp. 501–502.

38. J. G. A. Stanley to Jackson, 28 May 1883, Jackson Papers (Part I, Box 2, fd. 6), Charles Leaming Tutt Library. The entire text of his report is reprinted in "Report," pp. 507–508.

39. Stanley to Teller, 23 June 1883 (NA, RG 75, OIA, LR, #11939—1883).

40. Copy of Lawson's letter to Stanley (in Jackson's hand), 23 May 1883, Jackson Papers (Part I, Box 2, fd. 7), Charles Leaming Tutt Library.

41. Undated draft of letter from Jackson to Stanley, Jackson Papers (Part I, Box 2, fd. 8), Charles Leaming Tutt Library. This letter would had to have been written either in late May or early June 1883. For the statement of her illness, see draft of Jackson to Lawson, written 31 May but sent 1 June 1883, Jackson Papers (Part I, Box 2, fd. 8), Charles Leaming Tutt Library.

42. Lawson to Jackson, 2 March 1883, Jackson Papers (Part I, Box 2, fd. 4), Charles Leaming Tutt Library.

43. All quotes Lawson to Price, 1 June 1883 (NA, RG 75, OIA, SC 31, LR, #10808—1883, but included in #10049—1883). See also Lawson to Jackson, 7 June 1883, Jackson Papers (Part I, Box 2, fd. 4), Charles Leaming Tutt Library. This letter was in Jackson's hand.

44. Lawson to Price, 22 June 1883 (NA, RG 75, OIA, SC 31, LR, #11732—1883).

45. Rough draft of Jackson to Lawson, 8 May 1883, Jackson Papers (Part I, Box 2, fd. 8), Charles Leaming Tutt Library.

46. Affidavit of Patricio Soberano and Felipe Jogua relating to claims of Arthur Golsh, 1 May 1883, Jackson Papers (Part I, Box 3, fd. 3), Charles Leaming Tutt Library.

47. Lawson to Jackson, 9 May 1883, Jackson Papers (Part I, Box 2, fd. 4), Charles Leaming Tutt Library.

48. Jackson to Lawson, 12 May 1883, Jackson Papers (Part I, Box 2, fd. 4), Charles Leaming Tutt Library. See also Jackson to Price, 5 May 1883 (NA, RG 75, OIA, SC 31, LR, #8650—1883).

49. Lawson to Jackson, 13 and 21 May 1883, Jackson Papers (Part I, Box 2, fd. 4), Charles Leaming Tutt Library.

50. Draft of Jackson to Lawson, written 31 May but sent 1 June 1883, Jackson Papers (Part I, Box 2, fd. 8), Charles Leaming Tutt Library. For more on the legal suit see Lawson to Price, 1 June 1883 (NA, RG 75, OIA, SC 31, LR, #10808—1883).

51. Lawson to Jackson, 6 June 1883 (in Jackson's hand), Jackson Papers (Part I, Box 2, fd. 4), Charles Leaming Tutt Library.

52. Draft of Jackson to Lawson, n.d. but in answer to his letters of 6 and 7 June 1883, Jackson Papers (Part I, Box 2, fd. 8), Charles Leaming Tutt Library.

53. Jackson to Price, 27 July 1883 (NA, RG 75, OIA, LR, #14177—1883). See also Jackson to the Coronels, 19 August 1883, Coronel Collection, Seaver Center, Los Angeles County Museum, for mention of Lawson's resignation and statements by various California newspapers regarding it.

54. First quotation from Jackson to Aldrich, 1 April 1883, the second from Jackson to Aldrich, 4 May 1883, both in Aldrich Papers, Houghton Library, Harvard University.

55. Jackson to Mary Sheriff, 13 and 20 May 1883, Jackson manuscripts (HM 14209, 14210), Huntington Library. The original legal opinion can be found in Brunson and Wells to Abbot Kinney, 12 May 1883 (NA, RG 75, OIA, LR, SC 31, #10062—1883), enclosed with Jackson to Teller, 16 May 1883 (Ibid., #10049—1883). The legal opinion of Brunson and Wells was reprinted in "Report," pp. 475–479.

See Felix S. Cohen, "Section 9. Tribal Title Derived from other Sovereignties," *Handbook of Federal Indian Law*, p. 303. The Mexican cession was a result of the 1848 Treaty of Guadalupe Hidalgo, and land grants would have been recognized by the American government.

56. All quotes from Jackson to Price, 5 May 1883, (marked Personal) (NA, RG 75, OIA, SC 31, LR, #9103—1883). See also Jackson to Price, 5 May 1883 (Ibid., #8650—1883).

57. Price to Jackson, 16 May 1883, Jackson Papers (Part I, Box 2, fd. 5), Charles Leaming Tutt Library. For the removal order for Capitán Grande see L. Q. C. Lamar to the Commissioner of Indian Affairs, 3 November 1886 (NA, RG 75, OIA, SC 31, LR, #14110—1886).

58. Jackson to Price, 17 May 1883 (NA, RG 75, OIA, SC 31, LR, #9440—1883).

59. Jackson, "Exhibit B: Saboba," "Report," p. 480. See also Jackson to Price, 9 May 1883 (NA, RG 75, OIA, SC 31, LR, #8994—1883).

60. Price to Teller, 21 May 1883 (NA, RG 75, OIA, SC 31, LR, #11342—1883). In March, Lawson had recommended that part of an area outside of Saboba be set aside by an executive agreement. This area was included

within the executive order mentioned in Price to Teller, May 21. See E. L. Stevens to Teller, 24 April 1883, Ibid.

61. Draft of Jackson to Teller, n.d., Jackson Papers (Part I, Box 2, fd. 8), Charles Leaming Tutt Library.

62. Jackson to Teller, 16 May 1883 (NA, RG 75, OIA, SC 31, LR, #10049—1883). A draft of this letter can be found in Jackson Papers (Part I, Box 2, fd. 8), Charles Leaming Tutt Library. In a 26 June 1883 letter from the Attorney General of the United States to Teller (NA, RG 75, OIA, SC 31, LR, #11698—1883), the attorney general informed the secretary of the appointment of Brunson and Wells as special assistants to the United States attorney on behalf of the Mission Indians.

63. All quotes Jackson to Morse, 13 June 1883, Phelan Collection, San Francisco Public Library.

64. Jackson to Teller, 6 June 1883 (NA, RG 75, OIA, LR, #10823—1883).

65. Jackson to Price, 25 June 1882 (NA, RG 75, OIA, SC 31, LR, #11782—1883).

66. Ibid.

67. Jackson to Sheriff, 9 and 26 June and 2 August 1883, Jackson manuscripts (HM 14211, 14212, 14213), Huntington Library. See Sheriff to Jackson, 23 July 1883, in Jackson to Teller, 5 August 1883 (NA, RG 75, OIA, LR, #17750—1883).

68. Both quotes Jackson to Teller, 5 August 1883 (NA, RG 75, OIA, LR, #17750—1883).

69. Jackson to Price, 11 October 1883 (NA, RG 75, OIA, LR, #19173—1883).

70. Jackson to Gilder, 12 March 1883, Gilder Papers, New York Public Library.

71. Jackson to Warner, 13 August 1883, Warner Collection, Watkinson Library.

72. Brunson and Wells, in answer to a request by Kinney, gave an opinion that the Indians and descendents who occupied lands within specific Mexican grants legally possessed those lands and could hold the claim against others filing on it. See Brunson and Wells to Kinney, 12 May 1883, and a 26 June 1883 letter from the attorney general of the United States to Teller, formally appointing Brunson and Wells as special assistants to the United States attorney (NA, RG 75, OIA, SC 31, LR, #11698—1883).

73. Bishop Mora was willing to sell the Pauma Ranch to the government for $31,000. See Francis Mora to Jackson, 21 May 1883, Jackson, "Exhibit P: The Pauma Ranch," "Report," pp. 512–513. See also Mora to Jackson, 14 May 1883, Jackson Papers (Part I, Box 2, fd. 6), Charles Leaming Tutt Library.

74. Price to Jackson, 19 November 1883, Jackson Papers (Part I, Box 2, fd. 5), Charles Leaming Tutt Library.

75. Jackson, "Report," p. 464; Jackson to Price, 25 November 1883 (NA, RG 75, OIA, SC 31, LR, #21830—1883).

76. Jackson to Price, 25 November 1883 (NR, RG 75, OIA, SC 31, LR, #22018—1883).

77. U.S. Department of the Interior. Office of Indian Affairs, *Annual Report 1883*, p. XLVI.

78. Jackson to Ward, 30 September 1883, Jackson Collection (#7080-a), Clifton Waller Barrett Library.

79. As early as 6 June 1883 she had requested payment. See Price to Jackson, 21 June 1883, Jackson Papers (Part I, Box 2, fd. 5), Charles Leaming Tutt Library; see also Jackson to Teller, 14 October 1883, and Jackson to Price, 6 November 1883 (NA, RG 75, OIA, LR, #19638—1883 and #20695—1883).

80. Jackson to Price, 25 November 1883 (NA, RG 75, OIA, SC 31, LR, #22018—1883).

81. Jackson to Price, 16 January 1884 (NA, RG 75, OIA, SC 31, LR, #1285—1884).

82. United States Congress, Senate, "Message from the President of the United States," S. Ex. Doc. 49, 48th Cong. 1st Sess., 1884, pp. 1–7. (The complete text of the Jackson/Kinney report followed, see pp. 7–37.)

83. United States Congress, Senate, "Message from the President of the United States," S. Ex. Doc. 15, 49th Cong. 1st Sess., 1885, pp. 1–4. (The complete text of the Jackson/Kinney Report followed, see pp. 4–33.) See also "Mission Indians in California," U.S. Department of the Interior, Office of Indian Affairs, *Annual Report of the Commissioner of Indian Affairs to the Secretary of the Interior for the Year 1885*, p. XLVIII.

84. See "Mission Indians in California," *Annual Report of the Commissioner of Indian Affairs to the Secretary of the Interior for the Year 1886*, p. XLII; "Indians in California," *Nineteenth Annual Report of the Board of Indian Commissioners, 1887*, p. 13, and Kate Foote, *The Indian Legislation of 1888*, p. 5.

85. Lake Mohonk Conference, *Proceedings of the Ninth Annual Meeting of the Lake Mohonk Conference of Friends of the Indian, 1891*, p. 24. "An Act for the Relief of the Mission Indians in the State of California," Indian legislation passed during the second session of the Fifty-first Congress. U.S. Department of the Interior, Office of Indian Affairs, *Annual Report of the Commissioner of Indian Affairs to the Secretary of the Interior for the Year 1891*, pp. 612–614; also pp. 47–48. See also Garner, *Broken Ring*, pp. 115–118, and Prucha, *Policy in Crisis*, pp. 188–192.

5. *Ramona*, Its Successes and Failures

1. J. C. McCallum to Price, monthly report for November 1883, 10 December 1883 (NA, RG 75, OIA, SC 31, LR, #23116—1883). See "Report of Agents in California," U.S. Department of the Interior, Office of Indian Affairs, *Annual Report of the Commissioner of Indian Affairs to the Secretary of the Interior for the Year 1884*, pp. 12–15, and McCallum to Price, 12 January 1884 (NA, RG 75, OIA, SC 31, LR, #1441—1884).

2. Jackson to Gilder, 11 February 1881, Personal—Miscellaneous (Jackson), New York Public Library.

3. J. B. Gilder, "The Lounger," *Critic* NS 4 (22 August 1885): 91.

4. Jackson to Aldrich, 4 May 1883, Aldrich Papers, Houghton Library,

Harvard University. She used the same comparison in Jackson to Ward, 1 January 1884, Jackson manuscripts (HM 14197), Huntington Library. See also Valerie Sherer Mathes, "Parallel Calls to Conscience: Reformers Helen Hunt Jackson and Harriet Beecher Stowe," *Californians* 1 (July–August 1983): 32–40.

5. Jackson to Aldrich, 1 December 1884, Aldrich Papers, Houghton Library, Harvard University.

6. Jackson to Morse, 3 November 1883, Ephraim W. Morse Collection, Research Archives, San Diego Historical Society. See also Jackson to Morse, 7 February 1884, Phelan Collection, San Francisco Public Library. For Morse's reply to the 3 November 1883 letter see Morse to Jackson, 22 January 1884, Morse Letter Book, pp. 311–312, Research Archives, San Diego Historical Society.

7. Francis H. Whaley, "The Indian Agency," *San Luis Rey Star*, 4 August 1883. Clipping found in the Research Archives, San Diego Historical Society.

8. Jackson to the Coronels, 8 November 1883, in James, *Through Ramona's Country*, pp. 18–20. The text of this letter is reprinted in George Wharton James, "The Tender Heroine of Indian Friendship, Helen Hunt Jackson," in *Heroes of California*, pp. 367–370.

9. Jackson to Sheriff, 1 December 1883 and 20 January 1884, Jackson manuscripts (HM 14214, 14215), Huntington Library.

10. Jackson to Aldrich, 24 November 1883, Aldrich Papers, Houghton Library, Harvard University.

11. Brunson and Wells to Price, 8 January 1884 (NA, RG 75, OIA, SC 31, LR, #848—1884).

12. Price to Brunson and Wells, 29 January 1884 (NA, RG 75, OIA, LS, Land Division, Volume 61–LB 121, pp. 247–250).

13. Lamar to John D. C. Atkins, commissioner of Indian affairs, 3 November 1886 (NA, RG 75, OIA, SC 31, LR, #14110—1886).

14. Jackson to Kinney, 20 February 1884, in James, *Through Ramona's Country*, pp. 336–337.

15. Jackson to Price, 27 February 1884 (NA, RG 75, OIA, SC 31, LR, #4038—1884).

16. All quotes Thomas Wentworth Higginson, "How Ramona was Written," *Atlantic Monthly* 86 (November 1900): 712–714. This letter written in New York at the Berkeley Hotel on 5 February 1884 was, according to Evelyn Banning, *Helen Hunt Jackson*, p. 198, to Colonel Higginson. In a 4 December 1883 letter to Aldrich, Aldrich Papers, Houghton Library, Harvard University, Jackson noted the book was so predestined in her mind that she wrote one thousand to fifteen hundred words a day, which for her was miraculous. See also W. J. Harsha, "How 'Ramona' Wrote Itself," *Southern Workman* 59 (August 1930): 370–375, found in Hampton Institute Archives, Hampton, Virginia.

17. Charles Dudley Warner, "'H. H.' in Southern California," in *Fashions in Literature and Other Literary and Social Essays & Addresses*, p. 321. See also "Warner in Southern California made 'an estimate' of Ramona," *San Diego Union*, 18 March 1887; "Ramona: How the Book Was Written in a

Burst of Inspiration," *San Francisco Call*, 20 March 1887; James, *Through Ramona's Country*, p. 335; and Elaine Goodale Eastman, "Spinner in the Sun: The Story of Helen Hunt Jackson," unpublished, unpaged, typed manuscript in the Sophia Smith Collection, Women's History Archive, Smith College, Northampton, Massachusetts. Eastman also wrote a short sketch on Jackson entitled "The Author of Ramona," *Classmate* (21 January 1939): 6–7.

18. Jackson to Aldrich, 10 March 1884, Aldrich Papers, Houghton Library, Harvard University.

19. "Helen Hunt Jackson's Life and Writings," *Literary News*, p. 100. Copy in Special Collections, Milton S. Eisenhower Library, Johns Hopkins University. This statement was written to Mr. Niles at Roberts Brothers Publishers.

20. "A Case for Mrs. Helen Hunt Jackson," *San Diego Union*, 23 March 1884.

21. "Albert K. Smiley and General E. Whittlesey to Clinton B. Fisk, Chairman, Board of Indian Commissioners, May 1, 1884," in *Sixteenth Annual Report of the Board of Indian Commissioners, 1884*, pp. 18–19.

22. Brunson and Wells to E. S. Stevens, acting commissioner of Indian affairs, 24 May 1884 (NA, RG 75, OIA, SC 31, LR, #10477—1884).

23. Jackson to Aldrich, 10 March 1884, Aldrich Papers, Houghton Library, Harvard University.

24. James, *Through Ramona's Country*, p. 318.

25. Jackson to Aldrich, 1 December 1884, Aldrich Papers, Houghton Library, Harvard University.

26. Jackson to Scribner, 21 February 1885, Archives of Charles Scribner's Sons, Princeton University Library.

27. James, *Heroes of California*, p. 373.

28. This study does not attempt to be a literary analysis of *Ramona* or a discussion of the multitude of books and articles on the subject. For a complete analysis, see James, *Through Ramona's Country* (clearly one of the best studies); Carlyle Channing Davis and William A. Alderson, *The True Story of Ramona*; A. C. Vroman and T. F. Barnes, *The Genesis of the Story of Ramona*; Louis J. Stellman, "The Man who Inspired 'Ramona,'" *Overland Monthly* 50 (September 1907): 2–5; D. A. Hufford, *The Real Ramona of Helen Hunt Jackson's Famous Novel* (clearly apocryphal); Margaret V. Allen, *Ramona's Homeland* (one of the better studies); and Carter, *Some By-Ways*, pp. 57–76.

For additional information, see also Nevins, "Sentimentalist vs. Realist," pp. 269–285, and J. Frank Dobie, "Helen Hunt Jackson and Ramona," *Southwest Review* 44 (Spring 1959): 93–98 (written as an introduction to a limited-edition printing of *Ramona* in 1959). For an interesting comparison of *Ramona* and the Jackson/Kinney report, see John R. Byers, Jr., "The Indian Matter of Helen Hunt Jackson's *Ramona*: From Fact to Fiction," *American Indian Quarterly* 2 (Winter 1975–1976): 331–346. See also Edward B. Howell, "A Tragic Sequel to 'Ramona,'" *Review of Reviews* 10 (November 1894): 507–513, and *The Annotated Ramona*, intro. and notes by Antoinette May. Illustrations include original drawings by Henry Sandham who had accompanied Jackson on her tours, contemporary photographs, and scenes from various productions of the Ramona Pageant.

29. Starr, *Inventing the Dream*, pp. 60–61; see also pp. 55–63.

30. "Current Criticism: Something Very Rare," *Critic* NS 3 (10 January 1885): 22.

31. Milicent W. Shinn, "The Verse and Prose of 'H. H.,'" *Overland Monthly* 2d S, 6 (September 1885): 323.

32. Helen Gray Cone, "Women in American Literature," *Century Magazine* 40 (October 1890): 927–928.

33. *Southern Workman* (February 1885): 19.

34. "Book Reviews," *Overland Monthly* 2d S, 5 (March 1885): 330.

35. All quotes from Jackson to Warner, 25 December 1884, Warner Collection, Watkinson Library.

36. All quotes Jackson to Aldrich, 10 January 1885, Aldrich Papers, Houghton Library, Harvard University. For an interesting review, see Lawrence Clark Powell, "California Classics Reread: Ramona," *Westways* 60 (July 1968): 13–15.

37. Jackson to Frank Jewett Mather, 13 January 1885, Frank Jewett Mather Autograph Collection (Leaf 34), Princeton University Library, Princeton, New Jersey.

38. Jackson to Aldrich, 9 February 1885, Aldrich Papers, Houghton Library, Harvard University. The letter about the identity of the reviewer was Jackson to Aldrich, 8 March 1885, ibid.

39. "Recent American Fiction," *Atlantic Monthly* 55 (January 1885): 130.

40. All quotes Albion W. Tourgée, "Study in Civilization," *North American Review* 143 (August 1886): pp. 246, 251.

41. Minerva Louise Martin, "Helen Hunt Jackson in Relation to her Time" (Ph.D. dissertation, Louisiana State University, 1940), pp. 160–167. See also Raymond William Stedman, *Shadows of the Indian Stereotypes in American Culture*, pp. 194–196, 259, and William Oandasan, "*Ramona*: Reflected through Indigenous Eyes," *California Historical Courier*, February/March 1986, p. 7.

42. Nevins, "Sentimentalist vs. Realist," p. 280, and Albert Keiser, "The Mission Indians as Viewed by a Woman," in *The Indian in American Literature*, p. 251.

43. "Warner in Southern California . . . ," *San Diego Union*, 18 March 1887.

44. Jackson to Warner, 2 October 1884, Warner Collection, Watkinson Library. See also Jackson to Aldrich, 1 December 1884, Aldrich Papers, Houghton Library, Harvard University.

45. Jackson to Warner, 7 July 1884, Warner Collection, Watkinson Library; Jackson to Kinney, 16 July 1884, in James, *Through Ramona's Country*, pp. 337–338; Jackson to Aldrich, 22 September 1884, Aldrich Papers, Houghton Library, Harvard University; Jackson to Gilder, 23 July 1884, Personal—Miscellaneous, (Jackson) New York Public Library; Jackson to Mrs. Pratt, 6 August 1884, Morristown National Historical Park (LWS 2563),

Morristown, New Jersey; Jackson to Dawes, 27 August 1884, Dawes Papers (Box 26), Library of Congress; and Jackson to Conway, 28 October 1884, Conway Papers, Butler Library, Columbia University.

46. Jackson to Warner, 19 July 1884, Warner Collection, Watkinson Library. See also Jackson to her sister Ann, 25 July 1884, Jackson Family Papers (Part II, Box 3, fd. 31), Charles Leaming Tutt Library.

47. Sarah Chauncey [Susan Coolidge], "Biographical Sketch of H. H.," Jackson Collection (#7080-a), Clifton Waller Barrett Library.

48. Susan Coolidge, "H. H.," Critic NS 4 (3 October 1885): 164; this poem originally appeared in the 17 September 1885 issue of Christian Union.

49. All quotes from Jackson to Warner, 2 October 1884, Warner Collection, Watkinson Library. For a reminiscence of Jackson's love for the outdoors see "A. W. R. Writes from Monte Carneire Ranch," Critic NS 4 (19 September 1885): 139.

50. Jackson to Dawes, 27 August 1884, Dawes Papers (Box 26), Library of Congress.

51. Jackson to Conway, 28 October 1884, Conway Papers, Butler Library.

52. Jackson to Bowen, 15 October 1884, Jackson Collection (#7080-b), Clifton Waller Barrett Library.

53. Jackson to Teller, 14 November 1884 (NA, RG 75, OIA, SC 31, LR, #22736—1884). For the resignation of Ticknor, see McCallum to Price, 12 January 1884 (NA, RG 75, OIA, SC 31, LR, #1441—1884).

54. John S. Ward to A. B. Upshaw, acting commissioner of Indian affairs, 4 November 1885 (NA, RG 75, OIA, SC 31, LR, #26498—1885). See also Ward to Upshaw, 5 November 1885 (NA, RG 75, OIA, SC 31, LR, #26670—1885).

55. Jackson to Teller, 27 November 1884 (NA, RG 75, OIA, LR, #3278—1884).

56. Jackson to Kinney, 28 September 1884, James, Through Ramona's Country, p. 338.

57. Jackson to Alvah L. Frisbie, 28 December 1884, Miscellaneous Manuscripts, Amherst College Library, Amherst, Massachusetts.

58. Jackson to Aldrich, 8 to 21 March 1885, Aldrich Papers, Houghton Library, Harvard University. This letter begun in Los Angeles was completed in San Francisco. See also Jackson to Kinney, 1 April 1885, James Through Ramona's Country, p. 343; and Jackson to Edward Abbott, 22 June 1885, Abbott Memorial Collection: Edward Abbott Literary World, Lowell Tribute Scrapbook, Bowdoin College Library.

59. Jackson to William Sharpless Jackson, 29 March [1885], Jackson Family Papers (Part I, Box 1, fd. 5), Charles Leaming Tutt Library.

60. Ibid. Will Jackson does marry his wife's niece and does raise a family.

61. G. Wiley Wells to Jackson, 31 March 1885, in James, Through Ramona's Country, pp. 331–334.

62. Brunson and Wells to Hon. H. H. Markham, 20 June 1885 (NA, RG 75, OIA, SC 31, LR, #15095—1885). See also C. C. Painter, A Visit to the Mission Indians of Southern California and other Western Tribes, p. 17.

63. Jackson to Gilder, 6 May 1885, Personal—Miscellaneous (Jackson), New York Public Library.

64. Jackson to Gilder, 20 May 1885, Personal Miscellaneous (Jackson), New York Public Library. In her 3 June 1884 letter to Gilder, she thanked him for agreeing to withdraw the article.

65. This theme of evangelical Christianity permeates all of the books on nineteenth-century Indian reform. See Francis Paul Prucha, "Policy Reform and American Protestantism," and "Decline of the Christian Reforms," both in *Indian Policy in the United States*, pp. 229–262.

66. Wanken, "Woman's Sphere and Indian Reform," pp. 7–8, 9–11.

67. Jackson to John Muir, 8 June 1884, John Muir Papers, Holt-Atherton Pacific Center for Western Studies, University of the Pacific, Stockton, California. See also Jackson to Carr, 8 and 14 June 1885, Carr Collection (CA 195, 196), Huntington Library.

68. Muir to Jackson, 16 June 1885, William Frederick Bade, *The Life and Letters of John Muir*, II: 198–202. See her reply, Jackson to Muir, 20 June 1885, Muir Papers, Holt-Atherton Pacific Center for Western Studies.

69. Jackson to Sheriff, 17 July 1885, Jackson manuscripts (HM 14216), Huntington Library. To the Coronels, 27 June 1885, Coronel Collection, Seaver Center, Los Angeles County Museum, she noted that she had "been much cheered by an interview with Prof. Painter." See also C. C. Painter, *A Visit to the Mission Indians of Southern California and other Western Tribes*, pp. 11–12.

70. Jackson to Higginson, 27 July 1885, in Thomas Wentworth Higginson, "Helen Hunt Jackson," *Nation* 41 (20 August 1885): 151.

71. Jackson to Grover Cleveland, 8 August 1885, General Manuscripts (Boxes JA–JE, Folder: Jackson, H. H. 1830–1885, sub folder 2, H. H.), Princeton University Library. This letter has been reprinted in *Critic* NS 4 (3 October 1885): 167, and in *Century of Dishonor*, p. 515. See also Odell, *Helen Hunt Jackson (H. H.)*, p. 219, and E. Banning, *Helen Hunt Jackson*, p. 225.

72. Higginson, "The Last poems of Helen Jackson (H. H.), *Century Magazine* NS 31 (November 1885): 258.

73. William S. Jackson to Mrs. E. C. Banfield (Helen's sister), 12 August 1885, Jackson Family Papers (Part I, Box 1, fd. 5), Charles Leaming Tutt Library. For notices of her illness and death see *San Francisco Morning Call*, 5 August 1885, p. 3, and 12 August 1885, p. 13.

74. *The Letters of Emily Dickinson*, ed. Thomas H. Johnson, p. 889; Martha Dickinson Bianchi, *The Life and Letters of Emily Dickinson*, p. 373; and *Letters of Emily Dickinson*, ed. Mabel Loomis Todd, p. 363. For an interesting description of her grave at Cheyenne Mountain, see *Critic* NS 4 (21 November 1885): 251–252.

75. Higginson, *Contemporaries*, p. 142.

76. Higginson, "Helen Jackson," *Critic* NS 4 (22 August 1885): 86.

77. Flora Haines Apponyi, "Last Days of Mrs. Helen Hunt Jackson," *Overland Monthly* 2d S, 6 (September 1885): 310. For a mention of this touching story, see *Critic* NS 4 (19 September 1885): 144.

78. Joaquin Miller, "Helen Hunt Jackson: The Life Work of One of Our Most Gifted Writers," *San Francisco Morning Call*, 18 September 1892.

79. Susan Coolidge, "H. H.," *New York Independent*, 3 September 1885.

For a moving tribute, see "Helen Jackson," *Southern Workman*, October 1885.

80. Jackson to Reid, 4 April 1880, Papers of Whitelaw Reid, Library of Congress.

81. Quinton, "Care of the Indians," p. 374.

82. WNIA, *Fourth Annual Report* [1884], p. 63 for the honorary membership and p. 9 for the quotation.

83. Quinton, "Care of the Indian," p. 375.

84. Wanken, "Woman's Sphere and Indian Reform," pp. 310–321; and the WNIA, *The Ramona Mission and the Mission Indians.*

85. Francis Paul Prucha, "A 'Friend of the Indian' in Milwaukee: Mrs. O. J. Hiles and the Wisconsin Indian Association," *Historical Messenger of the Milwaukee County Historical Society* 29 (Autumn 1973): 80–84. Reprinted in Prucha, *Indian Policy in the United States*, pp. 214–228.

86. BIC, *Seventeenth Annual Report of the Board of Indian Commissioners for the Year 1885*, pp. 73, 105; Lake Mohonk Conference, *Proceedings of the Third Annual Meeting of the Mohonk Conference of the Friends of the Indians*, [1885], p. 69; and IRA, *Third Annual Report 1885*, p. 10.

87. Painter, *A Visit to the Mission Indians of Southern California*, p. 11.

88. Ibid.

89. Ubach to General W. S. Rosencrans, 4 September 1885 (NA, RG 75, OIA, SC 31, LR, #21068—1885).

90. These three quotes BIC, *Seventeenth Annual Report 1885*, pp. 104–106, and Lake Mohonk, *Third Annual Meeting* [1885], pp. 70–71. For Fletcher, see p. 105, for Fisk see pp. 106 and 71, and for Gates, see pp. 105 and 70.

91. Electa S. Dawes to Anna Dawes, 11 October 1885, Dawes Papers (Box 27), Library of Congress.

92. BIC "Third Annual Meeting of the Lake Mohonk Conference," *Seventeenth Annual Report 1885*, p. 104.

93. Floyd A. O'Neil, "Hiram Price, 1881–1885," in *The Commissioners of Indian Affairs, 1824–1977*, ed. Robert M. Kvasnicka and Herman J. Viola, pp. 176–178.

6. Indian Reform Organizations Carry On Jackson's Work

1. Wells to Lamar, 18 August 1885 (NA, RG 75, OIA, SC 31, LR, #19419—1885).

2. Ward to Upshaw, 11 November 1885 (NA, RG 75, OIA, SC 31, LR, #27366—1885).

3. L. D. McKisick to Commissioner J. D. C. Atkins, 29 October 1885 (NA, RG 75, OIA, SC 31, LR, #26011—1885); United States Attorney General to Secretary of the Interior, 14 January 1886 (ibid., #1447—1886). For Ward's acceptance, see Shirley C. Ward to Attorney General A. H. Garland, 16 March 1886 (NA, RG 75, OIA, SC 31, LR, #8672—1886).

4. John S. Ward to Hon. Banday Henley, 29 January 1886 (NA, RG 75, OIA, SC 31, LR, #4781—1886). For the Santa Ysabel Indians, see John S.

Ward to Atkins, 20 February and 12 March 1886 (NA, RG 75, OIA, SC 31, LR, #5935 and #8013—1886). For further information, see E. L. Lippitt (lawyer for the claimants) to the Secretary of the Interior, 12 August 1886 (NA, RG 75, OIA, SC 31, LR, #22378—1886).

5. Albert B. Weiner (secretary of the IRA) to Secretary Lamar, 15 February 1886 (NA, RG 75, OIA, SC 31, LR, #5194—1886).

6. Welsh to Atkins, 27 March 1886 (NA, RG 75, OIA, SC 31, LR, #8794—1886). See also Shirley C. Ward to Atkins, 10 June 1886 (NA, RG 75, OIA, SC 31, LR, #15947—1886), in which Ward informed the commissioner that he had been corresponding with Senator Dawes on the matter.

7. "*M. Byrnes vs. A. Alas*—Copy Findings," "*M. Byrnes vs. A Alas et als.*—Copy Judgment," included with J. M. Dodge to Leland Stanford, 7 August 1886 (NA, RG 75, OIA, SC 31, Box 24, LR, #6885—1886).

8. For a detailed discussion of the role of the IRA, see IRA, *The Case of the Mission Indians in Southern California and the Action of the Indian Rights Association in Supporting the Defense of their Legal Rights*, pp. 3–20. See also BIC, *Twentieth Annual Report of the Board of Indian Commissioners, 1888*, pp. 85–86.

9. U.S. Department of the Interior, Office of Indian Affairs, *Fifty-Seventh Annual Report of the Commissioner of Indian Affairs to the Secretary of the Interior, 1888*, pp. lxiv–lxx. See also IRA, *Sixth Annual Report of the Executive Committee of the Indian Rights Association*, [1889], pp. 30–31; Painter, *A Visit to the Mission Indians of California* [1887], pp. 3, 5. See also Charles C. Painter, *The Condition of Affairs in Indian Territory and California*, pp. 90–92; the text of the Byrnes case is reprinted on pp. 92–102.

10. Shirley C. Ward to Atkins, 21 February 1888 (NA, RG 75, OIA, SC 31, Box 24, LR, #5713—1888). For his legal services, see Ward to Col. Joseph W. Preston, 5 May 1888 (ibid., #12991—1888). See also Preston to Atkins, 9 May 1888 (ibid., #12991—1888), in which he recommends the payment of Ward's expenditures, and Shirley C. Ward to Welsh, 11 February 1888, *Indian Rights Association Papers (1864–1973)* (Reel 3); and BIC, *Twentieth Annual Report 1888*, pp. 85–86.

11. C. C. Painter, *A Visit to the Mission Indians of Southern California*, pp. 11–12. See also BIC, *Seventeenth Annual Report 1885*, p. 73, and *Eighteenth Annual Report of the Board of Indian Commissioners, 1886*, pp. 45–46.

12. Ubach to General W. S. Rosencrans, 4 September 1885 (NA, RG 75, OIA, SC 31, LR, #21068—1885).

13. For a general discussion of Painter's work with the Mission Indians, see William T. Hagan, *The Indian Rights Association*, pp. 68–71.

14. C. C. Painter, *A Visit to the Mission Indians of California*, [1887], pp. 3–18.

15. For a detailed report of his June activities in California see Painter to Joshua W. Davis, 30 June 1887, *Indian Rights Association Papers* (Reel 2), and Hagan, *Indian Rights Association*, p. 70. For additional information, see Painter, *The Condition of Affairs in Indian Territory and California*, pp. 49–102; BIC, *Nineteenth Annual Report 1887*, pp. 92–93, 130–132.

16. Helen Hunt Jackson, *Ramona*, p. 45.

17. Painter to Davis, 30 June 1887, *Indian Rights Association Papers* (Reel 2).

18. Ibid.

19. For information on this visit, see Painter to Davis, 12 July 1887, *Indian Rights Association Papers* (Reel 2).

20. For information on Saboba, see Painter to Davis, 17 July 1887, *Indian Rights Association Papers* (Reel 2).

21. Painter to Davis, 30 June 1887, *Indian Rights Association Papers* (Reel 2).

22. For background information on Hiles, see Prucha, "'Friend of the Indian' in Milwaukee," in *Indian Policy in the United States*, pp. 214–228.

23. For all quotes from the *Milwaukee Sentinel*, 9 August 1885, see the clipping accompanying Mrs. John Hiles to President Grover Cleveland, 12 August 1885 (NA, RG 75, OIA, LR, #19236—1885).

24. Ibid.

25. Lake Mohonk Conference, *Proceedings of the Fourth Annual Meeting of the Lake Mohonk Conference of Friends of the Indians*, [1886] p. 37. See also BIC, "Proceedings of the Mohonk Lake Conference: The Mission Indians of California," in *Eighteenth Annual Report 1886*, p. 81; but see also pp. 79–82.

26. Ibid.

27. BIC, *Nineteenth Annual Report 1887*, p. 91.

28. Lawson to Hiles, 2 December 1886 (NA, RG 75, OIA, SC 31, Box 24, LR, #1776—1886).

29. BIC, "Proceedings of the Fifth Annual Meeting of the Lake Mohonk Conference: Final Report of the Business Committee," in *Nineteenth Annual Report 1887*, p. 111.

30. For a negative discussion of the Dawes Act, particularly relative to a decline in farming, see Carlson, *Indians, Bureaucrats, and Land*, pp. 79–180. See also Washburn, *Assault on Indian Tribalism*, pp. 3–31.

31. BIC, "Proceedings of the Fifth Annual Meeting of the Lake Mohonk Conference: Final Report of the Business Committee," in *Nineteenth Annual Report 1887*, p. 111.

32. All quotes Hiles to Electa S. Dawes, 7 March 1887, Dawes Papers (Box 10), Library of Congress.

33. BIC, *Nineteenth Annual Report 1887*, p. 79.

34. Lake Mohonk Conference, *Proceedings of the Fifth Annual Meeting of the Lake Mohonk Conference of Friends of the Indians*, [1887] p. 93. See also BIC, *Nineteenth Annual Report 1887*, pp. 104–105.

35. Painter, *Visit to the Mission Indians* (1887), p. 4.

36. Hiles to William F. Vilas, 2 April 1888 (NA, RG 75, OIA, SC 31, Box 24, LR, #9592—1888).

37. Hiles to Atkins, 3 April 1888 (NA, RG 75, OIA, SC 31, #9572—1888).

38. Hiles to Vilas, 2 April 1888 (NA, RG 75, OIA, SC 31, Box 24, LR, #9592—1888).

39. Hiles to Atkins, 3 April 1888 (NA, RG 75, OIA, SC 31, LR, #9572—1888).

40. Jackson, "Report," p. 500.

41. Hiles to Atkins, 3 April 1888 (NA, RG 75, OIA, SC 31, Box 24, LR, #9572—1888).

42. Hiles to Vilas, 4 May 1888 (NA, RG 75, OIA, LR, #12918—1888).

43. Hiles to Atkins, 31 May 1888 (NA, RG 75, OIA, SC 31, Box 24, LR, #15206—1888). Atkins resigned on June 14, 1888. He was unsuccessful in his attempt to gain the nomination for the Senate seat from Tennessee and returned to farming.

44. Lake Mohonk Conference, *Proceedings of the Sixth Annual Meeting of the Lake Mohonk Conference of Friends of the Indians,* [1888] pp. 67, 83, 96.

45. WNIA, *Annual Report of the Women's National Indian Association* [1888], p. 24.

46. *Indian's Friend* 1 (December 1888): 3.

47. *Indian's Friend* 1 (November 1888): 4.

48. Hiles to John H. Oberly, 21 November 1888 (NA, RG 75, OIA, SC 143, LR, #28978—1888).

49. *Indian's Friend* 1 (June 1889): 1. For a report of the legislative work of the Wisconsin Indian Association presented by Hiles, who served as secretary, see *Indian's Friend* 2 (January 1890): 3.

50. Quotation from the newspaper clipping enclosed in Hiles to Noble, 13 May 1890 (NA, RG 75, OIA, LR, #15352—1890). See also Hiles to Thomas Morgan, 13 May 1890 (ibid., #15194—1890). For a slight change in attitude toward Agent Rust, see Hiles to Welsh, 24 December 1889, *Indian Rights Association Papers* (Reel 5).

51. Lewis himself sought the position as agent. See Lewis to Davis, 26 December 1888, *Indian Rights Association Papers* (Reel 4).

52. BIC, *Twentieth Annual Report 1888,* pp. 85–86.

53. U.S. Department of the Interior, Office of Indian Affairs, "The Mission Indians in California," in *Annual Report of the Commissioner of Indian Affairs to the Secretary of the Interior for the Year 1887,* p. li; see also "Reports of Agents in California," John S. Ward, 17 August 1887, ibid., p. 10.

54. U.S. Department of the Interior, Office of Indian Affairs, "Reports of Agents in California," in *Annual Report of the Commissioner 1888,* pp. 12–15.

55. Preston to Atkins, 20 February 1888 (NA, RG 75, OIA, SC 31, Box 24, LR, #5497—1888). McCallum dug a well in Taquitz Canyon that further reduced the Indians' supply of water and later built a canal to Palm Springs. For this and other detailed information on Agua Caliente to 1977, see Garner, *Broken Ring,* pp. 121–149.

56. All quotes Preston to Atkins, 20 February 1888 (NA, RG 75, OIA, SC 31, Box 24, LR, #5497—1888).

57. BIC, "Report of Albert K. Smiley, March 1, 1889," in *Twenty-First Annual Report of the Board of Indian Commissioners, 1889,* p. 11.

58. Jackson, "Report," pp. 508–511.

59. Garrett, Rust, Smiley, Shirley C. Ward to Thomas J. Morgan, 21 February 1890 (NA, RG 75, OIA, SC 31, Box 25, LR, #7188—1890). This entire report is reprinted in BIC, "Report of Albert K. Smiley, Los Angeles, February 21, 1890," in *Twenty-Second Annual Report of the Board of Indian Commissioners, 1890*, pp. 11–12.

60. Garrett to Morgan, 17 February 1890 (NA, RG 75, OIA, SC 31, Box 25, LR, #5723—1890). For Painter's approval of the arrangement, see Painter to Welsh, 6 March 1890, *Indian Rights Association Papers* (Reel 5).

61. Lewis to the Commissioner of Indian Affairs, 4 August 1890 (NA, RG 75, OIA, SC 31, Box 25, LR, #24182—1890).

62. Garrett, et al., 21 February 1890 (NA, RG 75, OIA, SC 31, Box 25, LR, #7188—1890).

63. IRA, *Ninth Annual Report of the Executive Committee of the Indian Rights Association*, [1892] p. 17.

64. Lake Mohonk Conference, *Proceedings of the Ninth Annual Meeting of the Lake Mohonk Conference of Friends of the Indian, 1891*, p. 24. See also U.S. Department of the Interior, Office of Indian Affairs, "An Act for the Relief of the Mission Indians in the State of California, Indian Legislation passed during the second session of the Fifty-first Congress," in *Sixtieth Annual Report of the Commissioner of Indian Affairs to the Secretary of the Interior for the Year 1891*, pp. 612–614, 47–48; and IRA, *Eighth Annual Report of the Executive Committee of the Indian Rights Association* [1891], p. 10.

65. Jackson could not foresee that the 1891 Act for the Relief of the Mission Indians, which Smiley had called her bill, would be detrimental to Pachanga. During the litigation of *Pechanga Band of Mission Indians v. Kacor Realty, Inc., et al.*, filed in 1978, the Ninth Circuit Court of Appeals decided that the "Mission Indian Relief Act of 1891 worked to extinguish whatever interest the Band had in the land pursuant to the Executive Order." Therefore, the Indians lost an estimated four hundred acres of land, which had been claimed in 1882 and 1885 by Peter Mouren. Christie, "Indian Land Claims," p. 241.

66. For authorization of this mission commission, see Noble to Thomas Jefferson Morgan, 24 January 1891 (NA, RG 75, OIA, SC 31, LR, #3101—1891). See also U.S. Department of the Interior, Office of Indian Affairs, "Mission Indian Commission," in *Sixtieth Annual Report, 1891*, pp. 47–48.

67. Painter noted he had received his commission on 28 January 1891. See Painter to Welsh, 28 January 1891, *Indian Rights Association Papers* (Reel 6).

68. Rust, agent for the Mission Indians, estimated their numbers in 1890 to be 2,895. See U.S. Department of the Interior, Office of Indian Affairs, "Report of the Mission Agency," in *Fifty-Ninth Annual Report of the Commissioner of Indian Affairs to the Secretary of the Interior, 1890*, p. 17.

69. All commission instructions are from Morgan to Smiley, Morse, and Painter, 31 January 1891 (NA, RG 75, OIA, SC 31, Box 25, LR, #3101—1891). The complete text of this letter was printed. A copy was included with George Chandler to Morgan, 9 February 1891 (ibid., #5319—1891). See also

Acting Commissioner R. V. Belt to Noble, 19 December 1891 (NA, RG 75, OIA, SC 31, Box 25, LR, #9299—1891). Painter in his report called one of his companions Joseph B. Moore while Morgan called him Joseph B. Morse.

70. Painter to Morgan, 12 February 1891 (NA, RG 75, SC 31, Box 25, LR, #5817—1891).

71. Smiley to Noble, 1 April 1891 (NA, RG 75, OIA, SC 31, Box 25, LR, #12973—1891).

72. Smiley, Painter, and Moore to Noble, 16 March 1891 (NA, RG 75, OIA, SC 31, Box 25, LR, #11277—1891). See also Smiley, Painter, and Moore to Noble, 1 April 1891 (ibid., #12973—1891).

73. Belt's reply to Smiley, Moore, and Painter, 1 April 1891, was included along with Smiley's original request (NA, RG 75, OIA, SC 31, Box 25, LR, #11277—1891).

74. Smiley, Painter, and Moore to Noble, 1 April 1891 (NA, RG 75, OIA, SC 31, Box 25, LR, #12973—1891).

75. Smiley and Moore to Noble, 14 April 1891 (NA, RG 75, OIA, SC 31, Box 25, LR, #14877—1891).

76. Painter to Noble, 14 April 1891 (NA, RG 75, OIA, SC 31, Box 25, LR, #14878—1891).

77. Painter to Welsh, 20 April 1891, *Indian Rights Association Papers* (Reel 7).

78. Smiley to Noble, 1 April 1891 (NA, RG 75, OIA, SC 31, Box 25, LR, #13939—1891). For Smiley's report before the Lake Mohonk Conference in 1891, see Lake Mohonk Conference, *Proceedings of the Ninth Annual Meeting 1891*, pp. 24–25.

79. For Painter's report with a general overview of the work of the commission, see IRA, *Ninth Annual Report* [1892], pp. 11–23. For more detail including letters from the commissioner of Indian affairs and the assistant attorney general of the United States, and extracts of the report of the Mission Indian commissioners, see "Mission Indians in California: Message from the President of the United States," U.S. Congress, House of Representatives, Ex. Doc. No. 96, 52d Congress, 1st Sess., 1892, pp. 1–18.

80. Painter to Morgan, 11 May 1891 (NA, RG 75, OIA, SC 31, Box 25, LR, #18195—1891). See also Painter to Welsh, 13 May 1891, *Indian Rights Association Papers* (Reel 7).

81. Painter to Noble, 4 June 1891 (NA, RG 75, OIA, SC 31, Box 25, LR, #20927—1891).

82. Painter to Morgan, 2 July 1891 (NA, RG 75, OIA, SC 31, Box 25, LR, #24215—1891). See also George Shield to Noble, 22 July 1891 (NA, RG 75, OIA, SC 31, Box 25, LR, #38241—1891).

83. To understand Painter's dislike of this work see Painter to Welsh, 8 June and 8 July 1891, *Indian Rights Association Papers* (Reel 7 and Reel 8).

84. Painter to Noble, 6 July 1891 (NA, RG 75, OIA, SC 31, Box 25, LR, #24778—1891). This is a detailed report listing new reservations and descriptions of each.

85. Painter to Morgan, 7 July 1891 (NA, RG 75, OIA, SC 31, Box 25, LR, #25081—1891).

86. Shield to Noble, 22 July 1891 (NA, RG 75, OIA, SC 31, Box 25, LR, #38241—1891). See also George Chandler to Morgan, 23 October 1891 (ibid.).

87. Painter to Morgan, 10 August 1891 (NA, RG 75, OIA, SC 31, Box 25, LR, #30088—1891).

88. Painter to Welsh, 6 October 1891, *Indian Rights Association Papers* (Reel 8).

89. Ibid.

90. Painter to Welsh, 12 November 1891, *Indian Rights Association Papers* (Reel 8).

91. Smiley to Whittlesey, 4 December 1891 (NA, RG 75, OIA, SC 31, Box 25, LR, #46165—1891).

92. For a description of the reservations, see Belt to Noble, 19 December 1891 (NA, RG 75, OIA, SC 31, Box 25, LR, #9299—1891). See also Painter's report in IRA, *Ninth Annual Report*, pp. 11–23.

93. Painter to Morgan, 15 December 1891 (NA, RG 75, OIA, SC 31, Box 25, LR, #44765—1891).

94. Painter to Welsh, 15 December 1891, *Indian Rights Association Papers* (Reel 8).

95. Rust on 7 September 1892 noted that allotments had not begun yet. See U.S. Department of the Interior, Office of Indian Affairs, "Report of Mission Agency," in *Sixty-First Annual Report of the Commissioner of Indian Affairs to the Secretary of the Interior, 1892*, p. 225.

96. Lake Mohonk Conference, "Report of Committee on Mission Indians," in *Proceedings of the Tenth Annual Meeting of the Lake Mohonk Conference of Friends of the Indians, 1892*, pp. 109–112. In 1893 over $1,900 was collected for the Mission Indian defense. See Lake Mohonk Conference, "Mission Indians," in *Proceedings of the Eleventh Annual Meeting of the Lake Mohonk Conference of Friends of the Indian, 1893*, p. 131.

97. U.S. Department of the Interior, Office of Indian Affairs, "Report of the Mission Tule River Agency," in *Sixty-Second Annual Report of the Commissioner of Indian Affairs to the Secretary of the Interior, 1893*, pp. 125–126, 128. For additional information on Kate Foote's allotment work, see "Association News and Notes," *Indian's Friend* 5 (February 1893): 1.

98. For Pachanga and Sequan see U.S. Department of the Interior, Office of Indian Affairs, "Report of Mission-Tule River Consolidated Agency," in *Annual Report of the Commissioner of Indian Affairs, 1894*, p. 121; for Capitán Grande, see "Report of Mission-Tule Agency," in *Annual Report of the Commissioner of Indian Affairs, 1895*, p. 133; and for Temecula, see "Report of Mission-Tule Agency," in *Annual Report of the Department of the Interior, 1898*, p. 135.

7. The WNIA at Cahuilla, El Potrero, and Saboba

1. "A Historical Sketch," *Indian's Friend* 9 (October 1896): 11.

2. WNIA, *Missionary Work of the Women's National Indian Association, and Letters of Missionaries*, p. 1.

3. Ibid., p. 17. See also WNIA, *Report of Missionary Work, November 1885 to November 1886,* pp. 7, 9, 11; WNIA, *Christian Civilization: Missionary Work of the Women's National Indian Association,* pp. 4, 5; and Wanken, "Woman's Sphere and Indian Reform," pp. 300–304.

4. Jackson to Dawes, 27 August 1884, Dawes Papers (Box 26), Library of Congress.

5. WNIA, *Report on Missionary Work* [1888], p. 9, and *Annual Report* [1888], p. 20.

6. Quinton to John H. Oberly, 18 February 1889 (NA, RG 75, OIA, LR, #4927—1889). See also "The New California Mission," *Indian's Friend* 1 (March 1889): 3. To acquaint WNIA members with the history of the Mission Indians, a series appeared in *Indian's Friend* during the months of March, April, May, and June 1889.

7. Quinton to Oberly, 12 April 1889 (NA, RG 75, OIA, LR, #1915—1889). See also Quinton to Oberly, 1 March 1889, and Noble to Oberly, 20 March 1889 (NA, RG 75, OIA, SC 143, LR, #19602[5839]—1889); Rust to Morgan, 22 October 1890, and Acting Secretary Chandler to Morgan, 6 November 1890 (NA, RG 75, OIA, SC 143, LR, #24792[33354]—1890); and Quinton to Weinland, 4 June 1889, William H. Weinland Collection (Box 7), Huntington Library.

8. For a brief history of the Indians at Saboba, Cahuilla, Warner's Ranch, San Ysidro, Pala, Temecula, Santa Ysabel, Mesa Grande, Capitán Grande, and the Los Coyotes, Sequans, and Conejos, see WNIA, *Ramona Mission and the Mission Indians,* pp. 1–18.

9. Quinton to Weinland, July [the letter was written sometime during the first two weeks of July] 1889, Weinland Collection (Box 7), Huntington Library.

10. Quinton to Weinland, July [no day] 1889, Weinland Collection (Box 7), Huntington Library.

11. Quinton to Weinland, 16 September 1890, Weinland Collection (Box 7), Huntington Library.

12. Quinton to Weinland, 23 December 1893, Weinland Collection (Box 7), Huntington Library.

13. WNIA, *Report of the Missionary Committee,* p. 13. See also Wanken, "Woman's Sphere and Indian Reform," pp. 307–308.

14. WNIA, *Report of the Missionary Committee* [1889], p. 14.

15. Quinton to Welsh, 5 July 1889, *Indian Rights Association Papers* (Reel 4).

16. Jackson to Sheriff, 17 July 1885, Jackson manuscripts (HM 14216), Huntington Library.

17. WNIA, *Report of the Missionary Committee* [1889], p. 10. Rust was not enthusiastic about Catholics purchasing more land near or on El Potrero Reservation. See Rust to Morgan, 26 November 1889 (NA, RG 75, OIA, SC 143, LR, #34628—1889). The WNIA also wrote kindly of Rust, see "Things Needed," *Indian's Friend* 2 (June 1890): 3.

18. U.S. Department of the Interior, Office of Indian Affairs, "Report of

the Mission Agency," *Fifty-Eighth Annual Report of the Commissioner of Indian Affairs to the Secretary of the Interior, 1889,* p. 125.

19. U.S. Department of the Interior, Office of Indian Affairs, "Report of Mission Agency," *Fifty-Ninth Annual Report 1890,* pp. 18–19.

20. WNIA, *Report of the Missionary Committee* [1889], pp. 15, 17.

21. Morgan to Quinton, 27 July 1889 (NA, RG 75, OIA, LS: Land Division, Vol. 94, LB 187, pp. 363–364).

22. Quinton to Weinland, 23, 25, and 29 July 1889, Weinland Collection (Box 7), Huntington Library.

23. WNIA, "The Ramona Mission," *Report of the Missionary Committee* [1889], pp. 8–9.

24. Quinton to Weinland, 25 and 30 September and 20 December 1889, Weinland Collection (Box 7), Huntington Library.

25. "From the Ramona Mission," *Indian's Friend* 2 (January 1890): 2.

26. Quinton to Weinland, 5 September 1890, Weinland Collection (Box 7), Huntington Library.

27. "News and Notes," *Indian's Friend* 3 (September 1890): 3; WNIA, "The Saboba Station," *Report of the Missionary Department* [1890], p. 12; WNIA, *Report of the Missionary Department* [1891], p. 7; and "A Letter from Saboba," *Indian's Friend* 3 (October 1890): 1. As early as February 1890 Quinton wrote Weinland that the WNIA would be able to sponsor Fowler at Saboba at $400 a year; see Quinton to Weinland, 5 February 1890, Box 7, Weinland Collection, Huntington Library; and also Quinton to Weinland, 23 May 1890, ibid.

28. Rust to Morgan, 31 October 1889 (NA, RG 75, OIA, SC 143, LR, #31742—1889).

29. "From the Ramona Mission," *Indian's Friend* 2 (January 1890): 2.

30. WNIA, "The Ramona Mission," *Report of the Missionary Department* [1890], pp. 10–11. See also WNIA, *Annual Report of the Women's National Indian Association* [1889], p. 18, and *Indian's Friend* 1 (February 1889): 4.

31. "Our New Ramona Mission," *Indian's Friend* 1 (June 1889): 2, and "From the Ramona Mission," *Indian's Friend* 2 (March 1890): 1.

32. "From the Ramona Mission," *Indian's Friend* 2 (January 1890): 2.

33. "From the Ramona Mission," *Indian's Friend* 2 (February 1890): 1, 3.

34. "Our New California Chapel," *Indian's Friend* 2 (May 1890): 3.

35. Quinton to Weinland, 3 May 1890, Weinland Collection (Box 7), Huntington Library; "Missions Transferred," *Indian's Friend* 2 (May 1890): 2. See also WNIA, *Report of the Missionary Department* [1890], pp. 4, 11, both of which state the transfer was made in the month of June. See also H. J. Bachman to the Commissioner, 12 February 1891 (NA, RG 75, OIA, SC 31, Box 25, LR, #46165—1891), and Quinton to Weinland, 17 January 1890, Weinland Collection (Box 7), Huntington Library in which Quinton asks if the Moravian Church would be interested in taking over the Potrero mission.

36. Quinton to Weinland, 7 August 1891, Weinland Collection (Box 7), Huntington Library; and WNIA, "Our Ramona Missions," in *Report of the Missionary Department* [1891], p. 8.

37. "Through Southern California: Letter Number Seven," *Indian's Friend* 4 (October 1891): 5.

38. In his first report Agent Rust recommended that Agua Caliente would be the most favorable location for a hospital. See U.S. Department of the Interior, Office of Indian Affairs, "Report of Mission Agency," in *Fifty-Eighth Annual Report of the Commissioner of Indian Affairs to the Secretary of the Interior, 1889*, p. 125.

39. "Letter Number Seven," *Indian's Friend* 4 (October 1891): 6.

40. "Letter Number Seven," p. 6.

41. "Letter Number Seven," p. 7. For her report, see Lake Mohonk Conference, *Ninth Annual Meeting 1891*, pp. 25–27. See also BIC, *Report of the Board of Indian Commissioners* [1891], pp. 1155–1156.

42. For the dates of the various organizations, see WNIA, *Annual Report of the Women's National Indian Association* [1891], pp. 17–18.

43. For information on the WNIA in Northern California, see Valerie Sherer Mathes, "Friends of the Indians: Women's National Indian Association in California," paper delivered 14 April 1984 at the California History Institute, University of the Pacific, Stockton, California; Valerie Sherer Mathes, "Indian Philanthropy in California: Annie Bidwell and the Mechoopda Indians," *Arizona and the West*, Summer 1983, pp. 153–166; Valerie Sherer Mathes, "Annie E. K. Biowell: Chico's Benefactress," *California History*, Spring–Summer 1989, pp. 14–25, 60–64; and Wanken, "Woman's Sphere and Indian Reform," pp. 324–339.

For a fascinating reminiscence of field matrons in Northern California, see Mary Ellicott Arnold and Mabel Reed, *In the Land of the Grasshopper Song: Two Women in the Klamath River Indian Country in 1908–09*. For a detailed study of the Greenville School, see William Allan Jones, "The Historical Development of the Greenville Indian Industrial School: Greenville, Plumas County California," (M.A. thesis, California State University, Chico, spring 1978).

44. WNIA, "Our Ramona Missions," *Report of the Missionary Department* [1891], p. 8, and "Association News and Notes," *Indian's Friend* 4 (September 1891): 1.

45. U.S. Department of the Interior, Office of Indian Affairs, "Report of Mission Agency," *Annual Report of the Commissioner 1888*, p. 17.

46. Quinton to Morgan, 28 June 1891 (NA, RG 75, OIA, LR, #24191–1891).

47. Quinton to Morgan, 4 August 1891 (NA, RG 75, OIA, LR, #29440–1891).

48. Both quotations are from U.S. Department of the Interior, Office of Indian Affairs, "Field Matrons," in *Annual Report of the Commissioner 1892*, p. 101. See also Elizabeth A. McKee, "Civilizing the Indian: Field Matrons under Hoopa Valley Agency Jurisdiction 1898–1919" (M.A. thesis, California State University, Sacramento, 1982); Elizabeth A. McKee, "Women's Beneficence and the Reform Mission of the Northern California Indian Association," paper read at the 37th California History Institute at the University of the Pacific, Stockton, California, 14 April 1984; Lisa E. Emmerick,

"Women among the Indians: Field Matrons and Civilization Policy in Action, 1890–1938," paper read at the Western History Association Conference, October 1984; "Field Matron," *Indian's Friend* 5 (December 1892): 2; "Field Matrons for Indians," *Indian's Friend* 6 (May 1894): 6; and "Field Matrons," *Indian's Friend* 6 (July 1894): 9–10. For the education of Indian girls, see Robert A. Trennert, "Educating Indian Girls at Nonreservation Boarding Schools, 1878–1920," *Western Historical Quarterly* 13 (July 1982): 271–290.

49. For a detailed discussion of the Home Building and Loan Department, see Wanken, "Woman's Sphere and Indian Reform," pp. 153–181.

50. "From a Missionary Report," *Indian's Friend* 4 (July 1892): 45; and WNIA, "Our Ramona Missions in California," in *Work of the Missionary Department of the Women's National Indian Association for the year Ending December 1892*, pp. 33–38. For Noble's concerns, see *Indian's Friend* 5 (November 1892): 1.

51. Quinton to Morgan, 1 November 1892 (NA, RG 75, OIA, LR, #39462—1892). See also Quinton to Weinland, 16 November 1892, Weinland Collection (Box 7), Huntington Library; WNIA, "The Ramona Missions in California," in *Work of the Missionary Department 1892*, p. 42; *Indian's Friend* 5 (November 1892): 4; and *Indian's Friend* 5 (December 1892): 3. For a letter from Johnson, see "Association News and Notes," *Indian's Friend* 5 (March 1893): 3.

52. Quinton to Morgan, 11 January 1893 (NA, RG 75, OIA, SC 143, LR, #1404—1893). See also Quinton to Weinland, 15 January 1893, Weinland Collection (Box 7), Huntington Library.

53. "Progress at Coahuilla," *Indian's Friend* 5 (April 1893): 1–3. See also "Coahuilla Again," *Indian's Friend* 5 (May 1893): 2.

54. "Association News and Notes," *Indian's Friend* 5 (June 1893): 3.

55. *Indian's Friend* 6 (June 1894): 3. For a report of the 1894 year at Cahuilla, see WNIA, "Coahuilla," *Sunshine Work*, December 1894, pp. 10–14.

56. Quinton to Weinland, 19 January 1893, Weinland Collection (Box 7), Huntington Library. See also Quinton to Weinland, 4 February 1893, ibid.

57. Quinton to Morgan, 16 January 1893 (NA, RG 75, OIA, LR, #2241—1893).

58. Quinton to Morgan, 4 February 1893 (NA, RG 75, OIA, SC 143, LR, #4665—1893).

59. Quinton to Weinland, 14 February 1893, Weinland Collection (Box 7), Huntington Library.

60. Quinton to Weinland, 17 June 1893, Weinland Collection (Box 7), Huntington Library.

61. Rust to Morgan, 6 February 1893 (NA, RG 75, OIA, LR, #5809—1893).

62. Rust to Morgan, 20 February 1893 (NA, RG 75, OIA, SC 143, LR, #7381—1893).

63. Ibid. For more on this incident, see Wanken, "Woman's Sphere and Indian Reform," pp. 310–16.

64. Quinton to Hoke Smith, 29 March 1893, Weinland Collection (Box 7), Huntington Library.

65. Quinton to Daniel M. Browning, 2 June 1893 (NA, RG 75, OIA, SC 143, LR, #20529—1893). In Quinton to Browning, 13 July 1893 (NA, RG 75, OIA, SC 143, LR, #28670[25849]—1893), Quinton enclosed the survey taken at Cahuilla and requested that the five acres described therein be granted to the association. She reminded the commissioner that the consent of the Indians had been obtained and the new Mission Agent Francisco Estudillo approved of their work. See also Quinton to Weinland, 13 April 1893, Weinland Collection (Box 7), Huntington Library.

66. Quinton to Belt, 3 April 1893 (NA, RG 75, OIA, LR, #11818—1893); see also Quinton to Belt, 22 March 1893 (ibid., #10514—1893).

67. For the first quotation, see Quinton to Weinland, 15 April 1893, and for the second, see Quinton to Weinland, 16 April 1893, Weinland Collection (Box 7), Huntington Library.

68. Estudillo to Browning, 12 July 1893 (NA, RG 75, OIA, SC 143, LR, #26444—1893).

69. Estudillo to Browning, 28 July 1893 (NA, RG 75, OIA, SC 143, LR, #28670[25849]—1893). In a second report to Browning, Estudillo changed some numbers of Indians either for or against the deed of land. Of those who had originally signed the land grant, three were school children under seventeen. See Estudillo to Browning, 11 September 1893 (NA, RG 75, OIA, SC 31, LR, #34928—1893).

70. Estudillo to Quinton, 25 July 1893 (NA, RG 75, OIA, LR, #34301—1893).

71. Quinton to Estudillo, 9 August 1893 (NA, RG 75, OIA, LR, #34301—1893).

72. Ibid.

73. Estudillo to Quinton, 18 August 1893 (NA, RG 75, OIA, LR, #34301—1893).

74. All quotes Quinton to Estudillo, 24 August 1893 (NA, RG 75, OIA, LR, #34301—1893).

75. Quinton to Browning, 17 August 1893 (NA, RG 75, OIA, SC 31, LR, #31665—1893).

76. All quotes Quinton to Browning, 17 August 1893 (NA, RG 75, OIA, SC 31, LR, #31665—1893). For a discussion of this issue at Cahuilla, see Wanken, "Woman's Sphere and Indian Reform," pp. 316–321.

77. Browning to Quinton, 14 August 1893 [copy of a letter sent and located on page 180, book 263] (NA, RG 75, OIA, SC 143, LR, #28670—1893). For a discussion of this letter, see Quinton to Weinland, 17 August 1893, Weinland Collection (Box 7), Huntington Library.

78. Quinton to Browning, 23 November 1893 (NA, RG 75, OIA, LR, #43864—1893).

79. Quinton to Browning, 27 February 1894 (NA, RG 75, OIA, LR, #9206—1894). See also Quinton to Weinland, 31 May 1894, Weinland Collection (Box 7), Huntington Library.

80. *Indian's Friend* 7 (February 1895): 9; and "News and Notes," *Indian's*

Friend 7 (August 1895): 3; and for Ritter's arrival, see "News and Notes," *Indian's Friend* 7 (March 1895): 2.

81. Quinton to Browning, 27 April 1896 (NA, RG 75, OIA, LR, #18032—1896). See also Quinton to Weinland, 24 February, 25 March, and 6 June 1896, Box 7, Weinland Collection, Huntington Library.

82. WNIA, *Annual Report of the Women's National Indian Association* [1896], p. 31. See also *Indian's Friend* 9 (May 1897): 5, and Quinton to Weinland, 1 October 1896, Weinland Collection (Box 7), Huntington Library.

83. WNIA, *Annual Report* [1896], pp. 21–22. See also Quinton to Weinland, 6 June 1896 and 15 April 1898, Weinland Collection (Box 7), Huntington Library.

84. Quinton to William A. Jones, 26 March 1901 (NA, RG 75, OIA, LR, #16352—1901).

85. Quinton to Weinland, 13 May 1901, Weinland Collection (Box 7), Huntington Library.

86. Quinton to Weinland, 5 July 1901, Weinland Collection (Box 7), Huntington Library.

8. The WNIA at Agua Caliente and Martínez

1. For a history of the Warner's Ranch Indians, see Hill, *History of Warner's Ranch*, pp. 135–142; for the legal history of the ranch, see pp. 143–154. See also Jackson, "Exhibit D: The Warner's Ranch Indians," "Report," pp. 485–488.

2. Quinton to Morgan, 1 September 1891 (NA, RG 75, OIA, LR, #40821—1891).

3. Quinton to Morgan, 18 December 1891 (NA, RG 75, OIA, LR, #44976—1891). See also Quinton to Smiley, 18 December 1891 (ibid.).

4. Quinton to Morgan, 8 January 1892 (NA, RG 75, OIA, LR, #904—1892).

5. Morgan to Quinton, 14 and 28 January 1892, included with Quinton to Morgan, 18 December 1891 (NA, RG 75, OIA, LR, #44976—1891).

6. Quinton to Morgan, 30 January 1892 (NA, RG 75, OIA, LR, #3897—1892).

7. Quinton to Morgan, 29 February 1892 (NA, RG 75, OIA, LR, #8669—1892).

8. Quinton to Weinland, 4 April 1892, Weinland Collection (Box 7), Huntington Library. See also Quinton to Weinland, 11 and 21 April 1892, ibid.

9. Quinton to Weinland, 15 May 1892, Weinland Collection (Box 7), Huntington Library.

10. Quinton to Weinland, 22 May 1892, Weinland Collection (Box 7), Huntington Library.

11. All quotes Quinton to Weinland, 16 May 1892, Weinland Collection (Box 7), Huntington Library.

12. Quinton to Rust, 23 May 1892, Weinland Collection (Box 7), Huntington Library.

13. Quinton to Weinland, 19 and 29 July 1892, Weinland Collection (Box 7), Huntington Library.

14. *Indian's Friend* 4 (August 1892): 48; 5 (October 1892): 2; and 5 (November 1892): 3. For more on the ejectment, see "Association News and Notes," *Indian's Friend* 6 (September 1893): 3; Lake Mohonk Conference, "Report of Committee on Mission Indians," in *Tenth Annual Meeting 1892*, pp. 111–113; and U.S. Department of the Interior, Office of Indian Affairs, "Report of Mission Tule River Agency," in *Annual Report of the Commissioner 1893*, pp. 126–127.

15. WNIA, *Annual Report of the Women's National Indian Association* [1892], p. 33.

16. Quinton to Weinland, 3 October 1892, Weinland Collection (Box 7), Huntington Library. See also Quinton to Josephine Babbitt, 3 October 1892, ibid.

17. Quinton to Weinland, 21 October 1892, Weinland Collection (Box 7), Huntington Library. See also Quinton to Weinland, 29 October 1892, ibid.

18. Quinton to Babbitt, 23 November 1892, Weinland Collection (Box 7), Huntington Library.

19. Quinton to Morgan, 24 November 1892 (NA, RG 75, OIA, LR, #42167—1892). See also Quinton to Weinland, 25 November 1892, Weinland Collection (Box 7), Huntington Library.

20. Quinton to Weinland, 30 January 1893, Weinland Collection (Box 7), Huntington Library. See also WNIA, "Agua Caliente," in *Work of the Missionary Department, 1892*, pp. 44–45; and "Association News and Notes," *Indian's Friend* 5 (February 1893): 5. For Hallowell's initial reaction to Agua Caliente, see "Letter from the New Mission," *Indian's Friend* 5 (March 1893): 2; see also "From Agua Caliente," *Indian's Friend* 5 (April 1893): 2.

21. Quinton to Weinland, 14 February 1893, Weinland Collection (Box 7), Huntington Library.

22. For Weinland's retirement see "Association News and Notes," *Indian's Friend* 5 (July 1893): 2, and "News and Notes," *Indian's Friend* 6 (February 1894): 5.

23. All quotes Quinton to Weinland, 15 August 1893, Weinland Collection (Box 7), Huntington Library. See also Quinton to Weinland, 4 September and 31 October 1893 (ibid.).

24. During 1893 the New York City association raised $1,627 for hospital work at Agua Caliente. See WNIA, *Annual Report of the Women's National Indian Association* [1893], p. 16. For information on the early stages of the Agua Caliente hospital, see WNIA, *Work of the Missionary Department, 1892*, pp. 43–46.

25. "From a New Correspondent," *Indian's Friend* 5 (May 1893): 3.

26. *Indian's Friend* 6 (March 1894): 6. For the general missionary report for 1894 at Agua Caliente, see "Agua Caliente," *Sunshine Work*, pp. 14–24. See also "The New York City Indian Mission," *Indian's Friend* 6 (May 1895): 7.

27. For information on the Committee on Temperance Appeals, see Wan-

ken, "Woman's Sphere and Indian Reform," pp. 150–152, and for Bailey's annual report, see WNIA, *Annual Report of the Women's National Indian Association* [1895], p. 37.

28. Quinton to Browning, 4 September 1893 (NA, RG 75, OIA, LR, #34301—1893).

29. Quinton to Browning, 22 August 1893 (NA, RG 75, OIA, LR, #31667—1893).

30. Estudillo to Quinton, 29 August 1893 (NA, RG 75, OIA, LR, #34301—1893).

31. Quinton to Estudillo, 6 September 1893 (NA, RG 75, OIA, LR, #34301—1893). See also Quinton to Weinland, 4 September 1893, Weinland Collection (Box 7), Huntington Library, and Wanken, "Woman's Sphere and Indian Reform," pp. 321–323.

32. "From California," *Indian's Friend* 7 (May 1895): 6. This letter begins on the inside cover, opposite the first page of the issue and continues on p. 6. See also Quinton to Weinland, 25 April 1895, Weinland Collection (Box 7), Huntington Library.

33. *Indian's Friend* 7 (July 1895): 3.

34. "From California," *Indian's Friend* 7 (June 1895): 8.

35. "Into the Desert," *Indian's Friend* 7 (July 1895): 6–8.

36. "News and Notes," *Indian's Friend* 8 (April 1896): 4.

37. For Quinton's California itinerary and her work among the WNIA affiliates see WNIA, *Annual Report* [1895], pp. 12–13, 23.

38. Lake Mohonk Conference, *Proceedings of the Thirteenth Annual Meeting of the Lake Mohonk Conference of Friends of the Indians, 1895,* pp. 89–90. The same report can be found in "Address of Mrs. A. S. Quinton," BIC, *Annual Report of the Board of Indian Commissioners, 1895,* p. 1050; see also p. 1077.

39. See, for example, Quinton to Weinland, 22 March 1898, Weinland Collection (Box 7), Huntington Library.

40. "From a Late Report: Rev. William H. Weinland," *Indian's Friend* 8 (June 1896): 8–9.

41. Quinton to Weinland, 14, 21, and 28 September 1896, Weinland Collection (Box 7), Huntington Library.

42. "The Desert Mission," *Indian's Friend* 9 (November 1896): 2, 4. See also WNIA, *Annual Report of the Women's National Indian Association* [1896], pp. 17, 30; "Dedication of the New Mission Church," *Indian's Friend* 9 (February 1897): 7; and Quinton to Weinland, 7 December 1895 and 21 February 1896, Weinland Collection (Box 7), Huntington Library. In a 22 December 1896 letter to Weinland, Quinton noted that the chapel was dedicated on December 6th.

43. "Desert Work," *Indian's Friend* 9 (July 1897): 11.

44. WNIA, "The Mission of the Brooklyn Indian Association," in *Our Missionary Report for 1897,* p. 37. For the entire report see pp. 35–37. See also WNIA, *Annual Report of the Women's National Indian Association* [1897], p. 20. For correspondence revealing the difficulty of the transfer to the Moravians, see Quinton to Weinland, 3 July, 2 August, 26 September,

and 18 December 1897, Weinland Collection (Box 7), Huntington Library. For an informative letter on the WNIA work in Southern California in general, see Quinton to Ethan Allen Hitchcock, 27 May 1899, Weinland Collection (Box 7), Huntington Library.

45. Quinton to Weinland, 7 December 1895, Weinland Collection (Box 7), Huntington Library. See also Quinton to Weinland, 4 September 1896 (ibid.).

46. Charles E. Shell to William A. Jones, 10 October 1903; David J. Woosley to Jones, 6 November 1903; Shell to Jones, 7 November 1903; Woosley to Jones, 12 January 1904; Paul deSchweinitz to Jones, 20 January 1904; Woosley to A. G. Tonner, 29 February 1904; Shell to Jones, 14 March 1904; and Hitchcock to Jones, 30 March 1904 (all in NA, RG 75, OIA, SC 143, LR, #87252—1904).

47. "News and Notes," *Indian's Friend* 8 (August 1896): 5, and WNIA, *Annual Report* [1896], pp. 16, 29.

48. *Indian's Friend* 12 (January 1900): 11.

49. For a brief discussion of the role of the IRA, see S. M. Brosius (agent for the IRA) to Weinland, 27 February 1901, Weinland Collection (Box 5), Huntington Library.

50. IRA, *The Pressing Needs of the Warner Ranch and other Mission Indians in Southern California,* passim, *Indian Rights Association Papers* (Reel 102).

51. For all of the detailed information on the Warner's Ranch case, see Hill, *History of Warner's Ranch,* pp. 143–165; IRA, "The Warner Ranch Case," in *Seventeenth Annual Report of the Executive Committee of the Indian Rights Association* [1900], pp. 4–5, 81–82; IRA, "The Warner Ranch Case," in *Fifteenth Annual Report of the Executive Committee of the Indian Rights Association* [1898], pp. 3–5; "A Most Unjust Decision," *Indian's Friend* 9 (February 1897): 3; WNIA, "The Mission of the New York City Indian Association," in *Our Missionary Report for 1897,* pp. 29–30; and "Agua Caliente," *Indian's Friend* 9 (July 1897): 3.

52. WNIA, *Annual Report of the Women's National Indian Association* [1898], p. 42, shows that a total of $930 was donated for the medical missionary from the New York City association.

53. Quinton to Weinland, 12 August 1898, Weinland Collection (Box 7), Huntington Library.

54. Quinton to Weinland, 28 January 1899, Weinland Collection (Box 7), Huntington Library.

55. WNIA, *Annual Report of the Women's National Indian Association* [1899], pp. 13, 20–21. See also WNIA, *Annual Report of the Women's National Indian Association* [1901], pp. 24–25. For more on the transfer to the Moravian Board, see Quinton to Weinland, 6 July and 1 August 1898, Weinland Collection (Box 7), Huntington Library.

56. Quinton to Weinland, 23 November 1898, Weinland Collection (Box 7), Huntington Library.

57. "News and Notes," *Indian's Friend* 11 (February 1899): 4.

58. *Indian's Friend* 10 (May 1898): 4; "News and Notes," *Indian's Friend* 10 (June 1898): 4. See also WNIA, *Annual Report* [1898], p. 14.

59. Cornelia Taber, "The Desert (Martínez) Riverside County—220 Indians," in *California and her Indian Children*, p. 51. These artesian wells were not a result of WNIA work.

60. WNIA, *Annual Report of the National Indian Association* [1902], pp. 18–19, and *Indian's Friend* 14 (June 1902): 2, 7; and 14 (July 1902): 2.

61. WNIA, *Annual Report of the National Indian Association* [1903], pp. 32–33.

62. WNIA, *Forty-Second Annual Report of the National Indian Association* [1921], p. 28.

63. WNIA, *Annual Report* [1901], p. 24.

64. Jackson, "Exhibit G: The Santa Ysabel Ranch," "Report," pp. 492–493.

65. IRA, "Our American 'Reconcentrados,'" in *The Eighteenth Annual Report of the Executive Committee of the Indian Rights Association*, [1901], p. 25.

66. Both quotations from Constance Goddard DuBois, *The Condition of the Mission Indians of Southern California*, p. 15.

67. Quinton to Weinland, 5 and 20 August 1901, Weinland Collection (Box 7), Huntington Library.

68. Quinton to Weinland, 11 August 1901, Weinland Collection (Box 7), Huntington Library.

69. U.S. Department of the Interior, Office of Indian Affairs, "Report of Mission-Tule Agency," in *Annual Report of the Department of the Interior* [1898], p. 135.

70. C. E. Kelsey, *Report of the Special Agent for California Indians to the Commissioner of Indian Affairs, March 21, 1906*, p. 15.

71. Kelsey, *Report of the Special Agent*, p. 24.

72. Jackson, "Exhibit M: The Pachanga Indians," "Report," p. 505.

73. IRA, "The California Indians," in *Twenty-Fifth Annual Report of the Executive Committee of the Indian Rights Association, for the Year ending December 12, 1907*, pp. 22–23.

74. For a brief history of these Indians through the 1970s, see Florence C. Shipek, "History of Southern California Mission Indians," in *Handbook of North American Indians*, vol. 8 *California*, ed. Heizer, pp. 610–618.

9. Retrospective

1. Jackson to Quinton, 2 April 1884, Pierpont Morgan Library (MA 4571), New York, New York.

2. Jackson to William Sharpless Jackson, 29 March [1885], Jackson Family Papers (Part I, Box 1, fd. 5), Charles Leaming Tutt Library.

3. Jackson probably to Higginson, 27 July 1885 in Higginson, "Helen Hunt Jackson," *Nation* 41 (20 August 1885): 151.

4. Nancy Meyer, *Chronology* "Ramona Episode," The Los Angeles History Project, 8 October 1987.

Bibliography

ARCHIVAL MATERIAL

Abbott Memorial Collection: Edward Abbott *Literary World*, Lowell Tribune Scrapbook. Bowdoin College Library. Brunswick, Maine.

Abbott Memorial Collection: Lyman Abbott Autograph Collection. Bowdoin College Library. Brunswick, Maine.

Aldrich, Thomas Bailey. Papers. Houghton Library, Harvard University. Cambridge, Massachusetts.

Alvord, William. Correspondence and Papers. The Bancroft, University of California. Berkeley, California.

Berg, Henry W. and Albert A. Collection. New York Public Library. Astor, Lenox, and Tilden Foundations. New York, New York.

Bowen, Henry Chandler. Collection. Huntington Library. San Marino, California.

Carr, Jeanne C. (Smith). Collection. Huntington Library. San Marino, California.

Chapin-Kiley Manuscripts. Amherst College Library. Amherst, Massachusetts.

Conway, Moncure D. Papers. Butler Library, Columbia University. New York, New York.

Coronel, Antonio F. Collection. Seaver Center for Western History Research, Los Angeles County Museum of Natural History. Los Angeles, California.

Dawes, Henry L. Papers. Library of Congress. Washington, D.C.

Dodge, Mary Mapes. Donald and Robert M. Dodge Collection. Princeton University Library. Princeton, New Jersey.

Fields, James Thomas. Collection. Huntington Library. San Marino, California.

Gilder, Joseph Benson. Papers. New York Public Library. Astor, Lenox, and Tilden Foundations. New York, New York.

Gilman, Daniel Coit. Papers. Milton S. Eisenhower Library, Johns Hopkins University. Baltimore, Maryland.

Hampton Institute Archives. Hampton, Virginia.

Harper & Brothers. Papers. Butler Library, Columbia University. New York, New York.

Higginson, Thomas Wentworth. Field Book. Houghton Library, Harvard University. Cambridge, Massachusetts.

Holmes, Oliver Wendell. Papers. Houghton Library, Harvard University. Cambridge, Massachusetts.

Houghton, Henry Oscar. Papers. Houghton Library, Harvard University. Cambridge, Massachusetts.

Indian Rights Association. Correspondence. Huntington Library. San Marino, California.

Jackson, Helen Maria Fiske Hunt. Collection. The Bancroft, University of California. Berkeley, California.

Jackson, Helen Maria (Fiske) Hunt. Collection. Boston Public Library. Boston, Massachusetts.

(Jackson), Helen Maria Fiske Hunt. Collection. Clifton Waller Barrett Library, University of Virginia. Charlottesville, Virginia.

Jackson, Helen Hunt. Manuscripts. Huntington Library. San Marino, California.

Jackson, Helen Hunt. Papers. Charles Leaming Tutt Library, Colorado College. Colorado Springs, Colorado.

Jackson, Helen Hunt. Papers. Jones Library. Amherst, Massachusetts.

Jackson, William Sharpless. Family Papers. Charles Leaming Tutt Library, Colorado College. Colorado Springs, Colorado.

Johnson, Robert Underwood. Papers. Butler Library, Columbia University. New York, New York.

Longfellow, Henry Wadsworth. Papers. Houghton Library, Harvard University. Cambridge, Massachusetts.

Mather, Frank Jewett. Autograph Collection. Princeton University Library. Princeton, New Jersey.

Miscellaneous Manuscripts. Amherst College Library. Amherst, Massachusetts.

Morristown National Historical Park. Morristown, New Jersey.

Morse, Ephraim W. Collection. San Diego Historical Society. San Diego, California.

Morse, Ephraim W. Letter Book, January 1883–August 19, 1884. San Diego Historical Society. San Diego, California.

Muir, John. Papers. Holt-Atherton Pacific Center for Western Studies, University of the Pacific. Stockton, California.

New Hampshire Historical Society. Concord, New Hampshire.

Oak, Henry. Correspondence and Papers. The Bancroft, University of California. Berkeley, California.

Office of Indian Affairs. Record Group 75. Letters Received, Letters Sent. National Archives. Washington, D.C.

Personal—Miscellaneous (Helen Hunt Jackson). New York Public Library. Astor, Lenox, and Tilden Foundations. New York, New York.

Pierpont Morgan Library. New York, New York.

Phelan Collection. San Francisco Public Library. San Francisco, California.

Quinton, Amelia Stone. Correspondence. Huntington Library. San Marino, California.

Reid, Whitelaw. Papers. Library of Congress. Washington, D.C.

Scribner's Sons, Charles. Archives. Princeton University Library. Princeton, New Jersey.

Smith, Sophia. Collection. Women's History Archive, Smith College. Northampton, Massachusetts.

Warner, Charles Dudley. Collection. Watkinson Library, Trinity College. Hartford, Connecticut.

Whipple, Henry B. Papers. Minnesota Historical Society. St. Paul, Minnesota.

Weinland, William H. Collection. Huntington Library. San Marino, California.

UNPUBLISHED WORKS

Bannan, Helen Marie. "Reformers and the 'Indian Problem' 1878–1887 and 1922–1934." Ph.D. dissertation, Syracuse University, 1976.

Burgess, Larry Y. "The Lake Mohonk Conference on the Indian, 1883–1916." Ph.D. dissertation, Claremont Graduate School, 1972.

Eastman, Elaine Goodale. "Spinner in the Sun: The Story of Helen Hunt Jackson." Unpublished, unpaged, typed manuscript, Sophia Smith Collection, Women's History Archive, Smith College, Northampton, Massachusetts.

Emmerick, Lisa E. "Women among the Indians: Field Matrons and Civilization Policy in Action, 1890–1938." Paper, Western History Association Conference, October 1984.

Fagan, George V. "Helen of Colorado Reexamined." Paper, meeting of the Colorado Springs Ghost Town Club, 28 October 1977. Special Collections, Charles Leaming Tutt Library, Colorado College, Colorado Springs, Colorado.

Friend, Ruth E. "Helen Hunt Jackson: A Critical Study." Ph.D. dissertation, Kent State University, 1985.

Hagan, William T. "Reformers' Images of the Native Americans: The Late 19th Century." Paper, Kent State University, Center for Native American Studies, Distinguished Lecturer Series, 25 February 1981.

Hoxie, Frederick E. "Beyond Savagery: The Campaign to Assimilate the American Indians, 1880–1920." Ph.D. dissertation, Brandeis University, 1977.

Hurtado, Albert L. "California Indian Demography, Sherburne F. Cook and

the Revision of American History." Paper, Western History Association
Meeting, Billings, Montana, 1986. Pp. 1–33.

————. "Ranchos, Gold Mines, and Rancherías: A Socioeconomic History
of Indians and Whites in Northern California, 1821–1860." Ph.D. dissertation, University of California, Santa Barbara, June 1981.

Jones, William Allan. "The Historical Development of the Greenville Indian Industrial School: Greenville, Plumas County, California." M.A. thesis, California State University, Chico, California, spring 1978.

McKee, Elizabeth A. "Civilizing the Indian: Field Matrons under Hoopa Valley Agency Jurisdiction 1898–1919." M.A. thesis, California State University, Sacramento, California, 1982.

————. "Women's Beneficence and the Reform Mission of the Northern
California Indian Association." Paper, California History Institute, University of the Pacific, Stockton, California, 14 April 1984.

Martin, Minerva Louise. "Helen Hunt Jackson in Relation to her Time."
Ph.D. dissertation, Louisiana State University, 1940.

Mathes, Valerie Sherer. "Friends of the Indians: the Women's National
Indian Association in California." Paper, California History Institute,
University of the Pacific, Stockton, California, 14 April 1984.

Meyer, Nancy. Chronology "Ramona Episode." The Los Angeles History
Project, 8 October 1987.

Ryan, Mary P. "American Society and the Cult of Domesticity, 1830–1860."
Ph.D. dissertation, University of California, Santa Barbara, 1971.

Thompson, Gregory Coyne. "The Origins and Implementation of the American Indian Reform Movement: 1867–1911." Ph.D. dissertation, University of Utah, 1981.

Wanken, Helen M. "Woman's Sphere and Indian Reform: The Women's
National Indian Association 1879–1901." Ph.D. dissertation, Marquette
University, 1981.

BOOKS, MONOGRAPHS, AND ARTICLES

Adams, John Quincy. Memoirs of John Quincy Adams, Comprising Portions of his Diary from 1795 to 1848. Ed. Charles Francis Adams. Vol. 10.
Philadelphia: J. B. Lippincott and Company, 1876.

Alderson, William A. The True Story of Ramona. New York: Dodge Publishing Company, 1914.

Allen, Margaret V. Ramona's Homeland. Chula Vista: Denrich Press, 1914.

The Annotated Ramona. Intro. and notes by Antoinette May. San Carlos,
Calif.: Wide World Publishing/Tetra, 1989.

Arnold, Mary Ellicott, and Mabel Reed. In the Land of the Grasshopper
Song: Two Women in the Klamath River Indian Country in 1908–09.
Lincoln: University of Nebraska Press, 1957.

Apponyi, Flora Haines. "Last Days of Mrs. Helen Hunt Jackson." Overland
Monthly 2d S, 6 (September 1885): 310–315.

"A. W. R. writes from Monte Carneire Ranch." *Critic* NS 4 (19 September 1885): 139.

Axtell, James. *The Invasion Within: The Contest of Cultures in Colonial North America.* New York: Oxford University Press, 1985.

Bade, William Frederick. *The Life and Letters of John Muir.* Boston: Houghton Mifflin Company, 1924.

Banning, Evelyn I. *Helen Hunt Jackson.* New York: Vanguard Press, 1973.

———. "Helen Hunt Jackson in San Diego." *Journal of San Diego History* 24 (Fall 1978): 457–467.

Bannan, Helen M. "The Ideal of Civilization and American Indian Policy Reformers in the 1880s." *Journal of American Culture* 1 (Winter 1978): 787–799.

———. "'True Womanhood' and Indian Assimilation." In *Selected Proceedings of the Third Annual Conference on Minority Studies,* ed. George E. Carter and James R. Parker, pp. 187–194. LaCross, Wis.: Institute for Minority Studies, 1976.

Beals, Ralph L. "The Anthropologist as Expert Witness: Illustrations from the California Indian Land Claims Case." In *Irredeemable America: The Indians' Estate and Land Claims,* ed. Imre Sutton, pp. 139–155. Albuquerque: University of New Mexico Press, 1985.

Berg, Barbara J. *The Remembered Gate: The Origins of American Feminism: The Woman and the City, 1800–1860.* New York: Oxford University Press, 1978.

Bianchi, Martha Dickinson. *The Life and Letters of Emily Dickinson.* Boston: Houghton Mifflin Company, 1924.

Board of Indian Commissioners. *Annual Reports of the Board of Indian Commissioners.* Washington, D.C.: Government Printing Office, 1872, 1876, 1880, 1884, 1885, 1886, 1887, 1888, 1889, 1890, 1891, 1895.

Bolton, Herbert E. "The Mission as a Frontier Institution in the Spanish-American Colonies." *American Historical Review* 23 (October 1917–July 1918): 42–61.

Bordin, Ruth. *Women and Temperance: The Quest for Power and Liberty, 1873–1900.* Philadelphia: Temple University Press, 1981.

Byers, John R. "Helen Hunt Jackson." *American Literary Realism: 1870–1910* 2 (Summer 1969): 143–148.

———. "The Indian Matter of Helen Hunt Jackson's *Ramona*: From Fact to Fiction." *American Indian Quarterly* 2 (Winter 1975–76): 331–346.

Byers, John R., and Elizabeth S. Byers. "Helen Hunt Jackson (1830–1885): A Critical Bibliography of Secondary Comment." *American Literary Realism: 1870–1910* 6 (Summer 1973): 197–241.

Carillo, Fr. J. M. *The Story of Mission San Antonio de Pala.* Oceanside, Calif.: North Country Printers, 1959.

Carlson, Leonard A. *Indians, Bureaucrats, and Land: The Dawes Act and the Decline of Indian Farming.* Westport, Conn.: Greenwood Press, 1981.

Carrico, Richard L. "San Diego Indians and the Federal Government: Years of Neglect, 1850–1865." *Journal of San Diego History* 26 (Summer 1980): 165–184.

Carter, Charles Franklin. "The Home of Ramona." In *Some By-Ways of California*, 2nd ed. pp. 57–76. San Francisco: Whitaker & Ray-Wiggin Co., 1911.

Christie, John C., Jr. "Indian Land Claims Involving Private Owners of Land: A Lawyer's Perspective." In *Irredeemable America: The Indians' Estate and Land Claims*, ed. Imre Sutton, pp. 233–246. Albuquerque: University of New Mexico Press, 1985.

Cohen, Felix. *Handbook of Federal Indian Law*. Albuquerque: University of New Mexico Press, n.d.

Cone, Helen Gray. "Women in American Literature." *Century Magazine* 40 (October 1890): 921–930.

Conway, Moncure Daniel. *Autobiography, Memories, and Experiences of Moncure Daniel Conway*. 2 vols. Boston and New York: Houghton Mifflin and Company, 1904.

Cook, Sherburne F. *The Conflict between the California Indian and White Civilization*. Berkeley: University of California Press, 1976.

Coolidge, Susan. "H. H." *Critic* NS 4 (3 October 1885): 164.

Costo, Rupert, and Jeannette Henry Costo. *The Missions of California: A Legacy of Genocide*. San Francisco: Indian Historian Press, 1987.

Cott, Nancy F. *The Bonds of Womanhood: "Woman's Sphere" in New England, 1780–1835*. New Haven: Yale University Press, 1977.

———. "Religion and the Bonds of Womanhood." In *Our American Sisters: Woman in American Life and Thought*, ed. Jean E. Friedman and William G. Shade, pp. 196–212. Lexington, Mass.: D. C. Heath and Company, 1982.

Crary, Margaret. *Susette LaFlesche: Voice of the Omaha Indians*. New York: Hawthorne Books, 1973.

"Current Criticism: Something Very Rare." *Critic*, 10 January 1885, p. 22.

Cutter, Donald C. "Books." *Californians* 6 (November/December 1988): 56.

Davis, Carlyle Channing, and William A. Alderson. *The True Story of Ramona*. New York: Dodge Publishing Company, 1914.

Dewey, Mary E. *Historical Sketch of the Formation and Achievements of the Women's National Indian Association in the United States*. Philadelphia: Women's National Indian Association, 1900.

Dickinson, Susan H. "Two Generations of Amherst Society." In *Essays on Amherst's History*, pp. 168–188. Amherst: Vista Trust, 1978.

Dobie, J. Frank. "Helen Hunt Jackson and Ramona." *Southwest Review* 44 (Spring 1959): 93–98.

Door, Julia C. R. "Emerson's Admiration of 'H. H.'" *Critic* 29 (August 1885): 102.

Douglas, Ann. *The Feminization of American Culture*. New York: Alfred A. Knopf, 1974.

Dubois, Constance Goddard. *The Condition of the Mission Indians of Southern California*. Philadelphia: Office of the Indian Rights Association, 1901.

Eastman, Elaine Goodale. "The Author of Ramona." *Classmate*, 21 January 1939, pp. 6–7.

Engelhardt, Zephyrin. *The Missions and Missionaries of California*. 5 vols. San Francisco: James H. Barry, 1908–1916.

———. *San Luis Rey Mission*. San Francisco: James H. Barry, 1921.

Epstein, Barbara Leslie. *The Politics of Domesticity: Women, Evangelism, and Temperance in Nineteenth Century America*. Middletown, Conn.: Wesleyan University Press, 1981.

Essays on Amherst's History. Amherst, Mass.: Vista Trust, 1978.

Flexnor, Eleanor. *Century of Struggle: The Woman's Rights Movement in the United States*. Cambridge: Harvard University Press, 1973.

Foote, Kate. *The Indian Legislation of 1888*. Philadelphia: Women's National Indian Association, 1888.

Fowler, William W. *Women on the American Frontier*. Williamstown, Mass.: Corner House Publishers, 1976.

Frazer, Robert W., ed. "Lovell's Report on the Cahuilla Indians 1854." *Journal of San Diego History* 22 (Winter 1976): 4–10.

Fritz, Henry E. "The Last Hurrah of Christian Humanitarian Indian Reform: The Board of Indian Commissioners, 1909–1918." *Western Historical Quarterly* 16 (April 1985): 147–162.

———. *The Movement for Indian Assimilation, 1860–1890*. Westport, Conn.: Greenwood Press, 1981.

Garner, Van H. *The Broken Ring: The Destruction of the California Indians*. Tucson: Westernlore Press, 1982.

Gilder, J. B. "The Lounger." *Critic* NS 4 (22 August 1885): 91.

Goodard, M. Le B. "A Century of Dishonor." *Atlantic Monthly* 47 (April 1881): 572–575.

Green, Norma Kidd. "Four Sisters: Daughters of Joseph LaFlesche." *Nebraska History* 45 (June 1964): 165–176.

———. *Iron Eyes' Family: The Children of Joseph LaFlesche*. Lincoln: Johnsen Publishing Company, 1969.

Hagan, William T. *The Indian Rights Association: The Herbert Welsh Years 1882–1904*. Tucson: University of Arizona Press, 1985.

Harsha, W. J. "How 'Ramona' Wrote Itself." *Southern Workman* 59 (August 1930): 370–375.

Hayes, Rutherford B. *Diary and Letters of Rutherford Hayes: Nineteenth President of the United States*. Ed. Charles Richard Williams. Ohio State Archaeological and Historical Society, 1924.

Hayter, Earl W. "The Ponca Removal." *North Dakota Historical Quarterly* 6 (July 1932): 263–275.

Heizer, Robert F., ed. *Handbook of North American Indians*. Vol. 8, *California*. Washington, D.C.: Smithsonian Institution, 1978.

"Helen Hunt Jackson's Life and Writings." In *Literary News*, pp. 97–102. Baltimore: Cushings & Bailey, Booksellers and Stationers, April 1887.

Higginson, Thomas Wentworth. *Contemporaries*. Boston: Houghton Mifflin and Company, 1899.

———. "Helen Jackson ('H. H.')." In *Short Studies of American Authors*, pp. 40–50. Boston: Lee and Shepard Publishers, 1880.

———. "Helen Jackson." *Nation* 41 (20 August 1885): 150–151.

——. "Helen Jackson." *Critic* NS 4 (22 August 1885): 85–86.
——. "How Ramona was Written." *Atlantic Monthly* 86 (November 1900): 712–714.
——. "Mrs. Helen Jackson ('H. H.')." *Century Magazine* 31 (November 1885): 251–257.
——. "The Last Poems of Helen Jackson (H. H.)." *Century Magazine* 31 (November 1885): 258.
——. "To the Memory of H. H." *Century Magazine* 32 (May 1886): 47.
Hill, Edward E. *The Office of Indian Affairs, 1824–1880: Historical Sketches.* New York: Clearwater Publishing Company, 1974.
Hill, Joseph John. *The History of Warner's Ranch and Its Environs.* Los Angeles, 1927.
Howell, Edward B. "A Tragic Sequel to 'Ramona.'" *Review of Reviews* 10 (November 1894): 507–513.
Hoxie, Frederick, E., ed. *Indians in American History.* Arlington Heights, Ill., 1988.
——. *A Final Promise: The Campaign to Assimilate the Indians, 1880–1920.* Lincoln: University of Nebraska Press, 1984.
Hubbard, Sara A. "Helen Hunt Jackson." *Dial* 6 (September 1885): 109–110.
Hufford, D. A. *The Real Ramona of Helen Hunt Jackson's Famous Novel.* 4th ed. Los Angeles: D. A. Hufford & Co., Publishers, 1900.
Hurtado, Albert L. *Indian Survival on the California Frontier.* New Haven: Yale University Press, 1988.
Indian Rights Association. *Annual Reports of the Executive Committee of the Indian Rights Association.* Philadelphia: Office of the Indian Rights Association, 1884, 1885, 1886, 1887, 1889, 1891, 1892, 1898, 1900, 1901, 1907.
——. *The Case of the Mission Indians in Southern California and the Action of the Indian Rights Association in Supporting the Defense of their Legal Rights.* Philadelphia: Office of the Indian Rights Association, 1886.
——. *Indian Rights Association Papers (1864–1973).* Glen Rock, N.J.: Microfilming Corporation of America, 1973.
——. *The Pressing Needs of the Warner Ranch and Other Mission Indians in Southern California.* Philadelphia: Office of the Indian Rights Association, October, 1901.
Jackson, Helen Hunt. *A Century of Dishonor: A Sketch of the United States Government's Dealings with Some of the Indian Tribes.* Boston: Roberts Brothers, 1888.
——. *Ah-Wah-Ne Days: A Visit to the Yosemite Valley in 1872.* San Francisco: Book Club of California, 1971.
——. ["H. H."] *Bits of Travel.* Boston: Roberts Brothers, 1893.
——. "Echoes in the City of Angels." *Century Magazine,* December 1883, pp. 194–210.
——. *Glimpses of Three Coasts.* Boston: Roberts Brothers, 1886.
——. *My Day in the Wilderness: Six California Tales.* San Francisco: Book Club of California, 1939.

———. *Ramona*. New York: Grosset & Dunlap, n.d.

———. "Report on the Condition and Needs of the Mission Indians of California, Made by Special Agents Helen Jackson and Abbot Kinney, to the Commissioner of Indian Affairs." In *A Century of Dishonor*, pp. 458–514.

———. ["H. H."] "The Wards of the United States Government." *Scribner's Monthly* 19 (March 1880): 775–782.

James, George Wharton. *Heroes of California*. Boston: Little, Brown & Co., 1910.

———. *Through Ramona's Country*. Boston: Little, Brown & Co., 1913.

Johnson, Thomas H., ed. *The Letters of Emily Dickinson*. Cambridge: Belknap Press of Harvard University Press, 1958.

Keiser, Albert. *The Indian in American Literature*. New York: Oxford University Press, 1933.

Keller, Robert H., Jr. *American Protestantism and United States Indian Policy, 1869–82*. Lincoln: University of Nebraska Press, 1983.

Kelsey, C. E. *Report of the Special Agent for California Indians to the Commissioner of Indian Affairs, March 21, 1906*. San Jose: Northern California Indian Association, 1906.

Kerber, Linda K. "Separate Spheres, Female Worlds, Woman's Place: The Rhetoric of Women's History." *Journal of American History* 75 (June 1988): 9–39.

King, James T. "A Better Way: General George Crook and the Ponca Indians." *Nebraska History* 50 (Fall 1969): 239–256.

Kroeber, A. L. *Handbook of the Indians of California*. New York: Dover Publications, 1976.

Lake Mohonk Conference of Friends of the Indian. *Proceedings of the Annual Meeting of the Lake Mohonk Conference of Friends of the Indian*. 1885, 1886, 1887, 1888, 1891, 1892, 1893, 1896.

Lerner, Gerda. "The Lady and the Mill Girl: Changes in the Status of Women in the Age of Jackson." In *Our American Sisters: Women in American Life and Thought*, ed. Jean E. Friedman and William G. Shade, pp. 83–195. Lexington, Mass.: D. C. Heath and Company, 1982.

McConnell, Virginia. "'H. H.,' and Colorado, and the Indian Problem." *Journal of the West* 12 (April 1973): 272–280.

McLoughlin, William G., ed. *The American Evangelicals, 1800–1900: An Anthology*. New York: Harper and Row Publishers, 1976.

McWilliams, Carey. *Southern California: An Island on the Land*. Santa Barbara: Peregrine Smith, 1973.

Mardock, Robert Winston. *The Reformers and the American Indian*. Columbia: University of Missouri Press, 1971.

———. "Standing Bear and the Reformers." In *Indian Leaders: Oklahoma's First Statesmen*, ed. H. Glenn Jordan and Thomas M. Holm, pp. 101–113. Oklahoma City: Oklahoma Historical Society, 1979.

Marriott, Katheryn. "Helen Hunt Jackson in Santa Barbara." *Noticias* 28 (Winter 1982): 84–92.

Marsden, Michael T. "A Dedication to the Memory of Helen Hunt Jackson, 1830–1885." *Arizona and the West* 21 (Summer 1979): 108–112.

Mathes, Valerie Sherer. "Annie E. K. Biowell: Chico's Benefactress." *California History*, Spring–Summer 1989, pp. 14–25, 60–64.

———. "Helen Hunt Jackson and the Campaign for Ponca Restitution, 1880–1881." *South Dakota History* 17 (Spring 1987): 23–42.

———. "Helen Hunt Jackson and the Ponca Controversy." *Montana: The Magazine of Western History* 39 (Winter 1989): 42–53.

———. "Helen Hunt Jackson: A Legacy of Indian Reform." *Essays and Monographs in Colorado History*, no. 4 (1986): 25–58.

———. "Helen Hunt Jackson: Official Agent to the California Mission Indians." *Southern California Quarterly* 63 (Spring 1981): 63–82.

———. "Indian Philanthropy in California: Annie Bidwell and the Mechoopda Indians." *Arizona and the West*, Summer 1983, pp. 153–166.

———. "Parallel Calls to Conscience: Reformers Helen Hunt Jackson and Harriet Beecher Stowe." *Californians* 1 (July–August 1983): 32–40.

May, Antoinette. *Helen Hunt Jackson: A Lonely Voice of Conscience*. San Francisco: Chronicle Books, 1987.

Milner, Clyde A., II. *Churchmen and the Western Indians 1820–1920*. Norman: University of Oklahoma Press, 1985.

———. *With Good Intentions: Quaker Work among the Pawnees, Otos, and Omaha in the 1870s*. Lincoln: University of Nebraska Press, 1982.

Myres, Sandra L. *Westering Women and the Frontier Experience, 1800–1915*. Albuquerque: University of New Mexico Press, 1982.

Nevins, Allan. "Helen Hunt Jackson, Sentimentalist v. Realist." *American Scholar* 10 (Summer 1941): 269–285.

Nye, Russell Blaine. *Society and Culture in America, 1830–1860*. New York: Harper and Row Publishers, 1974.

Oandasan, William. "*Ramona*: Reflected through Indigenous Eyes." *California Historical Courier*, February/March 1986, p. 7.

Odell, Ruth. *Helen Hunt Jackson (H. H.)*. New York: D. Appleton-Century Company, 1939.

O'Neil, Floyd A. "Hiram Price, 1881–1885." In *The Commissioners of Indian Affairs, 1824–1977*, ed. Robert M. Kvasnicka and Herman Viola, pp. 173–179. Lincoln: University of Nebraska Press, 1979.

Otis, D. S. *The Dawes Act and the Allotment of Indian Lands*. Ed. Francis Paul Prucha. Norman: University of Oklahoma Press, 1973.

Painter, C. C. *The Condition of Affairs in Indian Territory and California*. Philadelphia: Office of the Indian Rights Association, 1888.

———. *A Visit to the Mission Indians of Southern California and other Western Tribes*. Philadelphia: Office of the Indian Rights Association, 1886.

———. *A Visit to the Mission Indians of California*. Philadelphia: Office of the Indian Rights Association, 1887.

Phillips, George Harwood. *Chiefs and Challengers: Indian Resistance and Cooperation in Southern California*. Berkeley: University of California Press, 1975.

———. *The Enduring Struggle: Indians in California History*. San Francisco: Boyd & Fraser Publishing Company, 1981.

Powell, Lawrence Clark. "California Classics Reread: Ramona." *Westways* 60 (July 1968): 13–15.

Priest, Loring Benson. *Uncle Sam's Stepchildren: The Reformation of United States Indian Policy, 1865–1887.* Lincoln: University of Nebraska Press, 1981.

Prucha, Francis Paul. *American Indian Policy in Crisis: Christian Reformers and the Indian, 1865–1900.* Norman: University of Oklahoma Press, 1976.

———, ed. *Americanizing the American Indians: Writings by the "Friends of the Indian," 1880–1900.* Cambridge: Harvard University Press, 1973.

———, ed. *Documents of United States Indian Policy.* Lincoln: University of Nebraska Press, 1975.

———. "A 'Friend of the Indian' in Milwaukee: Mrs. O. J. Hiles and the Wisconsin Indian Association." *Historical Messenger of the Milwaukee County Historical Society* 29 (Autumn 1973): 78–95.

———. *The Great Father: The United States Government and the American Indians.* Lincoln: University of Nebraska Press, 1984.

———. *Indian Policy in the United States: Historical Essays.* Lincoln: University of Nebraska Press, 1981.

Quinton, Amelia Stone. "Care of the Indian." In *Woman's Work in America,* ed. Annie Hathan Meyer, pp. 373–391. New York: Henry Holt and Company, 1891.

———. "The Indian." In *The Literature of Philanthropy,* ed. Frances Goodale, pp. 116–140. New York: Harper & Brothers Publishers, 1893.

———. *Missionary Work of the Women's National Indian Association.* Philadelphia, n.d.

Rawls, James J. *Indians of California: The Changing Image.* Norman: University of Oklahoma Press, 1984.

———. "Recent American Fiction." *Atlantic Monthly* 55 (January 1885): 127–130.

Riley, Glenda. *Inventing the American Woman: A Perspective on Women's History.* Arlington Heights, Ill.: Harland Davidson, 1987.

———. *Women and Indians on the Frontier, 1825–1915.* Albuquerque: University of New Mexico Press, 1984.

Rogin, Michael Paul. *Fathers and Children: Andrew Jackson and the Subjugation of the American Indian.* New York: Vintage Books, 1976.

Ruether, Rosemary Radford, and Rosemary Skinner Keller, eds. *Women and Religion in America: The Nineteenth Century: A Documentary History.* Vol. I. San Francisco: Harper and Row, 1981.

Sandos, James A. "Junipero Serra's Canonization and the Historical Record." *American Historical Review* 93 (December 1988): 1253–1269.

Satz, Ronald N. *American Indian Policy in the Jacksonian Era.* Lincoln: University of Nebraska Press, 1975.

Schurz, Carl. *Speeches, Correspondence, and Political Papers of Carl Schurz.* Ed. Frederick Bancroft. New York: G. P. Putnam's Sons, 1913.

Sheehan, Bernard W. *Seeds of Extinction: Jeffersonian Philanthropy and the American Indian.* New York: W. W. Norton & Company, 1973.

Shinn, Milicent W. "The Verse and Prose of 'H. H.'" *Overland Monthly* 2d S, 6 (September 1885): 315–322.

Shipek, Florence C. "Mission Indians and Indians of California Land Claims." *American Indian Quarterly* 13 (Fall 1989): 409–420.

Sievers, Michael A. "Funding the California Indian Superintendency: A Case Study of Congressional Appropriations." *Southern California Quarterly* 59 (Spring 1977): 49–73.

Sklar, Kathryn Kish. *Catharine Beecher: A Study in American Domesticity.* New Haven: Yale University Press, 1973.

Starr, Kevin. *Inventing the Dream: California through the Progressive Era.* New York: Oxford University Press, 1985.

Stedman, Raymond William. *Shadows of the Indian Stereotypes in American Culture.* Norman: University of Oklahoma Press, 1982.

Stellman, Louis J. "The Man Who Inspired 'Ramona.'" *Overland Monthly* 50 (September 1907): 2–5.

Taber, Cornelia. *California and Her Indian Children.* San Jose: The Northern California Indian Association, 1911.

Thompson, Gerald. *Edward F. Beale & the American West.* Albuquerque: University of New Mexico Press, 1983.

Thornton, Russell. *American Indian Holocaust and Survival: A Population History since 1492.* Norman: University of Oklahoma Press, 1987.

Tibbles, Thomas Henry. *Buckskin and Blanket Days: Memoirs of a Friend of the Indians.* Lincoln: University of Nebraska Press, 1969.

———. *The Ponca Chiefs: An Account of the Trial of Standing Bear.* Ed. Kay Graber. Lincoln: University of Nebraska Press, 1972.

Todd, Mabel Loomis. *Letters of Emily Dickinson.* New York: World Publishing Company, 1951.

Tourgée, Albion W. "Study in Civilization." *North American Review* 143 (August 1886): 246–261.

"Treaty with the San Louis Rey, Etc. 1852." In *Irredeemable America: The Indians' Estate and Land Claims,* ed. Imre Sutton, pp. 390–392. Albuquerque: University of New Mexico Press, 1985.

Trennert, Robert A., Jr. *Alternative to Extinction: Federal Indian Policy and the Beginnings of the Reservation System, 1846–51.* Philadelphia: Temple University Press, 1975.

———. "Educating Indian Girls at Nonreservation Boarding Schools, 1878–1920." *Western Historical Quarterly* 13 (July 1982): 271–290.

U.S. Congress, House of Representatives. H.R. Rept. 3282, 50th Cong. 1st Sess., 1888.

U.S. Congress, Senate. S. Ex. Doc. 49, 48th Cong. 1st. Sess., 1884, S. Ex. Doc 15, 49th Cong. 1st Sess., 1885, S. Rept. 74, 50th Cong. 1st Sess., 1888.

U.S. Department of the Interior, Office of Indian Affairs. *Annual Report of the Commissioner of Indian Affairs to the Secretary of the Interior.* Washington, D.C.: Government Printing Office, 1875, 1877, 1879, 1880, 1881, 1882, 1883, 1884, 1885, 1886, 1887, 1888, 1889, 1890, 1891, 1892, 1893, 1894, 1895, 1898.

Utley, Robert M. "The Celebrated Peace Policy of General Grant." In *Amer-*

ican Indian Past and Present, ed. Roger L. Nichols and George R. Adams, pp. 183–199. Waltham, Mass.: Xerox College Publishing, 1971.

———. *Frontier Regulars: The United States Army and the Indian, 1866–1891*. New York: MacMillan Publishing Company, 1973.

———. *Frontiersmen in Blue: The United States Army and the Indians, 1848–1865*. New York: MacMillan Publishing Company, 1967.

Vickery, Joyce C. "Contradictory Realities: Helen Hunt Jackson's California." *California Historical Courier*, February/March 1986, p. 6.

Vroman, A. C., and T. F. Barnes. *The Genesis of the Story of Ramona*. Los Angeles: Kinsley-Barnes & Newner Company, 1899.

Warner, Charles Dudley. "'H. H.' in Southern California." In *Fashions in Literature and Other Literary and Social Essays & Addresses*, pp. 321–330. New York: Dodd, Mead & Company, 1902.

Washburn, Wilcomb E. *The Assault on Indian Tribalism: The General Allotment Law (Dawes Act) of 1887*. Philadelphia: J. B. Lippincott Company, 1975.

Weber, David J. *The Mexican Frontier 1821–1846: The American Southwest under Mexico*. Albuquerque: University of New Mexico Press, 1982.

Weber, Francis J., ed. *King of the Missions: A Documentary History of San Luis Rey de Francia*. Los Angeles: Timothy Cardinal Manning, n.d.

Welter, Barbara. *Dimity Convictions: The American Woman in the Nineteenth Century*. Athens: Ohio University Press, 1976.

Whitaker, Rosemary. *Helen Hunt Jackson*. Boise: Boise State University Western Writers Series, 1987.

Wilson, Dorothy Clarke. *Bright Eyes: The Story of Susette LaFlesche, an Omaha Indian*. New York: McGraw-Hill Book Company, 1974.

Women's National Indian Association. *Annual Meeting and Report of the Women's National Indian Association*. Philadelphia, 1883, 1884, 1886, 1888, 1889, 1891, 1892, 1893, 1895, 1896, 1897, 1898, 1899, 1901, 1902, 1903, 1921.

———. *Christian Civilization: Missionary Work of the Women's National Indian Association*. Philadelphia, November 1887.

———. *Indian's Friend* [Philadelphia]: November, December 1888; February, March, June 1889; January, February, March, May, June, September, October 1890; September, October 1891; July, August, October, November, December 1892; February, March, April, May, June, July, September 1893; February, March, May, June, July, December 1894; February, March, May, June, July, August 1895; April, June, August, October, November 1896; February, April, May, June, July, August 1897; April, May, June, September 1898; February 1899; January 1900, June, July 1902.

———. *Missionary Work of the Women's National Indian Association, and Letters of Missionaries*. Philadelphia, November 1885.

———. *Our Missionary Report for 1897*. Philadelphia, 1897.

———. *The Ramona Mission and the Mission Indians*. Philadelphia, May 1889.

———. *Report of the Missionary Committee*. Philadelphia, November 1889.

——. *Report of the Missionary Department.* Philadelphia, November 1890, November 1891.

——. *Report of Missionary Work, November 1885 to November 1886.* Philadelphia, 1886.

——. *Report on Missionary Work.* Philadelphia, November 1888.

——. *Sunshine Work.* Philadelphia, December 1894.

——. *Work of the Missionary Department of the Women's National Indian Association for the Year Ending December 1892.* Philadelphia, 1892.

Index